baking
sweets & treats

SCHOLASTIC

This edition published by Scholastic Inc., 557 Broadway, New York, NY 10012, by arrangement with McRae Publishing, Ltd.

Scholastic and associated logos are trademarks of Scholastic Inc.

Distributed by Scholastic Canada Ltd., Markham, Ontario

10 9 8 7 6 5 4 3 2 1

This book was conceived, edited and designed by McRae Publishing Ltd, London

Project Director Anne McRae
Art Director Marco Nardi

Photography Brent Parker Jones
Text Rachael Lane
Editing Christine Price, Anne McRae
Food Styling Lee Blaylock, Mark Hockenhull
Food Styling Assistant Rochelle Seator
Prop Styling Lee Blaylock

ISBN 978-0-545-85985-1

Printed in China

NOTE TO OUR READERS
Eating eggs or egg whites that are not completely cooked poses the possibility of salmonella food poisoning. The risk is greater for pregnant women, the elderly, the very young, and persons with impaired immune systems. If you are concerned about salmonella, you can use reconstituted powdered egg whites or pasteurized eggs.

Rachael Lane

baking
sweets & treats

SCHOLASTIC

contents

DON'T MISS

PISTACHIO BISCOTTI

DOUBLE CHOCOLATE MINT SLICE

DISCO BALL CAKE POPS

RED VELVET CAKE

PAIN AUX RAISINS

CHOCOLATE FONDANTS

At a Glance

This book has more than 200 baking recipes, ranging from cookies, brownies, and cakes, to pastries, desserts, and breads. On these pages you will find some ideas for unmissable, quick, classic, casual, favorite, easy, challenging, and celebratory dishes. Just to get you started!

EASY

ROSEWATER CUPCAKES

PEANUT BUTTER COOKIES

BUTTER CAKE

BANANA CAKE

PORTUGUESE TARTS

LINZERTORTE

APPLE TURNOVERS

PEACH COBBLER

APPLE & RHUBARB CRISP

SODA BREAD

OLD FAVORITES

CHOCOLATE CARAMEL SLICE

GINGERSNAPS

CHOCOLATE CAKE

SAINT HONORÉ

CHOCOLATE ÉCLAIRS

CHERRY CLAFOUTIS

CHERRY CLAFOUTIS

CASUAL ENTERTAINING

CRACKED CHEWY
CHOCOLATE COOKIES

SALTY PEANUT BARS

CHOCOLATE MUD CAKE

LEMON POPPY SEED
CAKE

LEMON TART

CROISSANTS

PASSIONFRUIT FOAM CAKE

QUICK

AFGHAN BISCUITS

PASSIONFRUIT YOYOS

COCONUT MACAROONS

LEMON MADELEINES

SWISS ROLL

PALMIERS

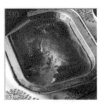

LEMON DELICIOUS
PUDDING

CLASSICS

SACHERTORTE

CHOCOLATE CHIP COOKIES

POUND CAKE

ANGEL FOOD CAKE

LEMON TART

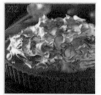

APPLE STRUDEL

CRÈME CARAMEL

SPECIAL OCCASIONS

BRANDY SNAPS

ORANGE CHIFFON CAKE

FRENCH FLAN

LEMON MERINGUE PIE

QUEEN OF PUDDINGS

QUEEN OF PUDDINGS

MARSHMALLOW PAVLOVA WITH FRESH BERRIES

CHALLENGING

DOBOS TORTE

DISCO BALL CAKE POPS

BATTENBURG CAKE

CLASSIC MILLE-FEUILLE

PARIS-BREST

RASPBERRY & VANILLA VACHERIN

RASPBERRY SOUFFLÉS

CELEBRATION

TRADITIONAL CHRISTMAS CAKE

GINGERBREAD PEOPLE

BRANDY SNAPS

LADY BALTIMORE CAKE

STRAWBERRY TARTLETS

CHRISTMAS MINCE PIES

PUMPKIN PIE

GALETTES DES ROIS

COFFEE CREAM
PROFITEROLES

KULICH

BELGIUM BISCUITS

RASPBERRY JELLY
CAKES

CARROT CAKE

FLOURLESS ORANGE
CAKE

VICTORIA SPONGE

TART AU CHOCOLAT

ALMOND JALOUSIE

CRÈME BRÛLÉE

SELF-SAUCING
CHOCOLATE PUDDING

EDITOR'S CHOICE

CHOCOLATE HAZELNUT DACQUOISE

ingredients

Baking delicious food for family and friends can be deeply satisfying, especially because you know exactly what ingredients have gone into each recipe. Store-bought baked goods often contain too much sugar and salt and are full of unhealthy trans fats, a major contributor to high cholesterol and coronary heart disease. When you bake at home, you can choose high quality, natural ingredients to ensure tastier and healthier food.

Fresh, wholesome ingredients ensure that the food you bake does not contain unhealthy preservatives, artificial flavorings, and trans fats.

Baking powder is added to make baked goods rise. Most commercial baking powders work well and will only let you down if they are old or have been left open.

Baking soda (bicarbonate of soda), a component of baking power, is also a leavener. It is activated by acidic ingredients, such as yogurt, sour cream, or lemon juice. Cook the baked goods soon after adding the baking soda. If the batter is left sitting, it will not work.

Butter is high in fat (most commercial brands contain 80–85 percent butter fat). Fat gives baked goods flavor, texture, and a flaky, tender crumb. Butter can be salted or unsalted. Except where otherwise specified, we suggest you use unsalted butter. Add salt as suggested in the recipes, or to taste.

Buttermilk is a cultured milk, not unlike yogurt. If preferred, you can make your own buttermilk by adding 1 tablespoon of white wine vinegar to each cup (250 ml) of whole milk.

Cocoa Powder is made from unsweetened chocolate. There are two types: regular and Dutch-processed. The Dutch-processed is less acidic and results in a darker color and better texture and flavor. Always sift before use to remove lumps.

Cornstarch (cornflour) is silky and smooth and is added to baked goods to improve texture.

Cream can be heavy (double) or light (single). Heavy cream has more fat (up to 48 percent), while light cream has less (about 18 percent). Fat levels vary, but if you want to whip the cream to fill a cake you will need a cream with at least 30–35 percent fat.

Eggs add flavor, structure, richness, and texture to baked goods and should always be as fresh as possible. Except where otherwise specified, we have used large eggs throughout. Large eggs weigh about 2 ounces (60 g) each. Eggs should always be at room temperature as cold eggs can curdle the batter. Take out of the refrigerator 1–2 hours ahead of time, or place in a bowl of warm water for 15 minutes.

Flour is the basic ingredient in most baked goods. There are several different types, including all-purpose (plain), whole-wheat (wholemeal), and strong bread flour. All of our recipes specify flour type, with most using ordinary all-purpose (plain) flour. A few recipes call for self-rising flour. If this is not available where you live, you can prepare it yourself by adding 2 teaspoons of baking powder to each cup (150 g) of all-purpose (plain) flour and sift several times before use. Normally you do not need to sift modern flour because it is all pre-sifted. Even so, in most of our recipes we suggest that you sift it anyway. A little bit of extra air will not do any harm!

Milk is used to moisten baked goods. We suggest that you use whole milk for best results.

Sugar adds flavor and texture to baked goods. There are several types. In this book, when the recipes list sugar, we mean ordinary granulated sugar; all other sugars are indicated by name—superfine (caster) sugar, confectioners' (icing) sugar, light brown sugar, dark brown sugar, and raw sugar.

Common, low-cost ingredients combined with just a little effort and skill allow you to bake a range of delicious cookies, cakes, and desserts for family and friends.

equipment

An ordinary well-stocked home kitchen will already have all the equipment required to prepare most of the recipes in this book. Here is a quick checklist of the basics.

Baking sheets (oven trays), also known as cookie sheets, are essential for baking cookies (biscuits). They can be shiny light silver or dark nonstick. Generally, the shiny silver sheets are better for cookies, giving them a crisp, golden finish on the bottoms.

Cake pans are essential for cakes. You will need several round ones. Buy them in sets of two. If you are just starting out, begin with two 8-inch (20-cm) and two 9-inch (23-cm) round springform pans. For special cakes, you will need kugelhopf, ring (Bundt), and angel food pans. For cake rolls (roulades), you will need a large jelly roll (Swiss roll) pan or two.

Muffin pans come in a variety of shapes and sizes. Most of our cupcake recipes call for standard 1/3 cup (90 ml) cups, but we have also included recipes for large (Texas) cupcakes and mini cupcakes.

Pie plates are made in glass, ceramic, and metal. Glass plates are useful if you are a beginner because you can see through the pan to check if the base is sufficiently browned. Glass, being nonreactive, is also good for storing acidic fruit pies since it won't flavor the fruit in any way.

Tart pans are available in a range of sizes. A 9-inch (23-cm) pan and an 11-inch (28-cm)

pan will do in most cases. The ones with removeable bottoms are very useful for getting tarts out of the pan without breaking the pastry case, and are not much more expensive. Mini tartlet pans are also available with removeable bottoms and make eyecatching mini tarts.

Specialty pans & items, including cookie cutters, madeleine molds, friand pans, patty pans, silicone whoopie pie and macaron baking matts, and cake pop sticks can be acquired gradually, as you bake the various recipes.

Pizza stones are a great buy if you make pizza or bread often at home. They provide intense, dry heat and will give your pizzas perfect, crisp crusts.

Stand mixers are the ultimate tool if you do a lot of baking. Even the most basic models will allow you to beat cake and cookie batter, knead pizza and bread dough, and whip egg whites and cream with a minimum of effort.

Handheld mixers are a must, especially if you don't have a stand mixer. They will do most things, but not bread or pizza dough.

Measuring cups & spoons are ideal if you don't have kitchen scales. All of our recipes list ingredients in cups and spoons and imperial weights where appropriate, as well as in metric

You won't need a lot of special or expensive equipment to make most of the recipes in this book. A few pans and bowls, some measuring cups and spoons, and a good oven are the essentials.

weight measurements. Don't mix the two; either follow the cups and imperial weights, or the metric, throughout each recipe.

Bowls are essential for mixing and you should have several in different sizes. Stainless steel is ideal for mixing, and glass and ceramic bowls are also good. It is best to avoid plastic bowls as they can flavor the food.

Kitchen scales provide the accuracy that many recipes require. If you do a lot of baking, we suggest you invest in some electronic scales with a digital display.

Pastry bags (piping bags) are cheap to buy and useful for so many different things, from piping éclairs, to filling fancy cakes, to decorating cookies. At a pinch, you can improvise a pastry bag by filling a plastic ziplock bag and cutting off a corner.

Plastic wrap (cling film) is essential for many recipes, and is used to wrap cookie dough and tart and pie crusts, as well as for keeping food covered and fresh in the refrigerator.

Parchment paper (greaseproof paper) is used for a variety of tasks, from lining baking sheets and cake pans to rolling doughs.

Whisks are used to combine ingredients, incorporate air, and remove lumps. You will need at least one medium metal whisk.

Most cookies need to rest on the baking sheets for a few minutes after they come out of the oven until they harden enough to move. This usually takes 2–3 minutes. Use a metal spatula to transfer the cookies to wire racks and let cool completely.

cookies

Cookies, along with bars & brownies, are among the most popular home-baked goods. They are usually simple and quick to prepare, and are good recipes to start with if you are a novice baker. On this page we show you the basic steps in classic cookie making. We also show you the key steps in baking biscotti and meringues.

Cookies

Cookies can be divided into two main types, drop cookies and cut-out cookies. Drop cookies are the simplest to make; the dough is dropped onto the baking sheets and baked. Cut-out cookies are chilled first and then rolled out and cut into shapes using cookie cutters.

1. LINE baking sheets with parchment paper. Preheat the oven to the temperature given in the recipe. It will take 10–15 minutes for the oven to reach the desired temperature.

2. BEFORE you begin mixing, set out all the ingredients listed in the recipe. Sift the flour and any other dry ingredients into a bowl and set aside, ready to add when you need them.

3. MOST cookies are based on a mixture of butter and sugar, which is beaten until pale and creamy. If beating by hand, use a wooden spoon and beat vigorously for several minutes.

4. IF you have an electric mixer, beat the butter and sugar on medium speed until pale and creamy. Beat in the remaining ingredients to form a dough.

DROP COOKIES

5. DROP spoonfuls of dough onto the prepared baking sheets, spacing about 2 inches (5 cm) apart.

CUT-OUT COOKIES

6. PRESS the dough into a disk, wrap in plastic wrap (cling film), and chill for 30 minutes (or the time given in the recipe).

7. UNWRAP the chilled dough and use a rolling pin to roll it out on a lightly floured work surface.

8. USE cookie cutters to cut out cookies. Use a metal spatula to transfer the cookies to the prepared baking sheet.

Meringues

Meringues can be colored with food dye to make pretty party cookies, or stuck together in pairs with cream. For perfect meringues, alway use a very clean bowl and make sure that the egg whites contain no traces of yolk. Add the sugar very gradually, beating it so that it dissolves into the whites as they firm into soft, glossy peaks.

1. COMBINE the egg whites and a pinch of salt in a prefectly clean bowl. Begin by whisking gently, gradually increasing speed as the whites increase in volume. You can use a whisk, hand-held beater, or stand mixer, as preferred.

2. WHEN the egg whites stand in soft peaks, begin adding the sugar a few tablespoons at a time. Whisk or beat until the meringue stands in soft, glossy peaks. Do not overbeat.

3. FILL a pastry bag about half full with the meringue and twist the top closed to stop the meringue from spilling out. Pipe out meringues onto the baking sheets, spacing about 2 inches (5 cm) apart.

Biscotti

Biscotti are crisply chewy Italian cookies. They get their name, and their chewiness, from being cooked twice: *bis* (meaning twice) and *cotti* (cooked). Biscotti originally come from the Tuscan city of Prato. Made with almonds, they are traditionally served with a glass of vin santo (holy wine) for dunking. Here we show you the key steps: preparing the cookie logs for the first baking time, then slicing them so that they can be returned to the oven for the second baking.

1. DIVIDE the cookie dough into thirds, and roll each third into a long roll or log about 1 inch (2.5 cm) in diameter.

2. PLACE the logs on baking sheets lined with parchment paper. Flatten each log slightly and brush the tops with egg white.

3. BAKE for about 20 minutes, until pale golden brown. Take out of the oven and let cool slightly. Move to a cutting board and cut diagonally into 1-inch (2.5-cm) thick slices. Arrange on parchment-lined baking sheets and bake until crisp and golden.

cakes

Cakes can include small offerings such as cupcakes, cake pops, and madeleines, as well as the larger and more traditional tea and coffee cakes, fancy layer cakes, roulades, and tortes. The larger cakes can be divided into two main groups: butter cakes (which contain butter or fat) and foam cakes (which do not).

SMALL CAKES

In recent years a host of smaller cakes have become fashionable. Cupcakes are a prime example, and now exist in a huge range of flavors and with more or less elaborate decoration. Cake pops are also popular, and are perfect for parties. We have also included recipes for whoopie pies, madeleines, fairy cakes, rochers, friands, financiers, and more.

Butter Cakes

These are the simplest cakes to make. A well-made butter cake has a moist, fine-grained crumb and an even texture. Success depends on incorporating enough air bubbles into the batter. Begin by creaming the butter and sugar together in a large bowl. Make sure that the butter is not cold; it should be softened at warm room temperature, not straight from the refrigerator. The eggs and milk (or other liquid) should also be at room temperature. Sometimes the eggs are added whole, other times the whites are beaten separately and folded in at the end. Folding is not stirring; you should lift the batter gently upward and fold it over the whites so that the mixture does not deflate. Repeat until just combined.

1. PREHEAT the oven to the temperature given in each recipe. It will take 10–15 minutes to reach the desired temperature. Grease a round or square cake pan and line the base with parchment (greaseproof) paper. Set aside. Sift the flour and other dry ingredients into a bowl and set aside.

2. BEAT the butter and sugar in a bowl with a hand-held mixer, stand mixer, or wooden spoon until pale and creamy. Add the eggs one at a time, beating until just combined after each addition. Gradually beat in the flour mixture, alternating with any liquids, such as milk.

3. SPOON the batter into prepared cake pan and bake for the time indicated in the recipe, until well risen and golden brown. Leave to cool in the pan for 10–15 minutes.

4. TURN OUT of the pan and let cool completely on a wire rack. Carefully remove the paper from the bottom of the cake before decorating, or slicing to serve.

Foam Cakes

Foam cakes, or sponge cakes, as they are known in the United Kingdom and many other parts of the world, are soft, light cakes made with no butter or fat (or very little). They often contain no baking powder and are leavened by beating the eggs and sugar together until they are very thick and as much as tripled in bulk. These cakes often form the basis of fancy layer cakes and gateaux, especially those filled with rich creams. They can be baked in one or two pans and then sliced horizontally into layers once cooled. In the sequence below you will find some general tips for best results.

1. SIFT the flour and any other dry ingredients into a bowl. You may want to sift them two or three rimes, to incorporate as much air as possible.

2. BEAT the eggs and sugar in a large bowl over a pan of barely simmering water until the sugar has dissolved. Remove from the heat and beat until cooled, pale, tripled in volume, and very thick.

3. USE a large rubber spatula to gradually fold the dry ingredients into the egg and sugar mixture, taking care not to deflate the mixture.

FOAM CAKE BASICS

Make sure the egg whites are at warm room temperature, and do not overbeat. Beat slowly at first to develop plenty of air cells, then beat faster as the foam develops. Beat in the sugar until the whites are almost stiff, then gently fold in the dry ingredients. Do not stir, or the fragile air cells will deflate. Gently pour the batter into the prepared pan as soon as it is ready; don't let it sit around before baking. Make sure the oven is heated to the right temperature ahead of time.

ANGEL FOOD CAKES

Angel food cakes are a type of foam cake. They are baked in a special pan with tiny "feet." When the cake comes out of the oven it is turned upside down and left to hang as it cools. If you don't have a special pan with little feet, hang the tube pan over a funnel or balance it on inverted coffee cups or mugs.

1. WHEN the cake is cooked, it will be risen and golden brown and a cake tester or toothpick inserted into the center will come out clean. The top will spring back when pressed gently.

2. AS SOON AS the cake is cooked, turn the pan upside down on its feet and let the cake hang until it is completely cool.

3. TO UNMOLD, run a long knife around the edges of the pan, taking care not to separate the golden crust from the cake. Use a serrated knife and a sawing motion to slice the cake. An ordinary knife pushed into the cake will crush it.

tarts & pies

Generally speaking, tarts have a sweet pastry crust covered with filling but are left open. Pies have a flaky pastry crust and topping with the filling enclosed. Tarts and pies can be either sweet or savory, although they are most often sweet and are served as dessert.

Tarts

Most tarts have a sweet pastry (*pâte sucrée*) crust. Here you can see how to mix the crust, transfer it to the pan, and pre-bake it (a technique known as "baking blind"). You can mix the dough in a food processor or by hand. The food processor method is easier and will make an excellent crust, but be sure not to overmix. For the skilled baker, the hand method will produce a lighter and flakier crust. When shaping the dough for chilling, check to see if there are tiny flakes of butter visible beneath the surface. If so, then it is not overmixed and will be flaky. We suggest that you use all-purpose (plain) flour. Some cooks use a mixture of all-purpose and pastry flour for a tender crust.

Sweet Tart Pastry

1. BY MACHINE: Put the flour, sugar, and salt in a food processor with a metal blade. Add the butter and pulse until coarse crumbs form. Add the egg and pulse until smooth.

2. BY HAND: Stir the flour, sugar, and salt in a bowl. Rub in the butter until coarse crumbs form. Stir in the egg until a smooth dough forms.

3. TURN the dough out onto a sheet of plastic wrap (cling film). Press into a 6-inch (18-cm) disk and wrap in the plastic. Chill for at least 30 minutes (or up to 48 hours).

4. LIGHTLY GREASE a tart pan with a removable bottom. Unwrap the dough and place on a cool work surface. Flour the dough lightly on both sides.

5. ROLL OUT between two sheets of plastic wrap until ⅛ inch (3 mm) thick. Remove the top layer of plastic. Dust the rolling pin with flour and roll the pastry around it, removing the other layer of plastic as you work.

6. UNROLL the pastry over the pan. Ease into the bottom and sides of the pan. Fold any excess dough at the top back on itself to create a rim. Preheat the oven to 400°F (200°C/gas 6) about 20 minutes before you bake.

7. LINE the crust in the pan with foil. Fill with pie weights or dried beans. Bake for 5 minutes. Lower the temperature to 375°F (190°C/gas 5) and remove the foil and weights. Bake for 5–10 minutes, until firm and golden.

8. THE CRUST should be pale golden brown, baked enough to be filled and eaten as is, or ready for more baking with the filling.

You can also make single portion tartlets or pies using the same techniques. Mini tarts and pies are slightly more time consuming to prepare, but they are very attractive to serve.

Pies

Most pies have a flaky pastry (*pâte brisée*) crust. The top can be plain or latticed. You can mix the dough in a food processor or by hand. When baking a pie with a smooth top and an enclosed filling, remember that the filling will produce steam during baking which must escape otherwise the top of the pie will puff up or the filling will burst the edges and seep out.
To prevent this from happening, cut vents into the top of the pie with a sharp knife or skewer so that the steam can escape.

Flaky Pastry

1. BY MACHINE: Put the flour and salt in a food processor. Add the butter and pulse until coarse crumbs form. Add the liquid and pulse until the dough comes together.

2. BY HAND: Combine the flour and salt in a bowl. Cut or rub in the butter until coarse crumbs form. Add the liquid and stir with a rubber spatula until a dough forms.

3. PRESS the dough into a disk. Wrap in plastic wrap and chill for 1 hour. Unwrap, divide in half, and roll out one piece into a large disk. Re-wrap the other piece and chill.

4. ROLL the pastry around the rolling pin and drape over a pie pan. Trim the top edge by running the rolling pin over it.

5. PREPARE the filling and spoon it into the crust. Roll out the remaining dough and place over the filling, tucking in the edges. Use a knife to cut vents in the top for steam to escape during baking.

6. FOR A LATTICE-TOPPED PIE, roll the remaining dough into a circle just slightly larger than the pan. Cut into 3/4-inch (2-cm) strips.

7. PLACE half the strips over the filling in one direction. Fold back every other strip a little past the center. Place a strip crosswise on top. Unfold the strips. Fold back the strips that were not folded back before. Lay a second strip crosswise on top.

8. CONTINUE until all the strips are on the pie. Trim the strips to a 1/2 inch (1 cm) overhang. Moisten with water and tuck the strips in under the crust.

pastries

In English, pastries is a hold-all term for a variety of preparations made with a flour and fat-based dough. The sweet tart pastry and the flaky pastry on the previous pages are both pastries, as are the tarts and pies they produce. Other pastries include puff pastry, strudel pastry, choux pastry, and the various pastries used to make breakfast "pastries," such as croissants.

Choux Pastry

Choux pastry (*pâte à choux*), is a light pastry dough used to make cream puffs (profiteroles), éclairs, croquembouches, beignets, St. Honoré cake, and gougères, among other things. (See pages 264–275 for our recipes using choux pastry.) It is made with butter, water, flour, and eggs and, instead of a raising agent, it employs high moisture content to create steam during cooking to puff the pastry. See page 264 for the exact ingredients.

1. PLACE the water, butter, and salt in a medium saucepan over medium heat and bring to a boil. Add the flour and cook, stirring vigorously with a wooden spoon, until the dough begins to come away from the sides of the pan, 1–2 minutes.

2. BY MACHINE: Transfer the hot water and butter mixture to the bowl of a stand mixer fitted with a beater attachment. Beat for 1 minute, until cooled slightly. Add the eggs gradually, beating until the dough is smooth, glossy, and drops off a spoon. You may not need all the egg. The mixture should hold its shape when piped.

3. BY HAND: Set the mixture aside for 5 minutes, to cool slightly. Add the first three eggs, one at a time, stirring vigorously to incorporate after each addition. Lightly beat the remaining egg in a small bowl and add, one tablespoon at a time, until smooth and glossy and drops off a spoon. You may not need all the egg. The mixture should hold its shape when piped.

Puff Pastry

Puff pastry is used in a huge variety of dishes, both sweet and savory. It is not simple or quick to make and easily available at the supermarket but it is fun sometimes to try your hand at some "real" cooking. Puff pastry is made by repeatedly rolling and folding layers of dough and solid fat (usually butter). The pastry rises during baking because the steam caught between the layers pushes it up. You will need to pierce the dough repeatedly with a fork to prevent it from rising too much. See page 224 for the exact ingredients.

1. PLACE the flour and chilled diced butter in a food processor and blend to resemble coarse crumbs. Combine the water and lemon juice in a small bowl. Gradually add the lemon water to the food processor, pulsing to roughly combine.

2. TURN OUT onto a clean work surface and gently knead until it comes together as a dough.

3. SHAPE the dough into a ball and cut a deep cross in the top. Wrap in plastic wrap (cling film) and chill for at least two hours.

4. LEAVE the butter at room temperature for 20 minutes. Dust with flour, place between two sheets of parchment paper, and roll into a 7 inch (18 cm) square, about $^2/_3$ inch (1.5 cm) thick. Wrap and chill until it is the same consistency as the pastry when it comes time to roll out.

5. LIGHTLY FLOUR a work surface and place the rested pastry on top. Using a lightly floured rolling pin, roll out to make a 12 inch (30 cm) square. Place the butter square in the center of the dough and rotate so it faces you like a diamond with the corners pointing to the sides of the dough.

6. TAKE the corners of the pastry and fold in to meet in the center of the butter square, slightly overlapping to completely enclose the butter. Press down firmly across the seams with a rolling pin to seal. Roll out lengthwise to increase by approximately three times in length to make a $^1/_2$-inch (1-cm) thick, 12 x 24-inch (30 x 60-cm) rectangle.

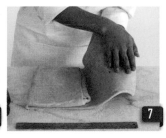

7. WITH the longest end facing you, fold the left third of the pastry into the center over the middle third. Fold the right third over to cover the two layers. Press lightly to seal. Turn 90 degrees clockwise, so that the seams are now pointing to the left and right of you. Roll out again to make a $^1/_2$-inch (1-cm) thick, 12 x 24-inch (30 x 60-cm) rectangle and fold as before. This completes the first two turns. Puff pastry requires six turns in total.

Wrap in plastic wrap (cling film) and chill for 30 minutes. Repeat the rolling and folding two more times, resting in the refrigerator for 30 minutes in between every two turns. For the final rest, wrap the pastry in plastic wrap and refrigerate for at least 2 hours, or overnight.

8. LEAVE OUT at room temperature for 20–30 minutes before rolling so that it is rollable but not too soft.

Croissant Dough

Croissant dough is prepared in much the same way as puff pastry, although unlike puff pastry, croissant dough contains yeast to help it rise. See page 241 for the exact ingredients.

1. IF MIXING BY MACHINE, combine the flour, sugar, and salt in the bowl of a stand mixer fitted with a dough hook. If using instant dried yeast, sprinkle it into the bowl. Mix on low speed to combine.

2. IF USING FRESH YEAST, mix with a little of the milk in a small bowl. Let rest until foamy, about 5 minutes. Add to the dough and mix on low speed for 1–2 minutes, until it comes away from the sides of the bowl. Increase the speed to medium-low and mix until soft and smooth, 2–3 minutes.

3. IF MIXING BY HAND, mix the ingredients together in a large bowl. Turn out onto a clean unfloured work surface. Knead until soft and smooth, 10–15 minutes. Place in a bowl, cover with plastic wrap, and rest in the refrigerator for 2 hours.

4. LEAVE the butter at room temperature for 20 minutes. Dust the butter with flour and place between two sheets of parchment paper. Roll out into a 5 x 8-inch (13 x 20-cm) rectangle about ⅔ inch (1.5 cm) thick. Wrap and chill until the same consistency as the pastry when it comes time to roll out.

5. FLOUR a clean work surface and flatten the dough, knocking out the air. Use a floured rolling pin to make a 10-inch (25-cm) square about ½ inch (1 cm) thick. Place the butter in the center and rotate so it faces you like a diamond. Take the corners of the dough and fold in to meet in the center of the butter square, slightly overlapping to enclose the butter. Press down across the seams with the rolling pin to seal.

6. ROLL the dough out to make a ½-inch (1-cm) thick, 12 x 16-inch (30 x 40-cm) rectangle, stretching out the dough to make the sides straight. With the longest end facing you, fold the left third of the pastry into the center over the middle third. Fold the right third over to cover the two layers, as if folding a letter to put into an envelope.

7. WRAP in plastic wrap (cling film) and chill for 1 hour. Place on a lightly floured work surface and turn the dough 90 degrees clockwise, so that the seams are pointing to the left and right of you. Roll out again to ½ inch (1 cm) thick and fold as before. Wrap and chill for 1 hour. Finally, roll out the dough as before. This time, to fold, bring the two ends into the center to meet and fold them together as if closing a book. Wrap the dough in plastic wrap and chill for 4 hours, or overnight.

8. LEAVE OUT at room temperature for 20–30 minutes, to soften slightly before using it to prepare the croissants.

Strudel Dough

Strudel is a filled pastry roll made using a very elastic layered pastry dough. Strudel was first made in Hungary, but is now usually linked to the famous apple strudel made in Austria. Many modern recipes suggest that you use filo (phyllo) pastry to make strudel, and if you are short of time, filo pastry can be a good alternative. However, if you have a little time and patience nothing beats strudel made with the traditional dough. See page 251 for the exact ingredients.

1. SIFT the flour and salt into a medium bowl and make a well in the center.

2. BEAT the egg, water, and oil in a small bowl and pour into the well. Using a fork, work the flour into the liquid to make a sticky dough.

3. TURN the dough out onto a floured work surface and knead until soft, smooth, and elastic, about 5 minutes. Shape into two balls and place in oiled bowls, rolling to coat. Cover with plastic wrap (cling film) and let rest at room temperature for 1 hour.

4. COVER a kitchen table with a clean cloth and lightly dust with flour. You need to be able to easily move around all four sides of the table as you stretch the dough out.

5. USING A ROLLING PIN, roll out one of the dough balls as thinly as possible. Brush with melted butter, to prevent it from drying out. Cover with a clean kitchen cloth and leave to rest for 30 minutes.

6. WORKING your way around the table, gently pull the edges of the dough to stretch it until very thin. Lightly flour your hands and curl your fingers under to make a loose fist. Place your hands with the backs facing up underneath the dough and, working from the center, gently pull and stretch the dough until it is paper thin. It should be almost transparent and thin enough that you could read a newspaper through it. Patch up any tears or holes.

7. USE scissors to cut off the thick edges and trim to make a rectangle. Drizzle with melted butter and gently brush or rub over the pastry, taking care not to tear it. Use immediately.

cookies,
bars & brownies

This chapter features 31 recipes,
from classic chocolate chip cookies and
shortbread, to crisp meringues and
macaroons and gooey chocolate brownies.

Makes: about 25 cookies
Preparation: 15 minutes
Cooking: 10–15 minutes
Level: 1

. . . . .

These delicious, chewy cookies come from Australia and New Zealand. They take their name from the Australian and New Zealand Army Corps (ANZAC) which was set up in World War I. Wives and mothers of soldiers serving overseas would bake these long-lasting cookies and send them to their husbands and sons.

ANZAC BISCUITS

³/₄   cup (125 g) all-purpose (plain) flour

³/₄   cup (150 g) sugar

¹/₂   cup (60 g) shredded (desiccated) coconut

1   cup (100 g) old-fashioned (rolled) oats

¹/₃   cup (90 g) salted butter

2   tablespoons light corn syrup (or golden syrup)

1   tablespoon boiling water

¹/₂   teaspoon baking soda (bicarbonate of soda)

Preheat the oven to 350°F (180°C/gas 4). Grease two large baking sheets and line with parchment paper.

Combine the flour, sugar, coconut, and oats in a bowl.

Melt the butter and corn syrup together in a small saucepan over medium-low heat.

Mix the boiling water and baking soda together in a small bowl. Add to the butter mixture and stir to combine. Pour the liquid into the dry ingredients and mix well to form a stiff dough.

Roll heaped tablespoons of the dough into balls and place about 1¹/₂ inches (4 cm) apart on the prepared baking sheets. Flatten slightly with the back of a fork.

Bake for 10–15 minutes, until golden brown. Rotate the baking sheets halfway through for even baking.

Let the cookies cool on the baking sheets for 2–3 minutes, until they are firm enough to move. Transfer to a wire rack and let cool completely.

. . .

If you liked this recipe, you will love these as well.

CHOCOLATE CHIP COOKIES   GINGERSNAPS   AFGHAN COOKIES

CHOCOLATE CHIP COOKIES

1½	cups (225 g) all-purpose (plain) flour
1	teaspoon baking powder
½	cup (120 g) unsalted butter, softened
½	cup (100 g) firmly packed light brown sugar
1	teaspoon vanilla extract (essence)
1	large egg, lightly beaten
1	cup (180 g) dark or milk chocolate chips

Preheat the oven to 350°F (180°C/gas 4). Grease two large baking sheets and line with parchment paper. Sift the flour and baking powder into a bowl.

Beat the butter, brown sugar, and vanilla in a large bowl with an electric mixer on medium speed until creamy. Add the egg and beat until just combined. With the mixer on low speed, beat in the flour mixture, scraping down the sides occasionally, until just combined. Stir in the chocolate chips by hand.

Roll tablespoons of dough into balls and place 1 inch (2.5 cm) apart on the prepared baking sheets. Flatten slightly with the back of a fork.

Bake for 10–15 minutes, until golden. Rotate the baking sheets halfway through for even baking. Let the cookies cool on the baking sheets for 2–3 minutes, until they are firm enough to move. Transfer to a wire rack and let cool completely.

Makes: about 20 cookies Preparation: 15 minutes Cooking: 10–15 minutes Level: 1

GINGERSNAPS

1½	cup (225 g) all-purpose (plain) flour
1	tablespoon ground ginger
1	teaspoon baking soda (bicarbonate of soda)
1	teaspoon ground cinnamon
½	teaspoon pumpkin pie (mixed) spice
½	cup (120 g) unsalted butter, softened
½	cup (100 g) firmly packed light brown sugar
⅓	cup (80 ml) light corn (golden) syrup
	Raw sugar, to sprinkle

Preheat the oven to 350°F (180°C/gas 4). Grease two large baking sheets and line with parchment paper. Sift the flour, ginger, baking soda, cinnamon, and spice into a bowl.

Beat the butter, brown sugar, and corn syrup in a bowl with an electric mixer on medium speed until creamy. With the mixer on low speed, beat in the flour mixture, until just combined.

Roll the mixture into twenty-four even balls and place ¾ inch (2 cm) apart on the prepared baking sheets. Flatten slightly with the palm of your hand and sprinkle with raw sugar.

Bake for 10–15 minutes, until golden. Rotate the baking sheets halfway through for even baking.

Let the cookies cool on the baking sheets for 2–3 minutes, until they are firm enough to move. Transfer to a wire rack and let cool completely.

Makes: about 24 cookies Preparation: 15 minutes Cooking: 10–15 minutes Level: 1

Chocolate chip cookies were invented in Massachusetts in the 1930s. When restaurant owner and chef Ruth Wakefield ran out of baker's chocolate she replaced it in her cookies with chunks of dark chocolate that did not melt during baking. The cookies were so delicious that they quickly became a hit.

Gingersnaps, or gingernuts as they are known in the United Kingdom and many other parts of the world, should be dense and chewy. Every oven is different, so you must learn to adjust the baking time for your oven to achieve the perfect point of chewiness.

Makes: 16–24 pieces
Preparation: 30 minutes
+ 30 minutes to chill
Cooking: 35–40 minutes
Level: 1

Shortbread is a classic Scottish cookie, traditionally made with one part sugar, two parts butter, and three parts flour. Its high fat content gives it a crumbly texture and a delicious, rich flavor. There are many variations on the classic recipe.

SHORTBREAD

2½   cups (375 g) all-purpose (plain) flour
½   cup (75 g) rice flour
1   cup (250 g) salted butter, softened
1   cup (150 g) confectioners' (icing) sugar
1   large egg white, lightly beaten
1–2   tablespoons granulated sugar, to sprinkle

Mark 8-inch (20-cm) circles onto two pieces of parchment paper. Grease two large baking sheets and line with the parchment paper, marked-side facing down. Sift both flours into a bowl.

Beat the butter and confectioners' sugar in a bowl with an electric mixer on medium speed until pale and creamy. With the mixer on low speed, beat in the flour mixture, scraping down the sides occasionally, until just combined.

Turn out onto a clean work surface and gently knead to form a dough. Divide in half and shape into disks.

Place the disks in the center of the marked circles and roll out, using a lightly floured rolling pin, to the size of the circles and an even thickness of about ⅔ inch (1.5 cm). Use your thumb and index finger to pinch around the edges to make a decorative border.

Mark eight or twelve wedges in the top of each shortbread circle with a sharp knife. Prick all over with a fork. Refrigerate for 30 minutes.

Preheat the oven to 300°F (150°C/gas 2). Brush the shortbread with egg white and sprinkle with sugar.

Bake for 35–40 minutes, until pale golden brown and firm to the touch. Rotate the baking sheets halfway through for even baking.

Leave on the baking sheets to cool completely. Cut through the markings using a sharp knife, and serve.

• • •

If you liked this recipe, you will love these as well.

ANZAC BISCUITS
CHOCOLATE CHIP COOKIES
PEANUT BUTTER COOKIES

Makes: about 30
    cookies
Preparation: 15 minutes
    + 2 hours to chill
Cooking: 8–10 minutes
Level: 1

The salt in these crisp cookies contrasts deliciously with the sweet peanut flavor of the rest of the dough. Be sure to use sea salt flakes; smooth salt won't create the same effect.

PEANUT BUTTER COOKIES

2   cups (300 g) all-purpose (plain) flour

1¹/₂   tablespoons sea salt flakes + extra, to sprinkle

1   teaspoon baking soda (bicarbonate of soda)

1   cup (250 g) unsalted butter, softened

1   cup (200 g) firmly packed light brown sugar

¹/₂   cup (100 g) superfine (caster) sugar

1   teaspoon vanilla extract (essence)

2   large eggs

1¹/₂   cups (350 g) unsalted, crunchy peanut butter

Sift the flour, salt, and baking soda into a bowl. Beat the butter, brown sugar, superfine sugar, and vanilla in a large bowl with an electric mixer on medium speed until creamy. Add the eggs one at a time, beating well between each addition. Add the peanut butter and beat to combine. With the mixer on low speed, beat in the flour mixture, scraping down the sides occasionally, until just combined. Refrigerate until firm, about 2 hours.

Preheat the oven to 375°F (190°C/gas 5). Grease four large baking sheets and line with parchment paper.

Roll 2 tablespoons of dough into balls and place about 2 inches (5 cm) apart on the prepared baking sheets. Flatten slightly with the back of a fork and sprinkle with extra sea salt flakes.

Bake for 8–10 minutes, until golden around the edges but still soft in the center. Rotate the baking sheets halfway through for even baking.

Let cool completely on the baking sheets.

. . .

If you liked this recipe, you will love these as well.

ANZAC BISCUITS

CHOCOLATE CHIP COOKIES

SHORTBREAD

Makes: about 20 cookies
Preparation: 30 minutes
 + time to cool
Cooking: 35 minutes
Level: 2

. . . . .

Biscotti are a classic Italian cookie. They are named for their cooking method; biscotti means "cooked twice" in Italian. See page 19 for detailed instructions on how to prepare them.

PISTACHIO BISCOTTI

2 cups (300 g) all-purpose (plain) flour

1 teaspoon baking powder

1 cup (200 g) superfine (caster) sugar

2 large eggs

Finely grated zest of 1 unwaxed lemon

1 cup (150 g) unsalted pistachio kernels

Granulated sugar, to roll

Preheat the oven to 350°F (180°C/gas 4). Grease two large baking sheets and line with parchment paper. Sift the flour and baking powder into a bowl.

Beat the sugar, eggs, and lemon zest in a large bowl with an electric mixer on medium speed until light and fluffy. With the mixer on low speed, beat in the flour mixture, scraping down the sides occasionally, until just combined. Stir in the pistachios by hand.

Turn out onto a clean work surface and gently knead to form a dough. Divide in half and shape into two 10 x 2-inch (25 x 5-cm) logs. Roll the logs in the granulated sugar to coat and place on the prepared baking sheets.

Bake for about 20 minutes, until firm and pale golden brown. Leave on the sheet until cool enough to handle.

Decrease the oven temperature to 300°F (150°C/gas 2).

Using a serrated knife, cut the half-baked cookie logs into $2/3$-inch (1.5-cm) thick slices. Arrange the slices on the baking sheets. Bake for about 15 more minutes, until crisp and golden. Rotate the baking sheets halfway through for even baking.

Let the cookies cool on the baking sheets for 2–3 minutes, until they are firm enough to move. Transfer to a wire rack and let cool completely.

. . .

If you liked this recipe, you will love these as well.

FLORENTINE COOKIES

PISTACHIO & ROSEWATER MACARONS

SALTY PEANUT BARS

Makes: 30 cookies

Preparation: 20 minutes

Cooking: 10–15 minutes

Level: 1

· · · · ·

Afghan biscuits (cookies) are a classic from New Zealand. These crunchy cookies have relatively little sugar in the base which is made with plenty of butter and cornflakes. The sweetness is given by the delicious chocolate frosting.

AFGHAN BISCUITS

Cookies

1¼	cups (180 g) all-purpose (plain) flour
¼	cup (30 g) unsweetened cocoa powder
½	teaspoon baking powder
¾	cup (180 g) unsalted butter, softened
½	cup (100 g) firmly packed light brown sugar
2	cups (60 g) cornflakes
20	walnut halves, to decorate

Chocolate Frosting

2	cups (300 g) confectioner's (icing) sugar
3	tablespoons unsweetened cocoa powder
1–2	tablespoons boiling water
½	teaspoon vanilla extract (essence)

Cookies: Preheat the oven to 350°F (180°C/gas 4). Grease two large baking sheets and line with parchment paper. Sift the flour, cocoa, and baking powder into a bowl.

Beat the butter and brown sugar in a large bowl with an electric mixer on medium speed until creamy. With the mixer on low speed, beat in the flour mixture, scraping down the sides occasionally, until just combined. Stir in the cornflakes by hand.

Shape the dough into 30 even balls and place about ¾ inch (2 cm) apart on the prepared baking sheets. Flatten slightly with your hand.

Bake for 10–15 minutes, until firm to the touch. Rotate the baking sheets halfway through for even baking.

Let the cookies cool on the baking sheets for 2–3 minutes, until they are firm enough to move. Transfer to a wire rack and let cool completely.

Chocolate Frosting: Sift the confectioners' sugar and cocoa into a bowl. Stir in enough boiling water to make a smooth frosting. Stir in the vanilla.

Spoon a dollop of frosting onto each cookie and top with a walnut half. Allow the frosting to set before serving.

· · ·

If you liked this recipe, you will love these as well.

CRACKED CHEWY
CHOCOLATE COOKIES

CHOCOLATE WALNUT
BROWNIES

CHOCOLATE CARAMEL
SLICE

. . . . .

These cookies should be cracked and chewy. The chewiness will depend on how long they are cooked and on how hot or true to temperature your oven is. Generally speaking, the longer you bake the cookies, the less chewy and crisper they will be. Experiment!

CRACKED CHEWY CHOCOLATE COOKIES

7	ounces (200 g) bittersweet dark chocolate, coarsely chopped
3/4	cup (120 g) all-purpose (plain) flour
1/4	cup (30 g) unsweetened cocoa powder
2	teaspoons baking powder
1/3	cup (30 g) almond meal (ground almonds)
1 1/2	cups (300 g) firmly packed light brown sugar
1/2	cup (120 g) unsalted butter, softened
1	teaspoon vanilla extract (essence)
2	large eggs
1	cup (150 g) confectioners' (icing) sugar

Melt the chocolate in a heatproof bowl set over a saucepan of barely simmering water, ensuring the base of the bowl does not touch the water. Set aside to cool slightly.

Sift the flour, cocoa, and baking powder into a bowl. Stir in the almonds. Beat the brown sugar, butter, and vanilla in a large bowl with an electric mixer on medium speed until creamy. Add the melted chocolate, beating to combine. Add the eggs one at a time, beating until just combined after each addition. With the mixer on low speed, beat in the flour mixture, scraping down the sides occasionally, until just combined.

Cover the bowl and refrigerate until the dough is firm enough to roll easily, about 1 hour.

Preheat the oven to 350°F (180°C/gas 4). Grease two large baking sheets and line with parchment paper.

Roll the cookie dough into 30 even balls. Roll the balls in confectioners' sugar, coating thoroughly, and place about 1 1/2 inches (4 cm) apart on the prepared baking sheets.

Bake for 10–12 minutes, until cracked and with a slightly firm crust. Rotate the baking sheets halfway through for even baking.

Let the cookies cool on the baking sheets for 2–3 minutes, until they are firm enough to move. Transfer to a wire rack and let cool completely.

. . .

If you liked this recipe, you will love these as well.

CHOCOLATE CHIP COOKIES

AFGHAN COOKIES

FLORENTINE COOKIES

Makes: 20 cookies
Preparation: 30 minutes
+ 1 1/2 hours to chill
Cooking: 8–10 minutes
Level: 2

. . . . .

Baking gingerbread in the shape of people is an ancient art dating back to the 16th century, if not before. An early fan, Queen Elizabeth I (1533–1603) of England had gingerbread men baked in the shape of some of her most famous party guests.

GINGERBREAD PEOPLE

Gingerbread

3	cups (450 g) all-purpose (plain) flour
3	teaspoons ground ginger
1	teaspoon baking soda (bicarbonate of soda)
1	teaspoon ground cinnamon
1/2	teaspoon ground nutmeg
1	cup (200 g) firmly packed light brown sugar
1/2	cup (120 g) unsalted butter, softened
1/2	cup (120 ml) corn (golden) syrup
1	large egg

Decoration

1	cup (150 g) confectioners' (icing) sugar
1–2	tablespoons boiling water
	Currants, to decorate
	Colored chocolate buttons, to decorate
	Few drops red food coloring

Gingerbread: Sift the flour, ginger, baking soda, cinnamon, and nutmeg into a bowl. Beat the brown sugar, butter, and corn syrup in a bowl with an electric mixer on medium speed until creamy. Add the egg and beat until just combined. With the mixer on low speed, beat in the flour mixture, scraping down the sides occasionally, until just combined. Divide the mixture in half and shape into disks. Wrap in plastic wrap (cling film) and refrigerate for 1 hour.

Preheat the oven to 350°F (180°C/gas 4). Grease two large baking sheets and line with parchment paper.

Roll the dough out between two sheets of parchment paper to 1/4 inch (5 mm) thick. Use a 3 1/2-inch (9-cm) gingerbread-person-shaped cutter to cut out the cookies and place about 3/4 inch (2 cm) apart on the prepared baking sheets. Gather the dough scraps, shape into a disk, re-wrap in plastic wrap, and chill for 30 minutes. Re-roll, cut, and cook.

Bake for 8–10 minutes, until golden brown. Rotate the baking sheets halfway through for even baking.

Let the cookies cool on the baking sheets for 2–3 minutes, until they are firm enough to move. Transfer to a wire rack and let cool completely.

Decoration: Combine the confectioners' sugar with enough of the boiling water to make a smooth frosting. Decorate the gingerbread people with currants for eyes and three colored chocolate buttons down the center, placing a dot of frosting behind each to secure. Tint the remaining frosting red and pipe a smile on each gingerbread face. Allow to set before serving.

. . .

If you liked this recipe, you will love these as well.

GINGERSNAPS   GINGER KISSES   GINGERBREAD & PEAR
                                                    LOAF

Makes: about 20 cookies
Preparation: 30 minutes
Cooking: 10–15 minutes
Level: 2

These slender cookies are a mix of flaked almonds, candied fruit, and caramel baked until crisp and then spread with dark chocolate. For a change, you can also spread them with melted milk or white chocolate.

FLORENTINE COOKIES

2	cups (160 g) flaked almonds
¹⁄₂	cup (100 g) red candied (glacé) cherries, coarsely chopped
2	tablespoons candied (glacé) mixed peel, coarsely chopped
¹⁄₄	cup (60 g) unsalted butter
¹⁄₄	cup (50 g) firmly packed light brown sugar
1	tablespoon honey
¹⁄₃	cup (50 g) all-purpose (plain) flour
4	ounces (120 g) dark chocolate, coarsely chopped

Preheat the oven to 350°F (180°C/gas 4). Grease four large baking sheets and line with parchment paper.

Combine the almonds, cherries, and mixed peel in a bowl, mixing well.

Melt the butter, brown sugar, and honey in a small saucepan over medium-low heat. Remove from the heat, sift in the flour and stir to combine. Pour into the almond mixture and stir to combine. Drop teaspoons of the mixture about 3 inches (8 cm) apart on the prepared baking sheets.

Bake for 10–15 minutes, until golden brown. Rotate the baking sheets halfway through for even baking.

Let the cookies cool on the baking sheets for 2–3 minutes, until they are firm enough to move. Transfer to a wire rack and let cool completely.

Melt the chocolate in a heatproof bowl set over a saucepan of barely simmering water, ensuring the base of the bowl does not touch the water.

Spread the chocolate on one side of the cookies and return to the rack chocolate-side up until set.

. . .

If you liked this recipe, you will love these as well.

PISTACHIO BISCOTTI

BRANDY SNAPS

ALMOND TUILES

. . . . .

Unfilled brandy snaps can be made in advance and stored in an airtight container for up to two days. Don't fill the cookies until just before serving; if you fill them too far ahead of time they will become soggy.

BRANDY SNAPS

½ cup (75 g) all-purpose (plain) flour

1 teaspoon ground ginger

⅓ cup (70 g) firmly packed dark brown sugar

¼ cup (60 g) salted butter

3 tablespoons light corn syrup (or golden syrup)

1¼ cups (300 ml) light whipping cream

1 tablespoon confectioners' (icing) sugar

1 tablespoon brandy

Preheat the oven to 350°F (180°C/gas 4). Grease two large baking sheets and line with parchment paper. Sift the flour and ginger into a bowl.

Lightly grease the handle of a wooden spoon with oil spray.

Melt the brown sugar, butter, and corn syrup in a small saucepan over medium-low heat. Remove from the heat and stir in the flour mixture. Drop four tablespoons of mixture about 2 inches (5 cm) apart on each of the prepared baking sheets.

Bake for 7–10 minutes, until bubbled and golden brown. Rotate the baking sheets halfway through for even baking.

Working quickly, lift the circles, one at a time using a spatula, and loosely wrap around the handle of the greased wooden spoon to create a tube. Press lightly to seal. Leave for a moment, to cool and set. Slide off and place on the rack to cool completely. Repeat with the remaining mixture.

Whip the cream, confectioners' sugar, and brandy in a bowl until firm peaks form. Spoon the cream into a pastry (piping) bag fitted with a star nozzle.

Fill the cooled brandy snap tubes with cream when ready to serve.

. . .

If you liked this recipe, you will love these as well.

FLORENTINE COOKIES

CHOCOLATE-COATED ALFAJORES

ALMOND TUILES

Makes: 12 filled cookies

Preparation: 30 minutes + 3½ hours to cool, chill & set

Cooking: 3 hours + 8–10 minutes

Level: 3

. . . . .

Alfajores are classic cookies from Spain and many parts of Latin America. Their name suggests that they were originally of Arabic origin. There are many variations; ours is basic and classic (and delicious!)

Take care when simmering the sweetened condensed milk; the can should always be completely covered with water, otherwise it may explode.

CHOCOLATE-COATED ALFAJORES

1	(14-ounce/400-ml) can sweetened condensed milk
1½	cups (225 g) cornstarch (cornflour)
1	cup (150 g) all-purpose (plain) flour
½	cup (75 g) confectioners' (icing) sugar
1	cup (250 g) unsalted butter, melted and cooled
½	cup (120 ml) light (single) cream
7	ounces (200 g) bittersweet dark chocolate

To make the dulce de leche filling, place the unopened can of sweetened condensed milk in a medium saucepan, cover completely with water and bring to a boil. Simmer on low heat for 3 hours. Top up with boiling water as required to keep the can completely covered, otherwise it may explode. Drain and set aside to cool completely before opening, at least 1 hour.

Preheat the oven to 350°F (180°C/gas 4). Grease two large baking sheets and line with parchment paper.

Sift the cornstarch, flour, and confectioners' sugar into a medium bowl. Pour in the cooled butter and stir to combine. Knead to form a dough.

Roll the dough out between two sheets of parchment paper to ½ inch (1 cm) thick. Cut out rounds using a 2½-inch (6-cm) cookie cutter. Place about ¾ inch (2 cm) apart on the prepared baking sheets. Gather the dough scraps, shape into a disk, re-wrap in plastic wrap, and chill for 30 minutes. Re-roll, cut, and cook. You need twenty-four rounds in total.

Bake for 8–10 minutes, until golden. Rotate the baking sheets halfway through for even baking.

Let the cookies cool on the baking sheets for 2–3 minutes, until they are firm enough to move. Transfer to a wire rack and let cool completely.

Spread a thick layer of the dulce de leche on half of the cooled cookies and sandwich together with the other half.

Place the cream in a small saucepan and bring almost to a boil. Place the chocolate in a heatproof bowl, pour in the hot cream and set aside for a few minutes, until the chocolate has melted. Stir until smooth.

Spread the chocolate mixture over the cookies. Stand at room temperature until set, about 2 hours, before serving.

Makes: 30 filled cookies
Preparation: 30 minutes
  + 1 hour to chill
Cooking: 10–15 minutes
Level: 1

These cookies are a favorite in Australia and New Zealand.

BELGIUM BISCUITS

Cookies

3   cups (450 g) all-purpose (plain) flour
2   teaspoons baking powder
2   teaspoons pumpkin pie spice (mixed spice)
1   teaspoon ground cinnamon + extra, for dusting
1   teaspoon unsweetened cocoa powder
1   teaspoon ground ginger
1   cup (250 g) salted butter, softened
1   cup (200 g) firmly packed light brown sugar
1   large egg
½   cup (160 g) raspberry preserves (jam)

Frosting

2   cups (300 g) confectioners' (icing) sugar
1–2 tablespoons milk
     Few drops red food coloring

Cookies: Preheat the oven to 350°F (180°C/gas 4). Grease four large baking sheets and line with parchment paper. Sift the flour, baking powder, pumpkin pie spice, cinnamon, cocoa, and ginger into a bowl.

Beat the butter and brown sugar in a bowl with an electric mixer on medium speed until creamy. Add the egg and beat to combine. With the mixer on low speed, beat in the flour mixture until just combined. Divide the dough in half and shape into disks. Wrap in plastic wrap (cling film) and chill for 30 minutes.

Roll the dough out between two sheets of parchment paper to ¼ inch (5 mm) thick. Cut out rounds using a 2-inch (5-cm) cookie cutter. Place about ¾ inch (2 cm) apart on the prepared baking sheets. Gather the dough scraps, shape into a disk, re-wrap in plastic wrap, and chill for 30 minutes. Re-roll, cut, and cook. You need sixty rounds in total.

Bake for 10–15 minutes, until golden brown. Rotate the baking sheets halfway through for even baking.

Let the cookies cool on the baking sheets for 2–3 minutes, until they are firm enough to move. Transfer to a wire rack and let cool completely.

Spread raspberry preserves on half of the cookies and sandwich together with the others.

Frosting: Combine the confectioners' sugar with enough milk in a small bowl to make a smooth frosting. Add a few drops of food coloring to tint pale pink. Spread a teaspoon of frosting on each cookie and dust with ground cinnamon. Allow the frosting to set before serving.

. . .

If you liked this recipe, you will love these as well.

ANZAC BISCUITS   AFGHAN COOKIES   PASSIONFRUIT YOYOS

Makes: 20 filled cookies
Preparation: 30 minutes
Cooking: 10–15 minutes
Level: 1

• • • • •

The custard powder in these cookies gives them a deliciously smooth texture.

PASSIONFRUIT YOYOS

Cookies

1½ cups (225 g) all-purpose (plain) flour
½ cup (75 g) custard powder
1 cup (250 g) unsalted butter, softened
½ cup (75 g) confectioners' (icing) sugar
½ teaspoon vanilla extract (essence)

Passionfruit Filling

⅓ cup (90 g) salted butter, softened
2 cups (300 g) confectioners' (icing) sugar
   Pulp of 2 passionfruit, strained and seeds discarded

Cookies: Preheat the oven to 350°F (180°C/gas 4). Grease four large baking sheets and line with parchment paper. Sift the flour and custard powder into a bowl.

Beat the butter, sugar, and vanilla in a large bowl with an electric mixer on medium speed until pale and creamy. With the mixer on low speed, beat in the flour mixture, scraping down the sides occasionally, until just combined.

Roll the mixture into forty even-size balls and place about 1 inch (2.5 cm) apart on the prepared baking sheets. Flatten slightly with the back of a fork, leaving an imprint with the tines.

Bake for 10–15 minutes, until firm but not colored. Rotate the baking sheets halfway through for even baking.

Let the cookies cool on the baking sheets for 2–3 minutes, until they are firm enough to move. Transfer to a wire rack and let cool completely.

Passionfruit Filling: Beat the butter in a bowl with an electric mixer on medium speed until pale and creamy. Add the confectioners' sugar about ½ cup (75 g) at a time, beating on low speed and scraping down the sides occasionally, until combined. Add the passionfruit juice and beat until smooth and creamy.

Spread the passionfruit filling on the flat side of half of the cookies and sandwich together with the others. Let the filling set before serving.

• • •

If you liked this recipe, you will love these as well.

CHOCOLATE-COATED ALFAJORES

BELGIUM BISCUITS

PISTACHIO & ROSEWATER MACARONS

Makes: 12–16 meringues
Preparation: 30 minutes
    + 12 hours to cool
Cooking: 2 hours
Level: 2

. . . . .

You can make the meringues as large or small as you like. If you make small meringues, stick them together with whipped cream just before serving.

CRISP PASTEL MERINGUES

4	large egg whites
1¼	cups (250 g) superfine (caster) sugar
1	teaspoon vanilla extract (essence)
1–3	drops pink food coloring
1–3	drops blue food coloring

Preheat the oven to 250°F (130°C/gas ½). Grease two large baking sheets and line with parchment paper.

Combine the egg whites, sugar, and vanilla in a heatproof bowl and set over a saucepan of barely simmering water, ensuring the base of the bowl does not touch the water. Stir continuously and scrape down the sides occasionally, until the sugar dissolves and the whites are warm to the touch.

Transfer the mixture to the bowl of an electric mixer and whisk on medium-high speed for 10 minutes, until doubled in volume and stiff glossy peaks form.

Divide the meringue evenly between two bowls. Use the food coloring to tint one bowl pastel pink and the other pale blue.

Spoon the meringues into separate pastry (piping) bags fitted with large star-shaped nozzles and pipe large rosettes of each color onto the prepared baking sheets. If you do not have two pastry bags, spoon the meringue onto the prepared baking sheets.

Decrease the oven temperature to 230°F (110°C/gas ¼).

Bake for 2 hours, until crisp but not colored. Turn the oven off and leave the meringues in the oven overnight with the door ajar.

Peel the meringues off the parchment paper to serve.

. . .

If you liked this recipe, you will love these as well.

PISTACHIO & ROSEWATER MACARONS

COCONUT MACAROONS

MARSHMALLOW PAVLOVA WITH FRESH BERRIES

Makes: 30 macarons
Preparation: 30 minutes
  + 4-5 hours to form
  a crust
Cooking: 10-15 minutes
Level: 3

· · · · ·

Macarons are light, meringue-like French cookies. They come in many flavors, but the classics are pistachio, chocolate, and vanilla. Make sure that the egg whites are at room temperature before you start to beat them with the sugar.

PISTACHIO & ROSEWATER MACARONS

Shells

1½	cups (150 g) almond meal (ground almonds)
1¼	cups (180 g) confectioners' (icing) sugar
3½	ounces (100 g), approximately 4 large egg whites
¼	cup (50 g) superfine (caster) sugar
1-3	drops green food coloring
⅓	cup (40 g) pistachio kernels, finely chopped

Rosewater Filling

½	cup (120 ml) light (single) cream
5	ounces (150 g) good quality white chocolate
¼	teaspoon rosewater
1-2	drops pink food coloring

Shells: Cut two pieces of parchment paper large enough to line two large baking sheets. Mark out sixty 1¼-inch (3-cm) circles about 1 inch (2.5 cm) apart on the paper. Lightly grease two large baking sheets and line with the paper, marked-side facing down.

Combine the almond meal and confectioners' sugar in a food processor and blend to make a powder. Sift twice, discarding any large particles.

Beat the egg whites in a bowl with an electric mixer on medium-high speed until soft peaks form. Gradually add the sugar, beating constantly until the sugar has dissolved and stiff glossy peaks form. Add the food coloring a drop at a time to tint pale green.

Stir a large spoonful of the egg whites into the almond mixture. Fold in the remaining whites until the mixture is glossy and the whites have broken down slightly.

Spoon the mixture into a pastry (piping) bag fitted with a ½-inch (1-cm) nozzle and pipe to the size of the marked circles. Sprinkle with pistachios. Tap the sheets firmly once on a work surface to remove any air bubbles.

Set aside for 4-5 hours, until a crust forms and the shells are no longer sticky to the touch.

Preheat the oven to 275°F (140°C/gas 1). Bake for 10-15 minutes, until firm but not colored. Let cool completely on the baking sheets.

Rosewater Filling: Put the cream in a small saucepan and bring almost to a boil. Place the chocolate in a heatproof bowl, pour in the hot cream, then set aside for a few minutes until melted. Stir until smooth. Add the rosewater and enough food coloring to tint pink.

Refrigerate for 20 minutes, stirring occasionally, until cooled and thickened enough to hold its shape. Spoon or pipe the filling on the flat side of half of the macaron shells and sandwich together with the remaining shells.

COCONUT MACAROONS

4   large egg whites
      Pinch of salt
1   cup (200 g) superfine (caster) sugar
1   teaspoon vanilla extract (essence)
3   cups (375 g) shredded (desiccated) coconut

Preheat the oven to 325°F (170°C/gas 4). Grease two large baking sheets and line with parchment paper.

Beat the egg whites and salt in a large bowl with an electric mixer on medium-high speed until soft peaks form. Gradually add the sugar, beating constantly, until stiff glossy peaks form. Add the vanilla and beat to combine. Fold in the coconut.

Spoon 25 mounds of mixture about 1 inch (2.5 cm) apart on the prepared baking sheets.

Bake for 10–15 minutes, until firm and golden. Rotate the baking sheets halfway through for even baking.

Let the cookies cool on the baking sheets for 2–3 minutes, until they are firm enough to move. Transfer to a wire rack and let cool completely.

Makes: 25 macaroons Preparation: 20 minutes Cooking: 10–15 minutes Level: 1

ALMOND TUILES

2   large egg whites
1/3   cup (80 g) superfine (caster) sugar
1/3   cup (50 g) all-purpose (plain) flour
1/4   cup (60 g) unsalted butter, melted and cooled
1   cup (75 g) flaked almonds

Preheat the oven to 375°F (190°C/gas 5). Cut a piece of parchment paper large enough to line a large baking sheet. Mark out two 4-inch (10-cm) circles. Grease a large baking sheet and line with the paper, marked-side facing down. Lightly grease the length of one half of a rolling pin with oil spray.

Beat the egg whites in a medium bowl using an electric mixer on medium-high speed until frothy. Add the sugar, sift in the flour, and stir to combine. Stir in the butter and almonds, mixing to combine.

Use 1 tablespoon of the mixture to spread evenly to the size of the marked circles on the prepared baking sheet.

Bake for 5–10 minutes, until golden. Working quickly, lift the circles using a spatula and drape over the greased side of the rolling pin. Leave for 30 seconds, until hardened, to create curved cookies. Transfer to a wire rack to cool. Repeat with the remaining mixture.

Makes: 12 tuiles Preparation: 30 minutes Cooking: 30-60 minutes Level: 3

Crisp on the outside and chewy in the middle, coconut macaroons are an irresistible treat with a cup of tea or coffee.

Tuiles are thin, crisp cookies that are curved like the roof tiles they are thought to resemble. They are not hard to make, but you must learn to work quickly. Delicious on their own, they also go very well with ice cream or mousse-like desserts.

Makes: 25 crackers
Preparation: 30 minutes
   + 3 hours to chill
Cooking: 15–20 minutes
Level: 1

· · · · ·

These crisp yet crumbly crackers are perfect with a glass of wine before dinner. Spread with cheese and serve with a bowl of marinated olives.

PARMESAN & ROSEMARY CRACKERS

1	cup (150 g) all-purpose (plain) flour
1/2	cup (120 g) chilled unsalted butter, diced
1	cup (120 g) freshly grated Parmesan cheese
1	tablespoon finely chopped fresh rosemary leaves
2	teaspoons salt flakes
1	teaspoon coarsely ground black pepper
1/4	teaspoon cayenne pepper
1	tablespoon chilled water
3/4	cup (75 g) poppy seeds
1	large egg white, lightly beaten

Combine the flour, butter, Parmesan, rosemary, salt, pepper, and cayenne in a food processor and blend until the mixture resembles coarse bread crumbs. Add the water and blend until a dough begins to form.

Turn out onto a clean, lightly floured work surface and knead to combine. Divide the dough in half and shape into two 2-inch (5-cm) wide cylinders. Wrap in plastic wrap (cling film) and refrigerate for 2 hours.

Spread the poppy seeds out on a large plate. Unwrap the dough, brush with egg white, and roll in the poppy seeds to coat. Re-wrap the dough and refrigerate for another hour.

Preheat the oven to 350°F (180°C/gas 4). Grease two large baking sheets and line with parchment paper.

Cut the cylinders into 1/4-inch (5-mm) thick slices and place about 3/4 inch (2 cm) apart on the prepared baking sheets.

Bake for 15–20 minutes, until golden brown. Rotate the baking sheets halfway through for even baking.

Let the crackers cool on the baking sheets for 2–3 minutes, until they are firm enough to move. Transfer to a wire rack and let cool completely.

OAT CRACKERS

MULTIGRAIN CRACKERS

SALTY PEANUT BARS

Makes: 40 crackers
Preparation: 20 minutes
+ 30 minutes to chill
Cooking: 15 minutes
Level: 1

Oats are a nutritious grain packed with fiber that helps lower cholesterol. Serve these cookies as a healthy afterschool snack or with pre-dinner drinks.

OAT CRACKERS

1½ cups (150 g) old-fashioned (rolled) oats + extra, to sprinkle

1½ cups (225 g) whole-wheat (wholemeal) flour

2 teaspoons salt flakes + extra, to sprinkle

1 teaspoon superfine (caster) sugar

1 teaspoon baking powder

½ cup (120 g) chilled unsalted butter, diced

⅓ cup (90 ml) chilled water

Place the oats in a food processor and blend until coarsely chopped. Add the whole-wheat flour, salt, sugar, and baking powder and blend to combine. Add the butter and blend until the mixture resembles coarse crumbs. Pour in the water and blend until a dough begins to form.

Turn out onto a clean work surface and knead to combine. Divide the dough in half and shape into two disks. Wrap in plastic wrap (cling film) and refrigerate for 30 minutes.

Preheat the oven to 350°F (180°C/gas 4). Grease two large baking sheets and line with parchment paper.

Roll the dough out between two sheets of parchment paper to about ¼ inch (5 mm) thick to make an 8 x 10-inch (20 x 25-cm) rectangle. Trim the edges to straighten. Cut the dough in half lengthwise and then into five crosswise, to make ten rectangles. Cut each rectangle in half diagonally to make twenty triangles.

Place about ¾ inch (2 cm) apart on the prepared baking sheets. Sprinkle with extra oats and salt. Repeat with the remaining dough.

Bake for 15 minutes, until crisp and pale golden brown. Rotate the baking sheets halfway through for even baking.

Let the crackers cool on the baking sheets for 2–3 minutes, until they are firm enough to move. Transfer to a wire rack and let cool completely.

. . .

If you liked this recipe, you will love these as well.

PARMESAN & ROSEMARY CRACKERS

MULTIGRAIN CRACKERS

FRUIT & NUT MUESLI BARS

Makes: 20 crackers
Preparation: 30 minutes
   + 30 minutes to chill
Cooking: 20–25 minutes
Level: 1

. . . . .

Making your own crackers at home means being sure that they contain no unhealthy ingredients.

Gram flour is made from garbanzo beans, or chickpeas. You can buy it wherever Indian foods are sold, or from online suppliers.

MULTIGRAIN CRACKERS

½   cup (75 g) whole-wheat (wholemeal) flour
¼   cup (30 g) all-purpose (plain) flour
¼   cup (30 g) gram (besan) flour
¼   cup (20 g) fine polenta
1   tablespoon ground flaxseeds
2   teaspoons salt flakes
1   teaspoon ground cumin
1   teaspoon ground coriander
1   teaspoon sweet paprika
⅓   cup (90 ml) water
¼   cup (60 ml) extra-virgin olive oil
1   tablespoon honey
2   tablespoons sunflower seeds
2   tablespoons pumpkin seeds
2   tablespoons sesame seeds
1   tablespoon poppy seeds

Combine the whole-wheat, all-purpose, and gram flours with the polenta, ground flaxseed, salt flakes, cumin, coriander, and paprika in a food processor and blend to combine.

Combine the water, oil, and honey in a small bowl. With the motor running, gradually add the liquid to the dry ingredients and blend to combine. Transfer to a bowl, add the sunflower, pumpkin, sesame, and poppy seeds and stir and knead to combine.

Divide the dough in half and shape into two disks. Wrap in plastic wrap (cling film) and refrigerate for 30 minutes.

Preheat the oven to 350°F (180°C/gas 4). Lightly grease two large baking sheets.

Roll the dough out between two sheets of parchment paper to about ¼ inch (5 mm) thick to make an 8 x 10-inch (20 x 25-cm) rectangle. Trim the edges to straighten. Cut the dough in half lengthwise and then into five crosswise, to make ten rectangles.

Place about ¾ inch (2 cm) apart on the prepared baking sheets. Repeat with the remaining dough.

Bake for 20–25 minutes, until crisp and golden brown. Rotate the baking sheets halfway through for even baking.

Let the crackers cool on the baking sheets for 2–3 minutes, until they are firm enough to move. Transfer to a wire rack and let cool completely.

. . .

If you liked this recipe, you will love these as well.

PARMESAN & ROSEMARY CRACKERS

OAT CRACKERS

FRUIT & NUT MUESLI BARS

PECAN BLONDIES

1 cup (150 g) all-purpose (plain) flour
1/2 teaspoon baking powder
1 cup (200 g) firmly packed light brown sugar
1/2 cup (120 g) unsalted butter, melted
1 large egg
1 teaspoon vanilla extract (essence)
3/4 cup (90 g) pecans, coarsely chopped

Preheat the oven to 325°F (170°C/gas 3). Grease and line the base and sides of an 8-inch (20-cm) square deep cake pan with parchment paper. Sift the flour and baking powder into a bowl.

Beat the brown sugar and melted butter in a bowl with an electric mixer on medium speed until creamy. Add the egg and vanilla, beating until just combined. With the mixer on low speed, beat in the flour mixture, scraping down the sides occasionally, until just combined. Stir in the pecans by hand. Pour into the prepared pan and smooth to an even thickness.

Bake for 25–30 minutes, until just set. Leave in the pan to cool completely. Cut into sixteen squares, and serve.

Makes: 16 blondies Preparation: 15 minutes Cooking: 25–30 minutes Level: 1

CHOCOLATE WALNUT BROWNIES

1 1/4 cups (180 g) all-purpose (plain) flour
1/3 cup (50 g) unsweetened cocoa powder + extra, to dust
1/4 teaspoon baking powder
8 ounces (250 g) dark chocolate, chopped
3/4 cup (200 g) butter, coarsely chopped
1 1/4 cups (250 g) firmly packed light brown sugar
3 large eggs
1 teaspoon vanilla extract (essence)
2/3 cup (100 g) walnuts, coarsely chopped

Preheat the oven to 325°F (170°C/gas 3). Grease and line the base and sides of an 8 inch (20 cm) square cake pan with parchment paper. Sift the flour, cocoa, and baking powder into a bowl.

Melt the chocolate and butter in a heatproof bowl set over a saucepan of barely simmering water, ensuring the base of the bowl does not touch the water. Stir occasionally until smooth. Set aside to cool slightly.

Beat the brown sugar, eggs, and vanilla in a bowl with an electric mixer on medium speed until creamy. Gradually pour in the cooled chocolate mixture, beating until combined. With the mixer on low speed, beat in the flour mixture, scraping down the sides occasionally, until just combined. Stir in the walnuts by hand. Pour into the prepared pan and smooth to an even thickness.

Bake for 30–35 minutes, until just set. Let cool completely in the pan. Dust with cocoa, cut into sixteen squares, and serve.

Makes: 16 brownies Preparation: 20 minutes Cooking: 30–35 minutes Level: 1

Blondies are similar to brownies, but instead of being based on cocoa or dark chocolate, they are made with brown sugar or white chocolate. As their name suggests, they are usually a beautiful pale golden brown color.

Brownies should be firm and almost crisp on top but still gooey in the center. The secret lies in the cooking time and oven temperature. Experiment with this classic recipe until you get it just right.

Makes: 20 squares
Preparation: 30 minutes
+ 30 minutes to chill
Cooking: 25–30 minutes
Level: 2

. . . . .

Add a piece of this hearty and nutritious square to school lunch boxes, or serve with coffee at breakfast or brunch.

RAISIN SLICE

Pastry

2 cups (300 g) all-purpose (plain) flour
1/4 cup (50 g) superfine (caster) sugar
1 teaspoon baking powder
1/2 cup (120 g) chilled unsalted butter, diced
1/4 cup (60 ml) milk + extra, to brush
1 large egg
Granulated sugar, to sprinkle

Filling

3 cups (540 g) raisins
1/2 cup (120 ml) water
2 tablespoons freshly squeezed lemon juice
2 teaspoons dark corn syrup (or golden syrup)
Finely grated zest of 1 unwaxed lemon

Pastry: Grease the base and sides of a 1¼-inch (3-cm) deep, 8 x 12-inch (20 x 30-cm) cake pan. Line with parchment paper, extending the paper 2 inches (5 cm) above the rim of the pan.

Combine the flour, sugar, and baking powder in a food processor and pulse until well mixed. Add the butter and pulse until the mixture resembles coarse crumbs. Lightly beat the milk and egg in a small bowl. With the motor running, gradually add the egg mixture. Turn out onto a clean work surface and bring the mixture together, to form a dough. Divide in half and shape into two disks. Wrap in plastic wrap (cling film) and refrigerate for 30 minutes.

Filling: Combine the raisins, water, lemon juice, corn syrup, and lemon zest in a medium saucepan and simmer over low heat for 5–10 minutes, until the mixture is thick and the raisins are plump. Set aside to cool.

Preheat the oven to 350°F (180°C/gas 4).

Roll the pastry out between two sheets of parchment paper to make a rectangle large enough to line the base of the prepared pan. Line and press into the pan.

Spread the filling over the base, making an even layer.

Roll out the remaining pastry disk to the same size as the base and cover the filling. Brush with milk and sprinkle with sugar. Bake for about 20 minutes, until golden brown.

Set aside to cool in the pan on a wire rack. Cut into twenty pieces to serve.

. . .

If you liked this recipe, you will love these as well.

RASPBERRY & COCONUT MERINGUE SLICE

FRUIT & MUESLI BARS

SALTY PEANUT BARS

. . . . .

For a slightly different flavor, replace the raspberry preserves with the same amount of cherry preserves or orange marmalade.

RASPBERRY & COCONUT MERINGUE SLICE

Base
1⅓ cups (200 g) all-purpose (plain) flour
1 teaspoon baking powder
⅓ cup (90 g) unsalted butter, softened
¼ cup (50 g) superfine (caster) sugar
2 large egg yolks

Filling
½ cup (160 g) raspberry preserves (jam), warmed

Topping
2 large egg whites
½ cup (100 g) superfine (caster) sugar
½ cup (60 g) shredded (desiccated) coconut
½ teaspoon vanilla extract (essence)

Base: Preheat the oven to 350°F (180°C/gas 4).

Grease the base and sides of a 1¼-inch (3-cm) deep, 8 x 12-inch (20 x 30-cm) cake pan. Line with parchment paper, extending the paper 2 inches (5 cm) above the rim of the pan.

Sift the flour and baking powder into a bowl. Beat the butter and sugar in a bowl with an electric mixer on medium speed until pale and creamy. Add the egg yolks one at a time, beating until just combined after each addition. With the mixer on low speed, beat in the flour mixture, scraping down the sides occasionally, until just combined.

Tip into the prepared pan and press down firmly to line the base. Use the back of a spoon to smooth and create an even layer.

Filling: Spread the warmed raspberry preserves over the base.

Topping: Beat the egg whites in a bowl with an electric mixer on medium-high speed until soft peaks form. Gradually add the sugar, beating constantly until stiff glossy peaks form. Add the vanilla and beat to combine. Fold in the coconut. Spread over the filling in an even layer.

Bake for 20 minutes, until golden brown.

Leave in the pan to cool completely. Cut into twenty pieces to serve.

. . .

If you liked this recipe, you will love these as well.

RAISIN SLICE

FRUIT & NUT MUESLI BARS

BERRY STREUSEL SLICE

Makes: 16 bars
Preparation: 20 minutes
Cooking: 35–45 minutes
Level: 1

. . . . .

Packed with healthy dried fruit and nuts, these bars can be served throughout the day, from breakfast and brunch to afterschool snacks.

FRUIT & NUT MUESLI BARS

2	cups (200 g) old-fashioned (rolled) oats
1/2	cup (75 g) almonds, coarsely chopped
1/2	cup (75 g) hazelnuts, coarsely chopped
1/2	cup (60 g) pecans, coarsely chopped
1/2	cup (75 g) sunflower seeds
1/4	cup (35 g) pumpkin seeds
1/2	cup (120 ml) honey
1/4	cup (50 g) firmly packed dark brown sugar
2	tablespoons (30 g) butter
1	teaspoon vanilla extract (essence)
1/2	teaspoon salt flakes
1/2	cup (60 g) flaked coconut
1/2	cup (90 g) finely diced dried apricots
1/3	cup (60 g) dried cranberries, coarsely chopped
1/3	cup (60 g) golden raisins (sultanas)
1/4	cup (25 g) ground flaxseed
1	tablespoon sesame seeds

Preheat the oven to 350°F (180°C/gas 4). Grease the base and sides of a 3/4-inch (2-cm) deep, 10 x 14-inch (25 x 35-cm) cake pan. Line with parchment paper, extending the paper 2 inches (5 cm) above the rim of the pan.

Combine the oats, almonds, hazelnuts, pecans, and sunflower and pumpkin seeds in a large bowl and mix well. Spread out on a large baking sheet and bake, stirring occasionally, for 20–25 minutes, until lightly toasted.

Melt the honey, brown sugar, and butter in a small saucepan over low heat. Stir in the vanilla and salt.

Combine the coconut, apricots, cranberries, golden raisins, flaxseed, and sesame seeds in a large bowl. Add the toasted mixture and stir to combine. Pour in the honey mixture and mix well.

Spread in the prepared pan, using the back of a spoon to press down and compact, creating a smooth even surface.

Bake for 15–20 minutes, until golden brown.

Leave in the pan to cool completely. Cut into sixteen bars to serve.

. . .

If you liked this recipe, you will love these as well.

RAISIN SLICE

RASPBERRY & COCONUT MERINGUE SLICE

BERRY STREUSEL SLICE

Makes: 20 bars
Preparation: 20 minutes
Cooking: 18–25 minutes
Level: 2

· · · · ·

The sweet and salty taste combo in these bars is very good. Serve with a cup of tea or coffee.

SALTY PEANUT BARS

Base

1½	cups (225 g) all-purpose (plain) flour
½	teaspoon baking powder
¼	teaspoon baking soda (bicarbonate of soda)
¼	teaspoon sea salt flakes
½	cup (120 g) unsalted butter, softened
½	cup (100 g) firmly packed light brown sugar
1	large egg

Topping

½	cup (100 g) firmly packed light brown sugar
⅓	cup (90 g) unsalted butter
1	tablespoon light corn (golden) syrup
1	teaspoon vanilla extract (essence)
2	cups (300 g) salted roasted peanuts

Base: Preheat the oven to 350°F (180°C/gas 4).

Grease the base and sides of a 1¼-inch (3-cm) deep, 8 x 12-inch (20 x 30-cm) cake pan. Line with parchment paper, extending the paper 2 inches (5 cm) above the rim of the pan.

Sift the flour, baking powder, baking soda, and salt into a bowl. Beat the butter and brown sugar in a separate bowl with an electric mixer on medium speed until creamy. Add the egg and beat to combine. With the mixer on low speed, beat in the flour mixture, scraping down the sides occasionally, until just combined.

Pour the mixture into the prepared pan and press down firmly to line the base. Use the back of a spoon to smooth and create an even layer.

Bake for 10–15 minutes, until golden. Set aside for 5 minutes, to cool slightly.

Topping: Heat the sugar, butter, corn syrup, and vanilla in a small saucepan over low heat. Simmer until the mixture thickens and darkens slightly, about 3 minutes. Stir in the peanuts. Pour over the base, spreading to create an even layer.

Bake for another 5 minutes, until just set.

Leave in the pan to cool completely. Cut into twenty bars to serve.

· · ·

If you liked this recipe, you will love these as well.

PEANUT BUTTER COOKIES

PISTACHIO BISCOTTI

PECAN BLONDIES

Makes: 20 bars
Preparation: 30 minutes
    + 2 hours to set
Cooking: 20 minutes
Level: 1

. . . . .

If you like ginger, you will love these bars.
Serve with tea or coffee.

GINGER CRISP BARS

Base

1²/₃	cups (250 g) all-purpose (plain) flour
¹/₂	cup (100 g) superfine (caster) sugar
1¹/₂	teaspoons ground ginger
1	teaspoon baking powder
³/₄	cup (180 g) chilled unsalted butter, diced

Topping

¹/₃	cup (90 g) unsalted butter
2	tablespoons light corn syrup (or golden syrup)
2¹/₄	cups (330 g) confectioners' (icing) sugar
1	tablespoon ground ginger

Base: Preheat the oven to 350°F (180°C/gas 4). Grease the base and sides of a 1¹/₄-inch (3-cm) deep, 8 x 12-inch (20 x 30-cm) cake pan. Line with parchment paper, extending the paper 2 inches (5 cm) above the rim of the pan.

Combine the flour, sugar, ginger, and baking powder in a food processor and pulse to combine. Add the butter and blend until the mixture resembles coarse crumbs. Pour into the prepared pan and press down firmly to line the base. Use the back of a spoon to smooth and create an even layer. Prick all over with a fork.

Bake for 20 minutes, until pale golden brown.

Topping: Prepare the topping while the base is oin the oven. Melt the butter and corn syrup in a medium saucepan over low heat. Sift in the confectioners' sugar and ginger and cook for 2–3 minutes, stirring until smooth.

Pour the topping over the hot base and leave at room temperature for 2 hours, until set.

Cut into twenty bars to serve.

. . .

If you liked this recipe,
you will love these as well.

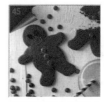

GINGERSNAPS   GINGERBREAD PEOPLE   GINGER KISSES

Makes: 14 slices

Preparation: 30 minutes
+ 30 minutes to
freeze

Cooking: 40 minutes

Level: 1

BERRY STREUSEL SLICE

1¹/₂ cups (225 g) all-purpose (plain) flour

1 cup (200 g) firmly packed light brown sugar

³/₄ cup (75 g) almond meal (ground almonds)

¹/₂ cup (60 g) shredded (desiccated) coconut

1 teaspoon ground cinnamon

1 cup (250 g) chilled unsalted butter, diced

Finely grated zest of 1 unwaxed lemon

3 cups (500 g) fresh or frozen mixed berries

Preheat the oven to 350°F (180°C/gas 4).

Grease the base and sides of a 1¹/₄-inch (3-cm) deep, 8 x 12-inch (20 x 30-cm) cake pan. Line with parchment paper, extending the paper 2 inches (5 cm) above the rim of the pan.

Place the flour, brown sugar, almond meal, coconut, and cinnamon in a food processor and pulse to combine. Add the butter and lemon zest and blend until the mixture resembles coarse crumbs. Pour half into the prepared pan and press down firmly to line the base. Use the back of a spoon to smooth and create an even layer.

Bake for 15 minutes, until pale golden brown. Set aside to cool.

Shape the remaining mixture into a log. Wrap in plastic wrap (cling film) and freeze for 30 minutes, until firm.

Scatter the berries over the base. Coarsely grate the frozen mixture over the top.

Bake for another 25 minutes, until golden brown.

Leave to cool completely in the pan. Cut into fourteen slices to serve.

. . .

If you liked this recipe, you will love these as well.

RAISIN SLICE

RASPBERRY & COCONUT
MERINGUE SLICE

FRUIT & MUESLI BARS

Makes: 18 pieces
Preparation: 30 minutes
+ 3 1/2 hours to chill
Cooking: 20 minutes
Level: 2

This luxurious chocolate peppermint slice is perfect for special occasions.

DOUBLE CHOCOLATE MINT SLICE

Base

1 1/2   cups (225 g) all-purpose (plain) flour

1/3   cup (50 g) confectioners' (icing) sugar

1/4   cup (30 g) unsweetened cocoa powder

1/2   cup (120 g) chilled unsalted butter, diced

2   tablespoons chilled water

1   large egg yolk

Filling

1/3   cup (90 ml) light (single) cream

6   ounces (180 g) good quality white chocolate, coarsely chopped

1 1/2   cups (225 g) confectioners' (icing) sugar

1   teaspoon peppermint extract (essence)

Topping

6   ounces (180 g) dark cooking chocolate, coarsely chopped

1   teaspoon vegetable oil

Base: Combine the flour, confectioners' sugar, and cocoa in a food processor and pulse to combine. Add the butter and blend until the mixture resembles coarse crumbs. Lightly beat the water and egg in small bowl. With the motor running, gradually add the egg mixture. Turn out onto a clean work surface and use your hands to press the mixture into a dough. Shape into a disk, wrap in plastic wrap (cling film), and refrigerate for 30 minutes.

Preheat the oven to 350°F (180°C/gas 4).

Grease the base and sides of a 1 1/4-inch (3-cm) deep, 8 x 12-inch (20 x 30-cm) cake pan. Line with parchment paper, extending the paper 2 inches (5 cm) above the rim of the pan.

Roll the pastry out between two sheets of parchment paper to make a rectangle large enough to line the base of the prepared pan. Line and press into the pan. Line with parchment paper and fill with baking weights, uncooked rice, or dried beans.

Bake for 15 minutes, until the edges are firm. Remove the parchment and baking weights and bake for 5 more minutes, until the pastry is cooked through. Set aside to cool.

Filling: Heat the cream in a small saucepan over low heat. Remove from the heat and add the white chocolate, stirring until the smooth. Sift in the confectioners' sugar, add the peppermint, and stir to combine. Pour over the base. Refrigerate until set, about 1 hour.

Topping: Melt the dark chocolate with the oil in a heatproof bowl set over a saucepan of barely simmering water, ensuring the base of the bowl does not touch the water. Stir until smooth. Set aside to cool to room temperature.

Pour the cooled chocolate over the filling, spreading to create an even layer. Refrigerate for 1 hour, until the chocolate begins to set but is still soft. Mark out eighteen pieces. Refrigerate for 1 more hour, until completely set. Cut through the markings using a sharp knife to serve.

Makes: 18 pieces
Preparation: 45 minutes
    + 4 hours to chill
Cooking: 30–45 minutes
Level: 2

. . . . .

The ultimate in wicked comfort food. Serve with a cup of tea or coffee.

CHOCOLATE CARAMEL SLICE

Base

1   cup (150 g) all-purpose (plain) flour
½   cup (100 g) firmly packed light brown sugar
¼   cup (25 g) old-fashioned (rolled) oats
¼   cup (30 g) shredded (desiccated) coconut
½   cup (120 g) unsalted butter, melted

Filling

1   (14-ounce/400-ml) can condensed milk
¼   cup (60 g) unsalted butter
2   tablespoons light corn syrup (or golden syrup)

Topping

7   ounces (200 g) dark chocolate, coarsely chopped
2   teaspoons vegetable oil

Base: Preheat the oven to 350°F (180°C/gas 4).

Grease the base and sides of a 1¼-inch (3-cm) deep, 8 x 12-inch (20 x 30-cm) cake pan. Line with parchment paper, extending the paper 2 inches (5 cm) above the rim of the pan.

Combine the flour, brown sugar, oats, and coconut in a medium bowl. Add the butter and mix well to combine. Pour into the prepared pan and press down firmly to line the base. Use the back of a spoon to smooth and create an even layer.

Bake for 10–15 minutes, until golden brown. Set aside until cool and firm.

Filling: Combine the condensed milk, butter, and corn syrup in a medium saucepan and simmer over low heat for 10–15 minutes, until golden. Pour over the cooled base, spreading to create an even layer. Bake for 10–15 minutes, until firm and the edges are golden. Set aside to cool slightly. Refrigerate until set, about 2 hours.

Topping: Melt the chocolate and oil together in a heatproof bowl set over a saucepan of barely simmering water, ensuring the base of the bowl does not touch the water. Stir until smooth.

Pour the cooled chocolate over the caramel filling, spreading to create an even layer. Refrigerate until the chocolate begins to set but is still soft, about 1 hour. Mark out eighteen pieces. Refrigerate until completely set, about 1 hour.

Cut through the markings using a sharp knife to serve.

. . .

If you liked this recipe, you will love these as well.

CHOCOLATE-COATED ALFAJORES

CHOCOLATE WALNUT BROWNIES

DOUBLE CHOCOLATE MINT SLICE

cakes

This chapter features 45 recipes,
from basics like butter and pound cakes
to classics, such as marble cake and Dobos
torte. It also includes roulades, sheet cakes,
and a selection of small cakes, such as
cupcakes, cake pops, and whoopie pies.

LEMON MADELEINES

1/4 cup (60 g) unsalted butter, melted and cooled + extra, to brush

3 large eggs

1/3 cup (70 g) superfine (caster) sugar

Finely grated zest of 1 unwaxed lemon

1/2 cup (75 g) all-purpose (plain) flour

Confectioners' (icing) sugar, to dust

Preheat the oven to 375°F (190°C/gas 5). Brush twenty madeleine molds with melted butter.

Beat the eggs and sugar in a bowl with an electric mixer on medium speed until pale and doubled in volume. Stir in the cooled butter and lemon zest. Sift in the flour and gently fold it in. Spoon batter into the prepared molds, filling each one three-quarters full.

Bake for 15 minutes, until the madeleines are risen, golden, and springy to the touch.

Leave in the pan for 5 minutes to cool slightly. Turn out onto a wire rack and let cool completely.

Dust with confectioners' sugar just before serving.

Makes: 20 madeleines Preparation: 20 minutes Cooking: 15 minutes Level: 1

RASPBERRY FRIANDS

1 1/4 cups (180 g) confectioners' (icing) sugar + extra, to dust

1/2 cup (75 g) all-purpose (plain) flour

1 cup (100 g) almond meal (ground almonds)

6 large egg whites, lightly beaten

3/4 cup (180 g) unsalted butter, melted and cooled

1 cup (150 g) fresh or frozen raspberries

Preheat the oven to 350°F (180°C/gas 4). Lightly grease 12 friand pans with melted butter.

Sift the confectioners' sugar and flour into a medium bowl. Add the almond meal and stir to combine. Add the egg whites and mix to combine. Stir in the butter. Fill the friand holes two-thirds full with batter. Scatter two or three raspberries on top of each friand.

Bake for 20–25 minutes, until golden and a toothpick inserted into the center comes out clean.

Leave in the pan for 5 minutes to cool slightly. Turn out onto a wire rack and let cool completely.

Dust with confectioners' sugar just before serving.

Makes: 12 friands Preparation: 20 minutes Cooking: 20–25 minutes Level: 1

Madeleines are a small French cake originally from Lorraine in northeastern France. They were immortalized in Marcel Proust's novels, *Remembrance of Things Past*.

Ours is a lemon recipe, but you could easily replace the lemon zest with vanilla or almond extract, or other flavors to your liking.

Buy the madeleine pan in kitchen supply stores or from online suppliers.

Friands are another small cake of French origin. They are usually made with ground almonds and eggs whites and can also be flavored with coconut, cocoa, fruit, and nuts.

You will need a 12-cup friand pan for this recipe. If you don't have one, use a standard 12-cup muffin pan instead.

Makes: 9 filled cakes
Preparation: 30 minutes
    + 2 hours to chill
Cooking: 10–15 minutes
Level: 2

. . . . .

These pretty cakes are perfect for dessert or a special occasion. You can change the way they look by using green, yellow, or other colored jelly crystals to make the dip.

RASPBERRY JELLY CAKES

Jelly Dip

1   (3-ounce/90-g) packet raspberry jelly (jello) crystals

1   cup (250 ml) boiling water

3/4 cup (180 ml) cold water

Cakes

1¼   cups (200 g) all-purpose (plain) flour

1   teaspoon baking powder

1/3 cup (90 g) unsalted butter, softened

1/2 cup (100 g) superfine (caster) sugar

1   teaspoon vanilla extract (essence)

1   large egg, lightly beaten

2/3 cup (150 ml) milk

2   cups (250 g) shredded (desiccated) coconut

Filling

3/4 cup (180 ml) heavy (double) cream

1   tablespoon confectioners' (icing) sugar

Jelly Dip: Combine the jelly crystals and boiling water in a heatproof bowl, stirring until the crystals dissolve. Add the cold water and stir to combine. Refrigerate until the jelly begins to set slightly, to about the consistency of egg whites, about 1 hour.

Cakes: Preheat the oven to 350°F (180°C/gas 4). Lightly grease 18 cups of two twelve-cup, 2-tablespoon capacity patty pans. Sift the flour and baking powder into a small bowl.

Beat the butter, sugar, and vanilla in a bowl with an electric mixer on medium speed until pale and creamy. Gradually add the egg, beating to combine. Add the flour mixture and milk in two batches, beating on low speed and scraping down the sides occasionally, until just combined. Divide the batter evenly among the prepared pans.

Bake for 10–15 minutes, until golden brown and the cakes bounce back when lightly pressed.

Leave in the pan for 5 minutes to cool slightly. Turn out onto a wire rack and let cool completely.

Using two forks, dip the cakes in the jelly dip, coating evenly. Roll in the coconut, shaking off any excess. Place on a plate and refrigerate for 1 hour until the jelly dip is set.

Filling: When ready to serve, whip the cream and confectioners' sugar in a medium bowl until firm peaks form.

Slice the cakes in half horizontally. Pipe or spoon cream onto the bases and sandwich together with the tops.

Makes: 12 cupcakes
Preparation: 15 minutes
Cooking: 15–20 minutes
Level: 1

. . . . .

Cupcakes are first mentioned in *American Cookery*, a recipe book published in 1796. They have become very popular in recent years, thanks in large part to the American sitcom *Sex in the City* which often featured the four heroines eating cupcakes from the Magnolia Bakery in Manhattan.

ROSEWATER CUPCAKES

Cupcakes

1½ cups (225 g) all-purpose (plain) flour

¼ cup (30 g) cornstarch (cornflour)

2 teaspoons baking powder

4 ounces (120 g) good quality white chocolate, coarsely chopped

¾ cup (150 g) superfine (caster) sugar

½ cup (120 g) unsalted butter, softened

1 teaspoon vanilla extract (essence)

2 large eggs, separated

Pinch of salt

2 tablespoons milk

Buttercream Frosting

3 ounces (90 g) good quality white chocolate, coarsely chopped

½ cup (120 g) unsalted butter

2 cups (300 g) confectioners' (icing) sugar

1 tablespoon milk

1 teaspoon rosewater

1–3 drops pink food coloring

Raspberry jelly crystals, to decorate (optional)

Cupcakes: Preheat the oven to 350°F (180°C/gas 4). Line a standard 12-cup muffin pan with paper liners. Sift the flour, cornstarch, and baking powder into a medium bowl.

Melt the white chocolate in a heatproof bowl set over a saucepan of barely simmering water, ensuring the base of the bowl does not touch the water. Stir occasionally, until smooth. Set aside to cool slightly.

Beat ½ cup (100 g) of sugar with the butter and vanilla in a bowl using an electric mixer on medium-high speed until pale and creamy. Beat in the egg yolks. Gradually pour in the melted chocolate, beating until combined. Gradually add the flour mixture, alternating with the milk, beating on low speed until combined.

Beat the egg whites and salt in a large bowl with an electric mixer on medium-high speed until soft peaks form. Beating constantly, gradually add the remaining sugar, until the sugar has dissolved and thick glossy peaks form. Stir a large spoonful of the whites into the cupcake batter. Fold in the remaining egg whites. Divide the batter evenly among the prepared muffin pans.

Bake for 15–20 minutes, until a toothpick inserted into the centers comes out clean. Remove the cupcakes from the pans, set aside on a wire rack, and let cool completely.

Buttercream Frosting: Melt the white chocolate in a heatproof bowl set over a saucepan of barely simmering water. Set aside to cool slightly.

Beat the butter in a bowl with an electric mixer on medium-high speed until pale and creamy. Gradually add the white chocolate, beating to combine. Sift in the confectioners' sugar in two batches, beating on low speed and scraping down the sides occasionally. Add the milk, rosewater, and enough food coloring to tint the frosting pale pink.

Spoon the frosting into a pastry (piping) bag fitted with a large star-shaped nozzle. Pipe onto the cupcakes and sprinkle with jelly crystals to decorate, if liked.

WHOOPIE PIES

2 cups (300 g) all-purpose (plain) flour
2 cups (300 g) unsweetened cocoa powder
2 teaspoons baking soda
1/2 teaspoon salt
1 1/4 cups (300 g) butter
1 1/2 cups (300 g) sugar
4 large eggs
2 teaspoons vanilla extract (essence)
1 1/2 cups (225 g) confectioners' (icing) sugar
12 ounces (350 g) cream cheese

Preheat the oven to 375°F (190°C/gas 5). Set out three 20-cavity silicone whoopie pie or macaroon baking mats. Alternatively, line four large baking sheets with parchment paper.

Sift the flour, cocoa, baking soda, and salt into a bowl. Beat ³/4 cup (180 g) of butter and sugar in a bowl with an electric mixer on medium-high speed until pale and creamy. Add the eggs one at a time, beating until just combined after each addition. Gradually beat in 1 teaspoon of vanilla and the flour mixture. The batter will be quite stiff.

Spoon or pipe walnut-size balls onto the mats or sheets, spacing well. Bake for 8–10 minutes, until firm. Let cool on wire racks.

Beat the remaining 1/2 cup (120 g) of butter, confectioners' sugar, cream cheese, and vanilla in a bowl until smooth and creamy. Sandwich the whoopies together with the filling. Chill until ready to serve.

Makes: 25–30 filled whoopie pies Preparation: 30 minutes Cooking: 8–10 minutes Level: 1

CHOCOLATE FAIRY CAKES

1 1/3 cups (200 g) all-purpose (plain) flour
2/3 cup (100 g) unsweetened cocoa powder
2 teaspoons baking powder
1/4 teaspoon salt
2/3 cup (150 g) unsalted butter, softened
1 cup (200 g) sugar
2 large eggs
1/2 cup (120 ml) milk
1 cup (250 ml) heavy (double) cream
1/2 cup (150 g) raspberry (jam)
Fresh raspberries

Preheat the oven to 350°F (180°C/gas 4). Set out 20 foil or paper baking cups. Sift the flour, cocoa, baking powder, and salt into a bowl.

Beat the butter and sugar in a bowl with an electric mixer on medium speed until pale and creamy. Add the eggs one at a time, beating until just combined after each addition. Gradually beat in the flour mixture, alternating with the milk. Spoon the batter into the prepared cups, filling each one two-thirds full.

Bake for 20–25 minutes, until a toothpick inserted into the centers comes out clean. Let cool in the pan for 5 minutes, then lift onto a wire rack to cool completely.

Beat the cream in a bowl until thick. Cut a small circle 1/2-inch (1-cm) deep from each cake. Fill with 1 teaspoon of preserves and top with cream. Cut the cake tops in half and arrange on each cake, like fairy wings. Decorate with the raspberries, and serve.

Makes: 20 fairy cakes Preparation: 30 minutes Cooking: 20–25 minutes Level: 2

Whoopie pies were first baked in the United States, and both Maine and Pennsylvania claim to have invented them. According to one theory, the Amish women of Pennsylvania made them first as a way of using up extra batter leftover from cake baking. Originally called gobs, they became known as whoopie pies because—the story goes—Amish children would exclaim "whoopie!" when they discovered one tucked into their lunch boxes.

Finish these pretty cakes by decorating them with 1–2 fresh raspberries or sliced strawberries.

Makes: 15 lamingtons
Preparation: 45 minutes
    + 1 hour to set
Cooking: 20 minutes
Level: 2

. . . . .

Lamingtons are a popular dessert cake in Australia and New Zealand. They are named after the English Lord Lamington who served as governor of Queensland from 1896 to 1901.

LAMINGTONS

Cake

1	cup (150 g) all-purpose (plain) flour
1/2	cup (75 g) cornstarch (cornflour)
1/2	teaspoon baking powder
6	large eggs
2/3	cup (140 g) superfine (caster) sugar
2	tablespoons (30 g) unsalted butter, melted and cooled
3/4	cup (240 g) raspberry preserves (jam), warmed
2	cups (250 g) shredded (desiccated) coconut

Frosting

1/2	cup (120 ml) milk
1/4	cup (60 g) unsalted butter
3	cups (450 g) confectioners' (icing) sugar
1/2	cup (75 g) unsweetened cocoa powder

Cake: Preheat the oven to 350°F (180°C/gas 4). Grease the base and sides of a deep, 10 x 12-inch (25 x 30-cm) lamington or jelly roll pan. Line with parchment paper, extending the paper 1½ inches (4 cm) above the sides.

Triple sift the flour, cornstarch, and baking powder into a bowl.

Beat the eggs and sugar in a bowl with an electric mixer on medium-high speed until pale and tripled in volume, about 10 minutes.

Fold the flour mixture into the batter one-third at a time. Pour the cooled melted butter down the side of the bowl and gently fold in. Spoon the batter into the prepared pan.

Bake for about 20 minutes, until a toothpick comes out clean when inserted into the center. Turn out onto a wire rack, cover with a clean kitchen cloth, and let cool completely.

Frosting: Heat the milk and butter in a small saucepan over low heat until the butter melts. Remove from the heat and sift in the confectioners' sugar and cocoa, stirring until smooth. Let cool slightly.

Cut the cake in half horizontally to create two even layers. Spread raspberry preserves over the cut side of one of the layers and cover with the remaining layer. Cut into fifteen squares.

Using two forks, dip the cake squares into the chocolate frosting, coating evenly. Roll in the coconut, shaking off excess. Place on a wire rack and leave for 1 hour for the frosting to set.

. . .

If you liked this recipe, you will love these as well.

RASPBERRY JELLY CAKES

COCONUT ROCHERS

COCONUT CAKE

COCONUT ROCHERS

3   cups (300 g) dried, unsweetened coconut flakes

$^3/_4$ cup (150 g) sugar

$^1/_4$ teaspoon salt

3   large egg whites

$^1/_2$ teaspoon vanilla extract (essence)

3   ounces (90 g) dark chocolate, to drizzle

Preheat the oven to 350°F (180°C/gas 4). Line a large baking sheet with parchment paper.

Stir the coconut, sugar, and salt in a bowl until well combined. Stir in the egg whites and vanilla. Continue stirring until well combined.

Shape and press the coconut dough into 24 balls and place on the prepared baking sheet. Pinch and shape each ball into a pyramid. The rochers can be placed close together on the baking sheet as they do not spread during baking.

Bake for about 12 minutes, until tinged with brown. Let cool on the baking sheet for 5 minutes. Transfer to a wire rack and let cool.

Melt the chocolate in a heatproof bowl set over a saucepan of barely simmering water, ensuring the base of the bowl does not touch the water. Drizzle over the cooled rochers and let set before serving.

Makes: 24 rochers   Preparation: 30 minutes   Cooking: 12 minutes   Level: 1

FINANCIERS

$^1/_2$ cup (120 g) salted butter + extra, to grease

$^1/_3$ cup (30 g) all-purpose (plain) flour

$1^1/_3$ cups (130 g) finely ground almonds

$^1/_2$ cup (100 g) superfine (caster) sugar

3   large egg whites, lightly beaten

$^1/_3$ cup (50 g) golden raisins (sultanas), soaked in 3 tablespoons rum

Butter and flour 24 financier molds or two 12-hole mini muffin pans and put them in the refrigerator so the butter sets.

Melt the butter in a pan over high heat until it starts to brown. Strain through a fine-mesh sieve and set aside to cool.

Mix the flour, almonds, and sugar in a bowl. Fold in the egg whites and stir in the golden raisins, rum, and butter. Chill for at least 1 hour, or overnight.

Preheat the oven to 390°F (190°C/gas 5).

Spoon the batter into the molds. Bake for 10–15 minutes, until golden brown and risen in the center.

Let cool in the pans before turning out of the pans to serve.

Makes: 24 financiers   Preparation: 20 minutes + 1–12 hours to chill   Cooking: 10–15 minutes   Level: 1

Coconut rochers are a small French cake closely related to macarons. They are usually formed into pyramid shapes. We have drizzled ours with dark chocolate for extra flavor.

Financiers are small, light French cakes similar to foam (sponge) cakes, although they are usually made with ground almonds. They are baked in rectangular molds which you can find in well-stocked baking supply stores and from online suppliers. Bake them in muffin pans if you can't get the financier molds.

Makes: 15 filled cakes
Preparation: 30 minutes
    + 30 minutes to chill
Cooking: 8–10 minutes
Level: 1

These little ginger cakes are perfect to serve with tea or coffee during the day.

GINGER KISSES

Cakes

1   cup (150 g) all-purpose (plain) flour
¼   cup (25 g) cornstarch (cornflour)
1   tablespoon ground ginger
1   teaspoon ground cinnamon
1   teaspoon baking powder
½   teaspoon baking soda (bicarbonate of soda)
½   cup (120 g) salted butter, softened
½   cup (100 g) firmly packed light brown sugar
2   large eggs
1   tablespoon light corn syrup (or golden syrup)
1   tablespoon boiling water
    Confectioners' (icing) sugar, to dust

Mock Cream Filling

¼   cup (60 g) salted butter, softened
1   teaspoon vanilla extract (essence)
2   cups (300 g) confectioners' (icing) sugar
2   tablespoons boiling water

Cakes: Lightly grease two large baking sheets and line with parchment paper.

Sift the flour, cornstarch, ginger, cinnamon, baking powder, and baking soda into a bowl.

Beat the butter and brown sugar in a bowl with an with an electric mixer on medium-high speed until creamy. Add the eggs one at a time, beating until just combined after each addition. Add the corn syrup and with the mixer on low speed, beat in the flour mixture, scraping down the sides occasionally, until just combined. Add the water and beat to combine. Cover and chill for 30 minutes.

Preheat the oven to 350°F (180°C/gas 4).

Using two spoons, shape the mixture into walnut-size balls and place about 1½ inches (4 cm) apart on the prepared baking sheets. You will need thirty cakes in total.

Bake for 8–10 minutes, until golden and the cakes spring back when pressed in the centers. Leave on the baking sheets for 5 minutes to cool slightly.

Transfer to a rack and leave to cool completely.

Mock Cream Filling: Beat the butter and vanilla in a bowl with an electric mixer on medium-high until pale and creamy. With the mixer on low speed, gradually beat in the confectioners' sugar. Gradually add the boiling water, beating until light and fluffy. Let cool a little.

Spoon the mock cream into a pastry (piping) bag fitted with a plain nozzle and pipe onto the flat side of half of the cakes. Sandwich together with the remaining cakes.

Dust with confectioners' sugar to serve.

Makes: 25 cake pops
Preparation: 1 hour
    + 2–3 hours to chill
    & set
Cooking: 1–1¼ hours
Level: 3

. . . . .

You will need 25 lollipop sticks to make these cake pops. Buy the 6-inch (15-cm) sticks if you can get them. You will also need a polystyrene foam block about 2 inches (5 cm) thick and measuring at least 12 x 18 inches (30 x 45 cm) to poke the lollipop sticks into after the pops have been dipped in the chocolate.

DISCO BALL CAKE POPS

Cake Pops

1	chocolate cake (see page 114)
1	(13-ounce/375-g) packet dark chocolate melts
2	(6½-ounce/190-g) packets colored sprinkles (100 & 1000's), to decorate
25	lollipop sticks
	Block polystyrene

Chocolate Buttercream

½	cup (120 g) unsalted butter, softened
1	teaspoon vanilla extract (essence)
1½	cups (225 g) confectioners' (icing) sugar
½	cup (75 g) unsweetened cocoa powder
2	tablespoons milk

Cake Pops: Make the chocolate cake and bake following the instructions on page 114. Trim off and discard the cake crust. Coarsely chop then crumble in a large bowl with your fingers to make coarse crumbs.

Chocolate Buttercream: Beat the butter and vanilla in a bowl with an electric mixer on medium-high speed until pale and creamy. Sift in the confectioners' sugar and cocoa and beat to combine. Add the milk and beat to incorporate.

Add the buttercream to the cake crumbs and mix well to combine.

Use your hands to shape the mixture into 25 walnut-size balls. Place on a large plate or board, cover, and chill for 1–2 hours, until firm.

Melt the chocolate in a heatproof bowl set over a saucepan of barely simmering water, ensuring the base of the bowl does not touch the water. Stir occasionally until smooth. Transfer to a deep mug.

Dip the lollipop sticks, one at a time, into the chocolate and push halfway into the center of the cake balls. Dip into the chocolate to coat, allowing the excess to drip off. Insert the stick into the polystyrene block and leave for 1–2 minutes, until the chocolate begins to set but is still soft.

Sprinkle with the colored sprinkles to coat. Insert the stick back into the polystyrene block and leave to set completely, at least 1 hour.

Repeat with the remaining cake balls.

. . .

If you liked this recipe, you will love these as well.

WHOOPIE PIES   LAMINGTONS   CHOCOLATE MINT KISSES

Makes: about 16 filled
    cakes
Preparation: 45 minutes
    + 1½–12½ hours to
    chill & rest
Cooking: 10–12 minutes
Level: 2

. . . . .

Peppermint and chocolate is a classic taste combination. Most people love it, but if you are not a fan you can still enjoy these pretty little cakes; just leave the peppermint extract out of the filling.

CHOCOLATE MINT KISSES

Cakes

1   cup (150 g)
       unsweetened cocoa
       powder
½   cup (75 g) + 2
       tablespoons all-
       purpose (plain) flour
½   cup (120 g) salted
       butter, softened
½   cup (100 g) sugar
1   large egg

Peppermint Ganache

½   cup (120 ml) heavy
       (double) cream
7   ounces (200 g)
       white chocolate,
       grated
¾   teaspoon
       peppermint extract
       (essence)

Cakes: Sift the cocoa and flour into a bowl. Beat the butter and sugar in a bowl with an electric mixer on medium-high speed until pale and creamy. Beat in the egg until well blended.

With the mixer on low speed, add the flour mixture, beating until just combined. Divide the dough in half and shape each half into a disk. Wrap in plastic (cling film). Chill for at least 1 hour, or overnight.

Preheat the oven to 350°F (180°C/gas 4). Line three baking sheets with parchment paper.

Transfer the dough to a work surface lightly dusted with flour. Roll out to ⅛ inch (3 mm) thick. Cut out rounds using a 2-inch (5-cm) cookie cutter. Transfer to the prepared baking sheets, spacing about ½ inch (1 cm) apart. Repeat with the remaining scraps of dough.

Bake for 10–12 minutes, until firm. Let cool completely on the baking sheets on wire racks.

Peppermint Ganache: Bring the cream to a boil in a small saucepan over medium-high heat. Add the chocolate. Simmer, stirring constantly, until the chocolate is melted and smooth. Stir in the peppermint extract. Let cool slightly, 10–15 minutes.

Spoon 1 teaspoon of ganache onto the bottom of half the cakes. Sandwich together with the remaining cookies. Chill until firm, about 10 minutes.

. . .

If you liked this recipe, you will love these as well.

DISCO BALL CAKE POPS

CHOCOLATE CAKE

CHOCOLATE MUD CAKE

Serves: 10
Preparation: 15 minutes
Cooking: 1–1¼ hours
Level: 1

. . . . .

This is a classic cake which can be enjoyed on its own with a cup of tea or coffee. It can also be sliced and filled with cream and fruit and served as dessert. If desired, you can flavor the batter with almond or other extracts to make a slightly different but equally delicious cake.

BUTTER CAKE

2⅓	cups (350 g) all-purpose (plain) flour
2	teaspoons baking powder
1	cup (250 g) unsalted butter, softened
1¼	cups (250 g) superfine (caster) sugar
1	teaspoon vanilla extract (essence)
3	large eggs
⅔	cup (150 ml) milk
	Confectioners' (icing) sugar, to dust

Preheat the oven to 350°F (180°C/gas 4). Lightly grease the base and sides of a deep 8-inch (20-cm) round cake pan. Line with parchment paper.

Sift the flour and baking powder into a bowl.

Beat the butter, sugar, and vanilla in bowl with an electric mixer on medium-high speed until pale and creamy. Add the eggs one at a time, beating until just combined after each addition. Sift the flour and baking powder into a medium bowl. With the mixer on low speed, gradually add the flour mixture alternating with the milk, scraping down the sides occasionally, and beating until just combined. Spoon the batter into the prepared pan.

Bake for 1–1¼ hours, until a toothpick inserted into the center comes out clean. Leave in the pan for 10 minutes to cool slightly.

Turn out onto a rack and leave to cool completely.

Dust with confectioners' sugar. Slice and serve.

. . .

If you liked this recipe, you will love these as well.

POUND CAKE

CINNAMON TEA CAKE

MADEIRA CAKE

Serves: 10

Preparation: 45 minutes
    + 1 hour to set

Cooking: 40 minutes

Level: 2

. . . . .

The chiffon cake is one of the few cakes whose invention can be precisely credited and dated. It was invented in 1927 by Californian caterer Harry Baker. The cake was a great success locally and he kept the recipe secret for 20 years before selling it to General Mills. The cake became widely known in 1948 when Betty Crocker published 14 variations on the basic theme.

ORANGE CHIFFON CAKE

Chiffon Cake

1   cup (150 g) all-purpose (plain) flour

1/2   cup (75 g) cornstarch (cornflour)

2   teaspoons baking powder

5   large eggs, separated

3/4   cup (180 ml) freshly squeezed orange juice, strained

1/3   cup (90 ml) vegetable oil

    Finely grated zest of 2 unwaxed oranges

3/4   cup (150 g) superfine (caster) sugar

    Pinch of salt

1/2   teaspoon cream of tartar

Orange Glaze

1 1/2   cups (225 g) confectioners' (icing) sugar

2–3   tablespoons freshly squeezed orange juice, strained

Chiffon Cake: Preheat the oven to 325°F (170°C/gas 3). Set aside a 4-inch (10-cm) deep, 10-inch (25-cm) tube pan with removable inner tube and base. Do not grease or line with parchment paper.

Sift the flour, cornstarch, and baking powder into a large bowl.

Beat the egg yolks, orange juice, oil, and orange zest in a bowl with an electric mixer on medium speed until combined. Add 1/2 cup (100 g) of the superfine sugar and beat to combine. Set aside.

Whisk the egg whites and salt in a large bowl with an electric mixer on medium speed until foamy. Add the cream of tartar and beat until soft peaks form. Gradually add the remaining sugar, beating continuously, until firm glossy peaks form and all the sugar has dissolved.

Fold one large spoonful of egg whites into the egg yolk and orange mixture. Gently fold in the remaining whites in two batches. Pour the batter into the prepared pan. Tap firmly on a work surface to remove any air bubbles.

Bake for 40 minutes, until the cake springs back when gently touched and a toothpick inserted into the center comes out clean.

Immediately invert the pan, resting the center tube on the base of an upside down bowl or cup, keeping the pan elevated from the work surface, allowing it to cool. Let cool completely in the pan.

Run a palette knife around the rim of the pan and around the tube to loosen the cooled cake. Lift the cake out of the pan using the removable tube. Run the palette knife between the cake and the base of the pan to free the cake. Invert onto a serving plate.

Orange Glaze: Sift the confectioners' sugar into a bowl. Add enough orange juice to make a smooth runny glaze. Pour the glaze over the cake so that it drips down the sides.

Leave for 1 hour for the glaze to set. Slice and serve.

. . . . .

Pound cake is named for the fact that traditionally it was made with a pound each of butter, sugar, eggs, and flour, with spices or nuts and seeds added for flavor. Originally, baking powder was not used and the leavening was provided by the eggs. Nowadays we use baking powder, and sometimes baking soda too, for reliable, easy leavening.

POUND CAKE

1³/₄ cups (275 g) all-purpose (plain) flour

¹/₄ cup (30 g) cornstarch (cornflour)

1 teaspoon baking powder

1 cup (250 g) unsalted butter, softened

1 cup (200 g) superfine (caster) sugar

2 teaspoons vanilla extract (essence)

4 large eggs

¹/₃ cup (90 ml) milk

Preheat the oven to 350°F (180°C/gas 4). Lightly grease the base and sides of a 9 x 5-inch (23 x 13-cm) loaf pan. Line with parchment paper.

Sift the flour, cornstarch, and baking powder into a bowl.

Beat the butter, sugar, and vanilla in bowl with an electric mixer on medium-high speed until pale and creamy. Add the eggs one at a time, beating until just combined after each addition. With the mixer on low speed, gradually add the flour mixture alternating with the milk, scraping down the sides occasionally, and beating until just combined. Spoon the batter into the prepared pan.

Bake for 50–60 minutes, until a toothpick inserted into the center comes out clean. Leave in the pan for 10 minutes to cool slightly.

Turn out onto a rack and leave to cool completely. Slice and serve.

. . .

If you liked this recipe, you will love these as well.

BUTTER CAKE

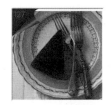

CINNAMON TEA CAKE

MADEIRA CAKE

Serves: 10
Preparation: 20 minutes
Cooking: 30 minutes
Level: 2

Angel food cakes are light, airy foam cakes made without egg yolks or fat of any kind. Food historians believe that they were invented in the 19th century by the Pennsylvania Dutch community as a way to use up leftover egg whites. There are many variations on the basic recipe; this one is our favorite.

ANGEL FOOD CAKE

1   cup (150 g) all-purpose (plain) flour

$1/4$ cup (30 g) cornstarch (cornflour)

$1^1/4$ cups (250 g) superfine (caster) sugar

12   large egg whites
     Pinch of salt

1   teaspoon cream of tartar

2   teaspoons vanilla extract (essence)
     Whipped cream, to serve
     Fresh berries, to serve

Preheat the oven to 325°F (170°C/gas 3). Set out a 4 inch (10 cm) deep, 10-inch (25-cm) tube pan with removable inner tube and base. Do not grease or line with parchment pan.

Sift the flour and cornstarch into a bowl Stir in $1/2$ cup (100 g) of sugar.

Beat the egg whites and salt in a large bowl with an electric mixer on medium speed until foamy. Add the cream of tartar and beat until soft peaks form. Gradually add the remaining sugar, beating continuously, until firm glossy peaks form and all the sugar has dissolved. Add the vanilla and beat to incorporate.

Gently fold the flour and sugar mixture into the whites in three batches. Spoon the batter into the pan. Tap firmly on a work surface to remove any air bubbles.

Bake for 30 minutes, until the cake springs back when gently touched and a toothpick inserted into the center comes out clean.

Immediately invert the pan, resting the center tube on the base of an upside down bowl or cup, keeping the pan elevated from the work surface, allowing it to cool. Let cool completely.

Run a palette knife around the rim of the pan and around the tube to loosen the cooled cake. Lift the cake out of the pan using the removable tube. Run the palette knife between the cake and the base of the pan to free the cake. Invert onto a serving plate.

Serve with whipped cream and fresh fruit.

. . .

If you liked this recipe, you will love these as well.

ORANGE CHIFFON CAKE

PASSIONFRUIT FOAM CAKE

SWISS ROLL

. . . . .

A classic chocolate cake, perfect for any occasion!

CHOCOLATE CAKE

Cake

1⅓ cups (200 g) all-purpose (plain) flour

½ cup (75 g) unsweetened cocoa

1 teaspoon baking powder

½ teaspoon baking soda

⅔ cup (150 g) salted butter, softened

1¼ cups (250 g) superfine (caster) sugar

1 teaspoon vanilla extract (essence)

2 large eggs

¾ cup (180 ml) milk

Chocolate Frosting

3 ounces (90 g) dark chocolate, coarsely chopped

2 tablespoons milk

2 tablespoons (30 g) butter

1 cup (150 g) confectioners' (icing) sugar

Cake: Preheat the oven to 350°F (180°C/gas 4). Lightly grease the base and sides of an 8-inch (20-cm) round cake pan. Line with parchment paper.

Sift the flour, cocoa, baking powder, and baking soda into a bowl.

Beat the butter, sugar, and vanilla in a large bowl using with an electric mixer on medium-high speed until pale and creamy. Add the eggs one at a time, beating until just combined after each addition. With the mixer on low speed, gradually add the flour mixture, alternating with the milk, scraping down the sides occasionally, and beating until just combined. Spoon the batter into the prepared pan.

Bake for 1–1¼ hours, until a toothpick inserted into the center comes out clean. Leave in the pan for 10 minutes to cool slightly.

Turn out onto a rack and leave to cool completely.

Chocolate Frosting: Place the chocolate, milk, and butter in a heatproof bowl and set over a saucepan of barely simmering water, ensuring the base of the bowl does not touch the water. Stir occasionally, until the chocolate and butter melt to make a smooth sauce. Remove from the heat and stir in the confectioners' sugar to make a smooth frosting.

Spread the frosting over the top of the cooled cake. Slice and serve.

. . .

If you liked this recipe, you will love these as well.

CHOCOLATE WALNUT BROWNIES

CHOCOLATE MUD CAKE

SACHERTORTE

Serves: 10
Preparation: 30 minutes
Cooking: 20 minutes
Level: 2

• • • • •

The slightly exotic flavor of the passionfruit frosting combines beautifully with the creamy filling and light-as-air foam (sponge) cake.

PASSIONFRUIT FOAM CAKE

Cake

3/4 cup (125 g) all-purpose (plain) flour

1/4 cup (30 g) cornstarch (cornflour)

1/2 teaspoon baking powder

4 large eggs

3/4 cup (150 g) superfine (caster) sugar

1 teaspoon vanilla extract (essence)

1/3 cup (90 ml) hot water

1 1/4 cups (300 ml) light whipping cream, whipped to soft peaks

Passionfruit Frosting

1 1/2 cups (225 g) confectioners' (icing) sugar

1/4 cup (60 g) unsalted butter, melted

Pulp of 4 passionfruit, strained and half of the seeds discarded

Cake: Preheat the oven to 350°F (180°C/gas 4). Lightly grease the base and sides of two 8-inch (20-cm) round cake pans. Line with parchment paper.

Triple sift the flour, cornstarch, and baking powder into a bowl.

Beat the eggs in a large bowl with an electric mixer on medium-high speed until light and fluffy. Add the sugar and vanilla and beat until pale and creamy and tripled in volume, about 10 minutes.

Gently fold the flour mixture into the egg mixture in three batches. Pour the hot water down the side of the bowl and into the mixture. Gently fold to combine. Divide the mixture evenly between the prepared pans.

Bake for 20 minutes, until well risen, golden brown, and beginning to shrink away from the sides of the pan slightly.

Cover two wire racks with sheets of parchment paper. Turn the cakes out onto the prepared racks and leave to cool completely.

Passionfruit Frosting: Sift the confectioners' sugar into a bowl, add the butter and passionfruit pulp, and stir until smooth.

To assemble, place one of the cakes on a serving plate. Spread with whipped cream. Cover with the remaining cake and spread the passionfruit frosting over the top.

Chill until the frosting sets, about 30 minutes. Slice and serve.

ORANGE CHIFFON CAKE

ANGEL FOOD CAKE

SWISS ROLL

Serves: 16

Preparation: 30 minutes
+ 1½ hours to cool
& set

Cooking: 1¼ hours

Level: 2

This cake is believed to have been invented in the state of Mississippi. According to legend, it is named after the mud that lines the banks of the famous Mississippi River—because it has the same texture!

CHOCOLATE MUD CAKE

Cake

1½	cups (300 g) superfine (caster) sugar
1	cup (250 g) salted butter, diced
7	ounces (200 g) bittersweet dark chocolate, coarsely chopped
1	cup (250 ml) milk
1	tablespoon instant coffee granules
1⅔	cups (250 g) all-purpose (plain) flour
¼	cup (30 g) unsweetened cocoa powder
1	teaspoon baking powder
3	large eggs, lightly beaten
1	teaspoon vanilla extract (essence)

Ganache

10	ounces (300 g) bittersweet dark chocolate
½	cup (120 ml) light (single) cream
2	tablespoons salted butter

Cake: Preheat the oven to 300°F (150°C/gas 2). Lightly grease the base and sides of a 9-inch (23-cm) round cake pan. Line with parchment paper.

Combine the sugar, butter, chocolate, milk, and coffee in a medium saucepan over low heat, stirring occasionally, until the sugar dissolves and the chocolate melts. Transfer to a large bowl and set aside for 15 minutes to cool slightly.

Sift the flour, cocoa, and baking powder into a bowl. Add the eggs and vanilla and stir to combine. Spoon the batter into the prepared pan.

Bake for 1¼ hours, until a toothpick inserted into the center comes out with just a few moist crumbs sticking to it but no raw cake batter. Leave in the pan to cool completely.

Ganache: Combine the chocolate, cream, and butter in a heatproof bowl and set over a saucepan of barely simmering water, ensuring the base of the bowl does not touch the water. Stir occasionally, until the chocolate and butter melt to make a smooth sauce. Remove from the heat and set aside until cooled and thickened slightly, about 15 minutes.

Spread the ganache evenly over the top and sides of the cake. Stand at room temperature for 1 hour, to set.

Slice and serve.

If you liked this recipe, you will love these as well.

CHOCOLATE CAKE　　　SACHERTORTE　　　BLACK FOREST CAKE

. . . . .

If liked, you can add a handful of golden raisins (sultanas) to this delicious cake. Serve with tea or coffee, or as a family dessert.

CARROT CAKE

Cake

1½	cups (225 g) all-purpose (plain) flour
2	teaspoons ground cinnamon
1½	teaspoons baking powder
1	teaspoon baking soda (bicarbonate of soda)
½	teaspoon ground nutmeg
¾	cup (150 g) superfine (caster) sugar
¾	cup (150 g) firmly packed light brown sugar
¾	cup (180 ml) vegetable oil
3	large eggs
10	ounces (300 g), about 3 medium carrots, peeled and coarsely grated
1	cup (120 g) walnuts, coarsely chopped
	Walnut halves, to decorate

Cream Cheese Frosting

8	ounces (250 g) cream cheese, softened
⅓	cup (90 g) unsalted butter, softened
2	cups (300 g) confectioners' (icing) sugar

Cake: Preheat the oven to 350°F (180°C/gas 4). Lightly grease the base and sides of a 9-inch (23-cm) round cake pan. Line with parchment paper.

Sift the flour, cinnamon, baking powder, baking soda, and nutmeg into a bowl.

Beat the superfine and brown sugars in a bowl with the oil and eggs until combined. Gradually beat in the flour mixture. Stir in the carrots and walnuts by hand. Spoon the batter into the prepared pan.

Bake for 50–60 minutes, until a toothpick inserted into the center comes out clean. Leave in the pan for 10 minutes to cool slightly.

Turn out onto a wire rack and let cool completely.

Cream Cheese Frosting: Beat the cream cheese and butter in a medium bowl with an electric mixer on medium-high speed until pale and creamy. Gradually add the confectioners' sugar, beating on low speed to combine. Beat on high speed until pale and creamy, 3–5 minutes.

Spread the frosting over the top and around the sides of the cake. Decorate with walnut halves.

Slice and serve.

. . .

If you liked this recipe, you will love these as well.

BANANA CAKE

COCONUT CAKE

LEMON POPPY SEED CAKE

LIGHT FRUIT CAKE

2¾ cup (500 g) mixed dried fruit
½ cup (120 ml) water
⅓ cup (90 ml) sherry
1½ cups (225 g) all-purpose (plain) flour
1 teaspoon mixed spice
½ teaspoon baking powder
½ teaspoon baking soda (bicarbonate of soda)
⅔ cup (150 g) unsalted butter, softened
¾ cup (150 g) firmly packed light brown sugar
2 large eggs
Finely grated zest of 1 unwaxed orange
Finely grated zest of 1 unwaxed lemon
½ cup (80 g) blanched almonds

Combine the mixed dried fruit and water in a medium saucepan, cover, and bring to a boil over medium heat. Remove from the heat, add the sherry, and set aside to cool.

Preheat the oven to 300°F (150°C/gas 2). Sift the flour, mixed spice, baking powder, and baking soda into a bowl.

Lightly grease the base and sides of an 8-inch (20-cm) round cake pan. Line with a double layer of parchment paper, extending the paper 2 inches (5 cm) above the rim.

Beat the butter and brown sugar in a bowl with an electric mixer on medium-high speed until creamy. Add the eggs one at a time, beating until just combined after each addition. Add the dried fruit mixture and the orange and lemon zest, beating to combine. Gradually beat in the flour mixture. Spoon the batter into the prepared pan and decorate the top with the almonds.

Bake for 1½–2 hours, until a toothpick inserted into the center comes out clean.

Wrap the hot cake in aluminum foil and a clean kitchen cloth. Set aside for at least 4 hours, until cooled completely.

Slice and serve.

· · ·

If you liked this recipe, you will love these as well.

CARROT CAKE

DATE & WALNUT ROLL

TRADITIONAL CHRISTMAS CAKE

Serves: 8–10

Preparation: 30 minutes
+ 1 hour to set

Cooking: 45–50 minutes

Level: 1

· · · · ·

This wonderful cake is a delicious way to use up bananas that are slightly too ripe to eat.

BANANA CAKE

Cake

1¹/₂ cups (225 g) all-purpose (plain) flour

1 teaspoon baking powder

¹/₂ teaspoon baking soda (bicarbonate of soda)

¹/₂ cup (120 g) unsalted butter, softened

³/₄ cup (150 g) superfine (caster) sugar

2 large eggs

1¹/₂ cups, about 3 large overripe bananas, mashed with a fork

Ground cinnamon, to dust

Lemon Frosting

1¹/₂ cups (225 g) confectioners' (icing) sugar

2 tablespoons freshly squeezed lemon juice

Cake: Preheat the oven to 350°F (180°C/gas 4). Lightly grease the base and sides of an 8-inch (20-cm) round cake pan. Line with parchment paper.

Sift the flour, baking powder, and baking soda into a bowl.

Beat the butter and sugar in a large bowl with an electric mixer on medium-high speed until pale and creamy. Add the eggs one at a time, beating until just combined after each addition. Add the banana and beat to combine. With the mixer on low speed, add the flour mixture and beat, scraping down the sides occasionally, until just combined. Spoon the batter into the prepared pan.

Bake for 45–50 minutes, until a toothpick inserted into the center comes out clean. Leave in the pan for 10 minutes to cool slightly.

Turn out onto a wire rack and let cool completely.

Lemon Frosting: Combine the confectioners' sugar and lemon juice in a small bowl and mix to make a smooth frosting.

Spread the frosting over the top of the cake and dust with cinnamon. Leave for 1 hour for the frosting to set.

Slice and serve.

· · ·

If you liked this recipe, you will love these as well.

CARROT CAKE

APPLE & CUSTARD TEA CAKE

LEMON POPPY SEED CAKE

Serves: 8
Preparation: 20 minutes
Cooking: 25–30 minutes
Level: 1

. . . . .

This light vanilla cake goes beautifully with the butter and spice topping. If preferred, you can use a mixture of spices, such as ginger, cinnamon, and nutmeg.

CINNAMON TEA CAKE

Cake

1¼ cups (180 g) all-purpose (plain) flour

1½ teaspoons baking powder

½ cup (100 g) superfine (caster) sugar

¼ cup (60 g) salted butter, softened

1 teaspoon vanilla extract (essence)

1 large egg

⅔ cup (150 ml) milk

Topping

1 tablespoon superfine (caster) sugar

1 teaspoon ground cinnamon

2 tablespoons salted butter, melted

Cake: Preheat the oven to 325°F (170°C/gas 3). Lightly grease the base and sides of an 8-inch (20-cm) round cake pan. Line with parchment paper.

Sift the flour and baking powder into a bowl.

Beat the sugar, butter, and vanilla in a bowl with an electric mixer on medium-high until pale and creamy. Add the egg and beat until just combined. With the mixer on low speed, gradually beat in the flour, alternating with the milk. Spoon the batter into the prepared pan.

Bake for 25–30 minutes, until golden brown and a toothpick inserted into the center comes out clean. Leave in the pan for 10 minutes to cool slightly while you prepare the topping.

Topping: Combine the sugar and cinnamon in a small bowl.

Turn the cake out onto a wire rack. Brush the warm cake with melted butter and dust with the cinnamon sugar.

Slice and serve.

BUTTER CAKE

BANANA CAKE

MADEIRA CAKE

. . . . .

This cake is a real treat for coconut lovers!

COCONUT CAKE

Cake

1½ cups (225 g) all-purpose (plain) flour

2 teaspoons baking powder

1 cup (100 g) shredded (desiccated) coconut

1 cup (200 g) superfine (caster) sugar

²/₃ cup (150 g) unsalted butter, softened

3 large eggs

1 cup (250 ml) coconut milk

Coconut Meringue Frosting

2 large egg whites

1 cup (200 g) superfine (caster) sugar

Few drops pink food coloring

1¼ cups (150 g) shredded (desiccated) coconut

Cake: Preheat the oven to 325°F (170°C/gas 3). Lightly grease the base and sides of a 9-inch (23-cm) round springform cake pan. Line with parchment paper.

Sift the flour and baking powder into a bowl. Stir in the coconut.

Beat the sugar and butter in a bowl with an electric mixer on medium-high speed until pale and creamy. Add the eggs one at a time, beating until just combined after each addition. With the mixer on low speed, gradually add the flour mixture, alternating with the coconut milk, scraping down the sides occasionally, and beating until just combined. Spoon the batter into the prepared pan.

Bake for about 40 minutes, until a toothpick inserted into the center comes out clean. Leave in the pan for 10 minutes to cool slightly.

Turn out onto a wire rack and let cool completely.

Coconut Meringue Frosting: Combine the egg whites and sugar in a heatproof bowl and set over a half-filled saucepan of barely simmering water, ensuring the base of the bowl does not touch the water. Stir continuously, until the sugar dissolves and the egg whites are warm to the touch.

Transfer to a large bowl and beat with an electric mixer on medium-high speed for 10 minutes, until doubled in volume, and stiff glossy peaks form. Whisk in enough food coloring to tint pale pink.
Stir in the shredded coconut.

Spread the frosting over the top of the cooled cake. Slice and serve.

Serves: 10
Preparation: 40 minutes
Cooking: 1–1¼ hours
Level: 2

This cake makes a great dessert for family meals or when entertaining friends casually.

APPLE & CUSTARD TEA CAKE

Custard

3   large egg yolks
⅓   cup (70 g) superfine (caster) sugar
2   teaspoons vanilla extract (essence)
¼   cup (30 g) all-purpose (plain) flour
1½   cups (375 ml) milk

Cake

1   cup (250 g) salted butter, softened + 1 tablespoon, melted
¾   cup (150 g) superfine (caster) sugar
3   large eggs
2   cups (300 g) all-purpose (plain) flour
2   teaspoons baking powder
¼   cup (60 ml) milk
2   medium cooking apples, such as Granny Smith, cored and thinly sliced
1   tablespoon raw sugar

Custard: Beat the egg yolks, sugar, and vanilla in a bowl with an electric mixer on medium-high until pale and thick. Stir in the flour.

Heat the milk in a small saucepan over low-medium heat until scalding. Gradually pour the milk into the egg mixture, stirring continuously, until combined.

Return the mixture to the pan and simmer over low-medium heat, whisking constantly, until it comes to a boil. Continue whisking while simmering for 1 minute. Transfer to a bowl and set aside to cool slightly. Cover the surface of the custard with a piece of parchment paper and refrigerate until cooled, about 30 minutes.

Cake: Preheat the oven to 325°F (170°C/gas 3). Lightly grease the base and sides of an 8-inch (20-cm) round springform cake pan. Line with parchment paper.

Sift the flour and baking powder into a bowl.

Beat 1 cup (250 g) of butter with the sugar in a bowl with an electric mixer on medium-high speed until pale and creamy. Add the eggs one at a time, beating until just combined after each addition. With the mixer on low speed, gradually add the flour mixture alternating with the milk, scraping down the sides occasionally, and beating until just combined.

Spoon half of the batter into the prepared pan. Pour the custard on top and spread in an even layer. Spread the remaining batter over the top to cover the layer of custard.

Arrange apple slices over the top in a circular, slightly overlapping fashion. Brush with the melted butter and sprinkle with the raw sugar.

Bake for 1–1¼ hours, until a toothpick inserted into the center comes out clean.

Let cool completely in the pan. Slice and serve.

Serves: 8–10

Preparation: 30 minutes + 1½–12½ hours to chill

Cooking: 35 minutes

Level: 2

· · · · ·

Gateau Basque is a traditional cake from the Basque region of southwestern France. It has two thick layers of almond (or almond-flavored) cake filled with pastry cream or cherry preserves.

GATEAU BASQUE

Cake

2	cups (300 g) all-purpose (plain) flour
⅓	cup (35 g) finely ground almonds
1½	teaspoons baking powder
½	teaspoon salt
¾	cup (180 g) unsalted butter, softened
1	cup (200 g) sugar
3	large egg yolks
½	teaspoon almond extract (essence)
	Confectioners' (icing) sugar, to dust

Custard Filling

¾	cup (180 ml) milk
½	cup (120 ml) heavy (double) cream
3	large egg yolks
⅓	cup (70 g) sugar
3	tablespoons cornstarch (cornflour)
1	teaspoon vanilla extract (essence)

Cake: Sift the flour, almonds, baking powder, and salt into a bowl.

Beat the butter and sugar in a bowl with an electric mixer on medium-high speed until pale and creamy. Add the egg yolks and vanilla, beating until just combined. With the mixer on low speed, gradually add flour mixture, beating until thoroughly combined and the mixture clings together when pressed against the side of bowl.

Divide into two portions, with one portion slightly larger than the other. Flatten each one into a disk, wrap in plastic wrap (cling film), and chill for at least 1 hour, or overnight.

Custard Filling: Heat the milk and cream in a medium saucepan over medium-low heat. Whisk the egg yolks, sugar, and cornstarch in a bowl. When the milk mixture is almost boiling, slowly drizzle it into the egg yolk mixture while vigorously whisking. Return to the saucepan and simmer over low heat, stirring constantly, until very thick. If lumps form, whisk until smooth. Stir in the vanilla.

Transfer the custard to a medium bowl. Place a sheet of plastic wrap directly on top. Chill 30 minutes.

Preheat the oven to 400°F (200°C/gas 6). Butter the base and sides of 9-inch (23-cm) springform pan.

Roll the larger portion of dough out on a lightly floured work surface into a 10½-inch (26-cm) round. It will be quite a thick piece of dough. Place in the prepared pan. Press the excess dough up the sides of the pan. Spoon in the custard filling, spreading it evenly.

Roll the remaining dough into a 9-inch (23-cm) round. Place on top of the filling in the pan. Press the edges of the dough to seal and form a rim. Place on a baking sheet.

Bake for 20 minutes. Reduce the oven temperature to 350°F (180°C/gas 4) and bake for more 15 minutes, until the cake is golden brown.

Let cool completely on a wire rack. Dust with confectioners' sugar and Slice and serve.

Serves: 8–10
Preparation; 30 minutes
    + 1 hour to set
Cooking: 45 minutes
Level: 1

· · · · ·

Poppy seeds are harvested from the opium poppy and are used to flavor a wide variety of foods, both sweet and savory. They are also pressed into a delicious oil.

LEMON POPPY SEED CAKE

Cake

2	cups (300 g) all-purpose (plain) flour
2	teaspoons baking powder
1	cup (200 g) superfine (caster) sugar
3/4	cup (180 g) salted butter, softened
	Finely grated zest of 2 unwaxed lemons
2	large eggs
1/2	cup (120 ml) plain yogurt
1/4	cup (60 ml) freshly squeezed lemon juice, strained
1/2	cup (75 g) poppy seeds

Lemon Drizzle Frosting

2	cups (300 g) confectioners' (icing) sugar
	Freshly squeezed juice of 1 lemon

Cake: Preheat the oven to 325°F (170°C/gas 3). Grease the base and sides of a 9-inch (23-cm) ring cake pan. Sift the flour and baking powder into a bowl.

Beat the sugar, butter, and lemon zest in a bowl with an electric mixer on medium-high speed until pale and creamy. Add the eggs one at a time, beating until just combined after each addition. With the mixer on low speed, gradually beat in the flour mixture. Add the yogurt and lemon juice, beating on low speed and scraping down the sides occasionally, until combined. Stir in the poppy seeds. Spoon the batter into the prepared pan.

Bake for 45 minutes, until a toothpick inserted into the center comes out clean. Leave in the pan for 10 minutes to cool slightly.

Turn out onto a wire rack and let cool completely.

Lemon Drizzle Frosting: Sift the confectioners' sugar into a medium bowl. Gradually stir in enough lemon juice to make a smooth, slightly runny frosting. Add a little hot water if necessary.

Pour the frosting over the cake, letting it run down the sides. Leave for 1 hour for the frosting to set.

Slice and serve.

· · ·

If you liked this recipe, you will love these as well.

CARROT CAKE

BANANA CAKE

FLOURLESS ORANGE CAKE

Serves: 10
Preparation: 30 minutes
Cooking: 2¼–2½ hours
Level: 2

This attractive and flavorsome cake is perfect if you suffer from gluten intolerance or are entertaining friends who don't eat gluten.

FLOURLESS ORANGE CAKE

2	large unwaxed or organic oranges
6	large eggs
1¼	cups (250 g) superfine (caster) sugar
2½	cups (250 g) almond meal (ground almonds)
1	teaspoon baking powder
½	cup (50 g) flaked almonds
	Confectioners' (icing) sugar, to dust

Preheat the oven to 325°F (170°C/gas 3). Lightly grease the base and sides of a 9-inch (23-cm) round springform cake pan. Line with parchment paper.

Place the oranges in a medium saucepan, cover with cold water, and simmer for 10 minutes. Drain. Cover again with cold water and simmer for 45 minutes. Drain and set aside to cool.

Coarsely chop the oranges, discarding any seeds.

Combine the oranges, eggs, and sugar in a food processor and blend until smooth. Transfer to a large bowl. Add the almond meal, sift in the baking powder, and stir to combine. Spoon the batter into the prepared pan and sprinkle with the flaked almonds.

Bake for 1¼–1½ hours, until a toothpick inserted into the center comes out clean. Leave in the pan to cool for 10 minutes.

Turn out onto a wire rack and let cool completely.

Dust with confectioners' sugar. Slice and serve.

. . .

If you liked this recipe, you will love these as well.

LEMON POPPY SEED CAKE

RHUBARB SOUR CREAM LOAF

CHOCOLATE & RASP-BERRY ROULADE

Serves: 8
Preparation: 25 minutes
Cooking: 1–1¼ hours
Level: 1

. . . . .

Rhubarb is packed with dietary fiber, anti-oxidants, minerals, and vitamins, making it a healthy food choice. Serve this cake for breakfast or brunch on lazy weekends.

RHUBARB SOUR CREAM LOAF

Loaf

1²/₃	cups (250 g) all-purpose (plain) flour
2	teaspoons baking powder
1	teaspoon ground cinnamon
1	cup (200 g) firmly packed light brown sugar
½	cup (120 g) salted butter, softened
1	teaspoon vanilla extract (essence)
3	large eggs
¾	cup (180 g) sour cream
14	ounces (400 g) rhubarb, about 4 stalks, trimmed and cut into 2-inch (5-cm) lengths

Topping

¼	cup (50 g) firmly packed brown sugar
1	teaspoon ground cinnamon

Loaf: Preheat the oven to 325°F (170°C/gas 3). Lightly grease the base and sides of a 9 x 5-inch (23 x 13-cm) loaf pan. Line with parchment paper, extending the paper 2 inches (5 cm) above the pan rim.

Sift the flour, baking powder and cinnamon into a bowl.

Beat the sugar, butter, and vanilla in a bowl with an electric mixer on medium-high speed until pale and creamy. Add the eggs one at a time, beating until just combined after each addition. Add the sour cream and beat to combine. With the mixer on low speed, gradually add the flour mixture alternating with the milk, scraping down the sides occasionally, and beating until just combined.

Spoon half of the batter into the prepared pan. Sprinkle with half of the rhubarb. Repeat the layering with the remaining batter and rhubarb.

Topping: Combine the brown sugar and cinnamon in a small bowl and sprinkle over the top of the loaf.

Bake for 1–1¼ hours, until a toothpick inserted into the center comes out clean. Leave in the pan for 10 minutes to cool slightly.

Lift out, set on a rack, and let cool completely.

Slice and serve.

. . .

If you liked this recipe, you will love these as well.

APPLE & CUSTARD
TEA CAKE

FLOURLESS ORANGE
CAKE

PLUM & ALMOND
SHEET CAKE

· · · · ·

You will need a tube pan (nut roll pan) to make this pretty cake. If you can't find one, just bake the loaf in a small rectangular loaf pan.

This cake is not too sweet and is perfect for breakfast or brunch.

DATE & WALNUT ROLL

3/4 cup (135 g) coarsely chopped dried dates

1/2 cup (120 ml) boiling water

2 tablespoons unsalted butter + extra, to serve (optional)

1/2 cup (100 g) firmly packed light brown sugar

1/4 teaspoon baking soda (bicarbonate of soda)

1 cup (150 g) all-purpose (plain) flour

1 teaspoon baking powder

1 large egg, lightly beaten

1/2 cup (60 g) coarsely chopped walnuts

Preheat the oven to 325°F (170°C/gas 3). Lightly grease the lids and inside of a 3 x 8-inch (8 x 20-cm) tube pan (nut roll pan) with melted butter. Put the base lid on the pan and place the pan upright on a baking sheet.

Combine the dates, boiling water, and butter in a medium bowl and set aside for 10 minutes, until the dates soften and the butter melts. Add the brown sugar and baking soda and stir to combine. Sift in the flour and baking powder. Add the egg and stir to combine. Mix in the walnuts.

Spoon the batter into the prepared pan and tap the base firmly on a work surface to remove any air pockets. Put the lid on and stand upright on a baking sheet.

Bake for 35–40 minutes, until a toothpick inserted into the center comes out clean. Leave in the pan for 10 minutes to cool slightly.

Remove the lid and turn out onto a wire rack. Let cool completely.

Slice and serve with butter, if desired.

· · ·

If you liked this recipe, you will love these as well.

LIGHT FRUIT CAKE

RHUBARB SOUR CREAM LOAF

GINGERBREAD & PEAR LOAF

MADEIRA CAKE

1½ cups (225 g) all-purpose (plain) flour

1 teaspoon baking powder

¾ cup (180 g) unsalted butter, softened

⅔ cup (150 g) superfine (caster) sugar + extra, to sprinkle

Finely grated zest of 1 unwaxed lemon

3 large eggs

2 tablespoons freshly squeezed lemon juice

Preheat the oven to 325°F (170°C/gas 3). Lightly grease the base and sides of a 9 x 5-inch (23 x 13-cm) loaf pan. Line with parchment paper. Sift the flour and baking powder into a bowl.

Beat the butter, sugar, and lemon zest in a bowl with an electric mixer on medium speed until pale and creamy. Add the eggs one at a time, beating until just combined after each addition. With the mixer on low speed, add the lemon juice and flour mixture and beat until just combined. Spoon the batter into the prepared pan. Sprinkle with sugar.

Bake for 40–50 minutes, until a toothpick inserted into the center comes out clean. Leave in the pan for 10 minutes to cool slightly.

Turn out onto a wire rack and let cool completely. Slice and serve.

Serves: 8 Preparation: 15 minutes Cooking: 40–50 minutes Level: 1

GINGERBREAD & PEAR LOAF

½ cup (120 g) butter

½ cup (120 ml) corn (golden) syrup + extra, to brush

½ cup (120 ml) water

⅓ cup (70 g) firmly packed light brown sugar

1¾ cups (275 g) all-purpose (plain) flour

1 tablespoon ground ginger

1 teaspoon ground cinnamon

½ teaspoon ground nutmeg

½ teaspoon baking soda

3 canned pear halves

Preheat the oven to 325°F (170°C/gas 3). Lightly grease the base and sides of a 9 x 5-inch (23 x 13-cm) loaf pan. Line with parchment paper, extending the paper 2 inches (5 cm) above the pan rim.

Heat the butter, corn syrup, water, and brown sugar in a saucepan over medium-low heat, stirring occasionally, until the butter has melted and the mixture combines. Bring to a boil. Remove from the heat and set aside for 5 minutes to cool slightly. Sift in the flour, ginger, cinnamon, nutmeg, and baking soda, stirring to combine.

Spoon the batter into the prepared pan. Thinly slice the pear halves and arrange decoratively on top.

Bake for 50–60 minutes, until a toothpick inserted into the center comes out clean. Brush the top of the hot loaf with corn syrup. Leave in the pan for 10 minutes to cool slightly. Lift out, set on a wire rack, and let cool completely. Slice and serve.

Serves: 8 Preparation: 20 minutes Cooking: 50–60 minutes Level: 1

Madeira cake is a traditional British offering. Very like a butter or pound cake, but flavored with lemon, it is usually served with a cup of tea.

The pears help keep this gingerbread loaf moist and flavorsome.

. . . . .

Sheet cakes, also known as traybakes, are simple, quick cakes that are baked in large rectangular pans. Serve directly from the pan. They are perfect for a crowd of visitors.

PLUM & ALMOND SHEET CAKE

3/4 cup (200 g) salted butter, softened

1 cup (200 g) superfine (caster) sugar

3 large eggs

1 cup (150 g) all-purpose (plain) flour

1 teaspoon baking powder

1 teaspoon ground cinnamon

1/4 cup (40 g) almond meal (ground almonds)

6 plums, halved and pitted

1/2 cup (50 g) flaked almonds

Preheat the oven to 350°F (180°C/gas 4). Grease the base and sides of a deep 8 x 12-inch (20 x 30-cm) cake pan. Line with parchment paper.

Sift the flour, baking powder, and cinnamon into a bowl. Stir in the almond meal.

Beat the butter and sugar in a bowl with an electric mixer on medium-low speed until pale and creamy. Add the eggs one at a time, beating until just combined after each addition. With the mixer on low speed, gradually beat in the flour mixture.

Spoon the batter into the prepared pan. Press the plums, cut-side up, into the batter and sprinkle with the almonds.

Bake for 40–45 minutes, until a toothpick inserted into the center comes out clean. Leave in the pan for 10 minutes to cool slightly.

Transfer to a wire rack to cool completely.

Slice into twelve pieces to serve.

APPLE & CUSTARD
TEA CAKE

RHUBARB SOUR CREAM
LOAF

TARTE TATIN

• • • • •

This cake makes a very good family dessert. Serve it warm with fresh cream or a scoop or two of vanilla ice cream.

UPSIDE-DOWN PINEAPPLE CAKE

1	(15-ounce/450-g) can pineapple rings, in syrup
7	Maraschino cherries
3/4	cup (180 g) + 1/3 cup (90 g) unsalted butter, softened
1/3	cup (70 g) firmly packed light brown sugar
1 1/2	cups (225 g) all-purpose (plain) flour
2	teaspoons baking powder
1	cup (200 g) superfine (caster) sugar
3	large eggs
1/2	cup (120 ml) milk

Preheat the oven to 350°F (180°C/gas 4). Lightly grease the base and sides of a 9-inch (23-cm) round cake pan. Line with parchment paper. If using a springform pan, wrap aluminum foil around the outside of the base to prevent the syrup from leaking.

Drain the pineapple, reserving the syrup. Place one pineapple ring in the center of the prepared pan and arrange six rings around it. Place a Maraschino cherry in the center of each ring.

Combine 1/3 cup (90 g) of the butter with the brown sugar and reserved pineapple syrup in a small saucepan and gently simmer, stirring occasionally, to make a thick syrup. Pour half of the syrup over the pineapple in the base of the pan, and set aside. Reserve the remaining syrup.

Sift the flour and baking powder into a medium bowl.

Beat the remaining 3/4 cup of butter and superfine sugar in a medium bowl with an electric mixer on medium-high until pale and creamy. Add the eggs one at a time, beating until just combined after each addition. With the mixer on low speed, gradually beat in the flour mixture, alternating with the milk. Spoon the batter into the prepared pan over the pineapple.

Bake for about 45 minutes, until golden brown and a toothpick inserted into the center comes out clean. Leave in the pan for 10 minutes to slightly.

Invert onto a serving plate and pour the remaining pineapple syrup over the top. Serve warm or at room temperature.

Serves: 8–10

Preparation: 30 minutes

Cooking: 20–25 minutes

Level: 1

The Victoria Sponge was named for Queen Victoria, who reigned over the United Kingdom for more than 63 years. She enjoyed a slice of cake for her tea in the late afternoon and this was one of her favorites.

VICTORIA SPONGE

Cake

- 1⅓ cups (200 g) all-purpose (plain) flour
- 2 teaspoons baking powder
- ¼ teaspoon salt
- ¾ cup (180 g) unsalted butter, softened
- 1 cup (200 g) superfine (caster) sugar
- 4 large eggs
- 2 tablespoons milk

Filling

- ½ cup (120 g) unsalted butter, softened
- 1 cup (150 g) confectioners' (icing) sugar + extra, to dust
- ½ teaspoon vanilla extract (essence)
- 1 cup (300 g) strawberry preserves (jam)

Cake: Preheat the oven to 325°F (170°C/gas 3). Butter two 8-inch (20-cm) round cake pans and line with parchment paper.

Sift the flour, baking powder, and salt into a bowl.

Beat the butter and sugar in a bowl with an electric mixer on medium-high speed until pale and creamy. Add the eggs one at a time, beating until just combined after each addition. With the mixer on low speed, gradually beat in the flour mixture and milk.

Spoon the batter into the prepared pans, smoothing the tops with the back of the spoon.

Bake for 20–25 minutes, until golden brown and springy to the touch. Let cool in the pans for 5 minutes, then turn out onto a wire rack and let cool completely.

Filling: Beat the butter, confectioners' sugar, and vanilla in a bowl until smooth and creamy.

Place one cake on a serving platter. Spread with the filling. Top the cream filling with the strawberry preserves and cover with the remaining cake.

Dust with confectioners' sugar. Slice and serve.

Serves: 8–10
Preparation: 30 minutes
+ 3–4 hours to set
Cooking: 40 minutes
Level: 2

. . . . .

This famous Austrian chocolate cake was invented by Franz Sacher for Prince Metternich in Vienna, in 1832.

SACHERTORTE

Cake

5 ounces (150 g) good quality bittersweet dark chocolate, coarsely chopped
1 tablespoon espresso coffee
$1/2$ cup (120 g) unsalted butter, softened
$1/2$ cup (100 g) superfine (caster) sugar
4 large eggs, separated
Pinch of salt
$3/4$ cup (120 g) all-purpose (plain) flour
$1/3$ cup (30 g) almond meal (ground almonds)
1 cup (325 g) apricot preserves (jam)
1 tablespoon dark rum

Ganache & Decoration

10 ounces (300 g) good quality semi-sweet dark chocolate, coarsely chopped
$1/2$ cup (120 ml) light (single) cream
2 tablespoons unsalted butter
$1^1/2$ ounces (50 g) good quality semi-sweet milk chocolate, coarsely chopped

Cake: Preheat the oven to 325°F (170°C/gas 3). Lightly grease the base and sides of a 9-inch (23-cm) cake pan. Line with parchment paper.

Place the chocolate and espresso in a heatproof bowl and set over a saucepan of barely simmering water, ensuring the base of the bowl does not touch the water. Stir occasionally until smooth. Remove from the heat and set aside for 10 minutes to cool slightly.

Beat the butter and sugar in a bowl with an electric mixer on medium-high until pale and creamy. Add the egg yolks one at a time, beating until just combined after each addition. Beat in the chocolate. Sift in the flour, add the almond meal, and stir to combine.

Beat the egg whites and salt in a bowl with an electric mixer on medium speed until firm peaks form. Fold one large spoonful of egg whites into the chocolate mixture. Fold in the remaining egg whites in two batches. Spoon the batter into the prepared pan. Tap the pan firmly on a work surface to remove any air bubbles.

Bake for about 40 minutes, until a toothpick inserted into the center comes out clean. Leave in the pan for 10 minutes to cool. Turn out onto a rack and let cool completely. Slice the cake in half horizontally.

Heat the apricot preserves and rum in a small saucepan over low heat. Strain through a fine mesh sieve. Spread half of the mixture over the cut side of the base. Cover with the other half and brush the remaining preserves over the top and sides. Let stand at room temperature until the preserves mixture sets, about 1 hour.

Ganache & Decoration: Combine the dark chocolate, cream, and butter in a heatproof bowl and set over a saucepan of barely simmering water, ensuring the base of the bowl does not touch the water. Stir often, until melted and smooth. Set aside for 15 minutes, until cooled and thickened slightly. Spread the ganache evenly over the top and sides of the cake. Let stand at room temperature until set, 2–3 hours.

Melt the milk chocolate. Spoon into a ziplock bag. Snip the corner off, to make a small hole, and pipe SACHER over the top of the cake.

Serves: 10
Preparation: 40 minutes
Cooking: 1 hour
Level: 1

. . . . .

This classic colored butter cake is easy to prepare and is always a success. If liked, you can use green or blue food coloring, instead of pink, to give the cake a slightly different appearance.

MARBLE CAKE

Cake

1³/₄	cups (275 g) all-purpose (plain) flour
¹/₄	cup (30 g) cornstarch (cornflour)
2	teaspoons baking powder
1	cup (250 g) unsalted butter, softened
1	cup (200 g) superfine (caster) sugar
1	teaspoon vanilla extract (essence)
3	large eggs
³/₄	cup (180 ml) + 2 tablespoons milk
2	tablespoons unsweetened cocoa powder
	Few drops pink food coloring

Butter Frosting

¹/₂	cup (120 g) unsalted butter, softened
1¹/₂	cups (225 g) confectioners' (icing) sugar
2	tablespoons + 1 teaspoon milk
¹/₂	teaspoon vanilla extract (essence)
2	teaspoons unsweetened cocoa powder
	Few drops pink food coloring

Cake: Preheat the oven to 350°F (180°C/gas 4). Lightly grease the base and sides of a 9-inch (23-cm) round cake pan. Line with parchment paper.

Sift the flour, cornstarch, and baking powder into a bowl.

Beat the butter, sugar, and vanilla in bowl with an electric mixer on medium speed until pale and creamy. Add the eggs one at a time, beating until just combined after each addition. With the mixer on low speed, add the flour mixture and ³/₄ cup (180 ml) of milk, scraping down the sides occasionally, until just combined.

Divide the batter among three bowls. Sift the cocoa powder into one bowl and add the remaining measure of milk, stirring to combine. Tint another bowl with pink with food coloring. Leave one bowl plain.

Drop alternate spoonfuls of batter into the prepared pan. Drag a butter knife through the batters to create a marbled effect.

Bake for 1 hour, until a toothpick inserted into the center comes out clean. Leave in the pan for 10 minutes to cool slightly.

Turn out onto a rack and leave to cool completely.

Butter Frosting: Beat the butter in a bowl with an electric mixer on medium speed until pale and creamy. Sift in the confectioners' sugar and add
2 tablespoons of milk in two batches, beating on low speed to combine.

Divide the frosting among three bowls. Sift the cocoa into one bowl, add the remaining measure of milk, and stir to combine. Tint another bowl pink, and leave the last bowl plain. Drop alternate spoonfuls on top of the cake and drag a knife through it to create a marbled effect.

Slice and serve.

Serves: 12–16

Preparation: 1 hour
+ 12 hours to soak,
4 hours to cool & 12
hours to set

Cooking: 3–3½ hours

Level: 2

. . . . .

A rich, fruity cake to celebrate Christmas is an old tradition in England, probably dating as far back as the 16th century. Ours is a classic recipe that you can use every year.

TRADITIONAL CHRISTMAS CAKE

Cake

2³/₄	cups (500 g) golden raisins (sultanas)
1²/₃	cups (300 g) raisins, coarsely chopped
1¹/₃	cup (240 g) currants
1	cup (180 g) candied (glacé) cherries, coarsely chopped
¹/₂	cup (100 g) mixed peel
1	cup (250 ml) + 2 tablespoons brandy or dark rum
1	cup (250 g) salted butter, softened
1	cup (200 g) light brown sugar
4	large eggs
2	cups (300 g) all-purpose (plain) flour
1	teaspoon ground ginger
1	teaspoon ground cinnamon
1	teaspoon mixed spice
¹/₂	teaspoon baking powder

Decoration

2	tablespoons brandy
¹/₃	cup (50 g) confectioners' (icing) sugar + extra, to dust
1¹/₂	pounds (750 g) ready-made marzipan
2¹/₃	pounds (1.2 kg) ready-made fondant
	Green and red food coloring

Cake: Combine the golden raisins, raisins, currants, cherries, mixed peel, and 1 cup (250 ml) of brandy in a bowl and mix well. Cover with plastic wrap and set aside at room temperature overnight, stirring often.

Preheat the oven to 300°F (150°C/gas 2). Lightly grease the base and sides of a deep 11-inch (28-cm) round cake pan and line with a triple layer of parchment paper, extending 2 inches (5 cm) above the rim.

Beat the butter and sugar in a bowl with an electric mixer on medium-high speed until pale and creamy. Add the eggs one at a time, beating until just combined after each addition. Add the soaked fruit mixture, beating to combine. Sift in the flour, ginger, cinnamon, mixed spice, and baking powder, beating to combine. Spoon the batter into the pan.

Bake for 3–3½ hours, until a toothpick inserted into the center comes out clean. Brush the hot cake with the remaining brandy. Wrap in aluminim foil and a clean kitchen towel. Let cool completely, 4 hours.

Decoration: Dust a work surface with confectioners' sugar and roll the marzipan out to make a ¹/₈ inch (3 mm) thick covering for the cake. Brush the cake with brandy and lay the marzipan over the top. Smooth down the sides to push out any air bubbles. Trim off any excess. Cover and let stand at room temperature overnight, to dry out.

Roll 2 pounds (1 kg) of fondant out to ¹/₄ inch (5 mm) thick. Brush the marzipan with brandy and lay the fondant on top. Smooth down the sides again, pushing out any air bubbles and trimming off excess.

Tint 5 ounces (150 g) of the remaining fondant dark green, kneading thoroughly to blend the color well. Roll out and cut out holly leaf shapes. Tint the remaining fondant red, kneading thoroughly. Roll small amounts into balls, like berries.

Combine the confectioners' sugar with enough water to make a paste. Brush the base of the holly leaves and berries with paste and stick decoratively on top of the cake.

Leave to stand at room temperature overnight, to set. Slice and serve.

Serves: 6–8
Preparation: 45 minutes
Cooking: 25 minutes
Level: 3

. . . . .

The Battenburg Cake was invented by chefs of the British royal family in 1884 to celebrate the marriage of Queen Victoria's granddaughter, Princess Victoria of Hesse, to Prince Louis of Battenburg.

BATTENBURG CAKE

3/4 cup (180 g) unsalted butter, softened

3/4 cup (150 g) superfine (caster) sugar

1 teaspoon vanilla extract (essence)

1/4 teaspoon almond extract (extract)

3 large eggs

1 cup (150 g) all-purpose (plain) flour

1 teaspoon baking powder

1/2 cup (50 g) almond meal (ground almonds)

Red food coloring

1/3 cup (110 g) apricot preserves (jam)

1 pound (500 g) ready-made marzipan

Confectioners' (icing) sugar, to dust

Preheat the oven to 350°F (180°C/gas 4). Lightly grease and line the base and sides of an 8-inch (20-cm) square cake pan with parchment paper. Make a divider for the pan using a piece of cardboard wrapped in aluminim foil and set across the middle of the pan, creating two halves.

Beat the butter, sugar, and vanilla and almond extracts in large bowl using an electric mixer on medium-high speed until pale and creamy. Add the eggs one at a time, beating until just combined after each addition. Sift in the flour and baking powder and add the almond meal, beating on low speed and scraping down the bowl occasionally, until combined. Spoon half the batter into one side of the cake pan. Beat enough red food coloring into the remaining batter to tint it dark pink. Spoon the pink batter into the other side of the pan.

Bake for 25 minutes, until a toothpick inserted into the center comes out clean. Leave in the pan for 10 minutes to cool slightly. Turn cakes out onto a wire rack and let cool completely.

Stack the cooled cakes on top of each other and trim off the browned edges. Trim the tops flat if they have risen in the middle, making sure they are the same thickness. Slice in half lengthwise to create four long rectangles.

Warm the apricot preserves and strain through a fine-mesh sieve. Brush the cake lengths with the preserves and stick together, two side by side and two on top, alternating colors to create a checkerboard pattern.

Lightly dust a clean work surface with confectioners' sugar and roll the marzipan out to about 1/4 inch (5 mm) thick in a rectangle large enough to cover the cake stack, leaving the ends exposed.

Brush the outside of the cake with preserves. Lay the marzipan over the cake and smooth down the sides, removing any air bubbles. Wrap the edges underneath, pressing to seal. Trim the ends to neaten and expose the checkerboard pattern. Make a criss-cross pattern on top of the cake using a sharp knife. Slice and serve.

Serves: 10
Preparation: 1 hour
    + 6-24 hours to chill
Cooking: 20–25 minutes
Level: 2

· · · · ·

Black Forest Cake, or *Schwarzwälder Kirschtorte* in German, originally comes from southern Germany. Brimming with cream, chocolate, cherries, and kirsch (a clear cherry brandy), it is perfect for all sorts of special occasions.

BLACK FOREST CAKE

1   (1½ -pound/750-g) jar Morello cherries, in syrup

¾   cup (150 g) superfine (caster) sugar

⅓   cup (90 ml) Kirsch

¼   cup (60 g) unsalted butter

4   large eggs

⅔   cup (100 g) all-purpose (plain) flour

⅓   cup (50 g) unsweetened cocoa powder

2½   cups (625 ml) heavy (double) cream

2   tablespoons confectioners' (icing) sugar

1   teaspoon vanilla extract (essence)

4   ounces (120 g) good quality bittersweet dark chocolate, made into shavings using a vegetable peeler

Preheat the oven to 350°F (180°C/gas 4). Lightly grease the base and sides of a 9-inch (23-cm) round cake pan. Line with parchment paper.

Strain the cherries, catching the juice in a small saucepan. Add ¼ cup (50 g) of sugar and the Kirsch and stir over low heat until the sugar dissolves. Simmer for 5 minutes. Set aside ten cherries. Combine the remaining cherries and the cherry Kirsch syrup in a bowl. Set aside. Melt the butter in a small saucepan, set aside, and keep warm.

Place the eggs and ½ cup (100 g) of sugar in a heatproof bowl and set over a saucepan of barely simmering water, ensuring the base of the bowl does not touch the water. Heat, stirring often, until lukewarm. Transfer to a bowl and whisk until very thick, 10–15 minutes. Sift the flour and cocoa into a bowl. Sift a second time, in three batches, into the egg mixture and gently fold to combine. Pour in the melted butter.

Pour the batter into the prepared pan. Bake for 20–25 minutes, until a toothpick inserted into the center comes out clean. Leave in the pan for 10 minutes. Turn out onto a rack and leave to cool completely. Wrap in plastic wrap and refrigerate for 4 hours, or overnight, until firm.

Slice the cake in half horizontally using a serrated knife. Whip the cream, confectioners' sugar and vanilla in a bowl using an electric mixer, until firm peaks form. Drain the cherries, reserving the syrup. Combine 1 cup of the whipped cream and the cherries in a medium bowl.

Place a cake on a serving plate. Drizzle with one-third of the syrup. Spread with the cherry and cream mixture, leaving a ¾ inch (2 cm) border. Drizzle another third of the syrup over the remaining cake, flip over and set on top of the cherry cream layer, syrup-side down. Drizzle the remaining syrup over the top.

Spoon 1 cup of cream into a piping bag fitted with a large star nozzle. Spread the remaining cream over the entire cake. Pipe ten rosettes around the top of the cake and top each with the reserved cherries. Press half of the chocolate shavings into the sides of the cake and scatter the rest on top. Chill for at least 2 hours, or overnight, to allow the flavors to develop. Slice and serve.

. . . . .

This is a classic American cake. The crumb is a deep reddish brown; originally the color was given by incorporating beets (beetroot) into the batter.

RED VELVET CAKE

Cake

1½ cups (300 g) superfine (caster) sugar

½ cup (120 g) unsalted butter, softened

2 teaspoons vanilla extract (essence)

2 large eggs

2¼ cups (330 g) all-purpose (plain) flour

¼ cup (30 g) cornstarch (corn flour)

¼ cup (30 g) unsweetened cocoa powder

1 teaspoon baking powder

½ teaspoon baking soda (bicarbonate of soda)

1 cup (250 ml) buttermilk

2 tablespoons red food coloring

Cream Cheese Frosting

1 pound (500 g) cream cheese, softened

⅓ cup (90 g) unsalted butter, softened

1 teaspoon vanilla extract (essence)

1 cup (250 ml) sour cream

3 cups (450 g) confectioners' (icing) sugar

Cake: Preheat the oven to 325°F (170°C/gas 3). Lightly grease the base and sides of two 9-inch (23-cm) round cake pans. Line with parchment paper.

Sift the flour, cornstarch, cocoa, baking powder and baking soda into a bowl.

Beat the sugar, butter, and vanilla in large bowl with an electric mixer on medium speed until pale and creamy. Add the eggs one at a time, beating until just combined after each addition. Blend the buttermilk and food coloring together in a small bowl. Add the flour mixture and the red buttermilk alternately in two batches, folding to combine.

Divide the batter evenly among the prepared pans.

Bake for 25–30 minutes, until a toothpick inserted into the center comes out clean. Leave in the pan for 10 minutes to cool slightly.

Turn out onto a rack and leave to cool completely.

Wrap the cakes in plastic wrap and refrigerate for at least 4 hours, or overnight, until firm.

Cream Cheese Frosting: Beat the cream cheese, butter and vanilla in a large bowl with an electric mixer on medium speed until pale and creamy. Add the sour cream and beat to incorporate. Add the confectioners' sugar 1 cup (150 g) at a time, beating on low speed and scraping down the sides occasionally, to combine.

To assemble the cake, slice the cakes in half horizontally using a serrated knife. Spread a large spoonful of frosting over one of the halves and sandwich another half on top. Repeat with the remaining cake disks, creating three frosting layers. Spread the remaining frosting over the entire cake, using a spatula to smooth.

Slice and serve.

Serves: 16
Preparation: 2 hours
Cooking: 15–20 minutes
Level: 3

. . . . .

This famous Hungarian cake was created by master chef Jósef Dobos in the second half of the 19th century. He presented it officially at a national show in 1885. No one else could quite get it right until 1906, when chef Dobos finally released the recipe.

DOBOS TORTE

Cake

8   large eggs, separated

3¹/₂   cups (525 g) confectioners' (icing) sugar

1   cup (150 g) all-purpose (plain) flour

2   tablespoons milk

    Pinch of salt

Chocolate Buttercream

10   ounces (300 g) bittersweet dark chocolate, coarsely chopped

1¹/₄   cups (300 g) unsalted butter, softened

2   large egg yolks

2   tablespoons espresso coffee

1   teaspoon vanilla extract (essence)

¹/₂   cup (75 g) confectioners' (icing) sugar

Toffee Layer

³/₄   cup (150 g) sugar

2   tablespoons water

Decoration

1   cup (100 g) coarsely grated dark chocolate

16   whole roasted hazelnuts, peeled

Cake: Preheat the oven to 350°F (180°C/gas 4). Grease and line the bases of seven 9-inch (23-cm) springform pans with parchment paper.

Beat the egg yolks and 3 cups (450 g) of the confectioners' sugar in a bowl with an electric mixer on medium speed until pale and very thick, 5–10 minutes. Sift in the flour. Add the milk, beating to combine.

Beat the egg whites and salt in a bowl until soft peaks form. Gradually beat in the remaining sugar until firm glossy peaks form. Stir one large spoonful of whites into the yolk mixture. Fold in the rest. Weigh the batter and divide into seven portions. Spoon a portion of batter into each prepared pan in an even layer. Bake for 5–7 minutes, until springy to the touch. Invert onto a rack, peel away the paper and let cool.

Chocolate Buttercream: Melt the chocolate in a heatproof bowl set over a saucepan of barely simmering water, ensuring the base of the bowl does not touch the water. Set aside to cool. Beat the butter in a bowl until pale and creamy. Add the egg yolks, coffee, and vanilla and beat to combine. Pour in the cooled chocolate and beat to combine. Fold in the sifted confectioners' sugar. Weigh and divide into eight portions.

Place one of the cakes on a serving plate. Spread with one portion of the buttercream. Continue layering to create six cake and buttercream layers. Set the remaining cake aside. Spread the remaining buttercream over the top and sides of the cake to completely cover using a spatula to create a smooth surface. Mark sixteen wedges on the top of the cake using a sharp knife. Press the grated chocolate around the edge of the cake. Refrigerate.

Toffee Layer: Line a rack with a piece of greased parchment paper and set over a pan to catch any drips. Cut the remaining cake down by ²/₃ inch (1.5 cm) around the edge and place on the rack. Combine the sugar and water in a small saucepan and heat over medium-low, swirling occasionally, but without stirring, for 3 minutes, until the sugar dissolves. Boil for 3 minutes, until it turns a deep caramel. Pour over the cake and quickly spread to make an even layer. Transfer immediately to a chopping board and cut into sixteen wedges. Arrange toffee wedges down the center of each marked portion of the cake, using a hazelnut to prop up each one slightly so they sit on an angle. Slice and serve.

Serves: 10–12
Preparation: 45 minutes
    + 1 hour to chill
Cooking: 25–30 minutes
Level: 3

. . . . .

This classic American cake has been served at genteel gatherings for many years. The origins of its name are disputed but according to one theory it was described in a popular novel published in 1906 and sounded so delicious that readers clamored for the recipe, which was duly produced.

LADY BALTIMORE CAKE

Filling

$1/2$	cup (90 g) coarsely chopped dried figs
$1/4$	cup (45 g) golden raisins, coarsely chopped
$1/4$	cup (45 g) dried cranberries
$1/4$	cup (60 ml) brandy or Grand Marnier
$1/2$	cup (60 g) pecans, coarsely chopped

Cake

$1^1/3$	cups (270 g) superfine (caster) sugar
$3/4$	cup (180 g) unsalted butter, softened
2	teaspoons vanilla extract (essence)
$2^1/2$	cups (375 g) all-purpose (plain) flour
$1/2$	cup (75 g) cornstarch (corn flour)
3	teaspoons baking powder
1	cup (250 ml) milk
6	large egg whites Pinch of salt

Frosting

2	cups (400 g) sugar
$3/4$	cup (180 ml) water
4	large egg whites Pinch of salt
2	teaspoons vanilla extract (essence)

Filling: Combine the figs, raisins, and cranberries in a bowl. Add the liqueur, stir to combine, and set aside.

Cake: Preheat the oven to 350°F (180°C/gas 4). Lightly grease and line the base and sides of three 8-inch (20cm) springform pans with parchment paper.

Beat the sugar, butter, and vanilla using an electric mixer on medium-high speed until pale and creamy. Sift the flour, cornstarch, and baking powder into a medium bowl. Add the flour mixture and milk alternately in three batches, folding to combine.

Whisk the egg whites and salt together in a large bowl, using an electric mixer, until stiff peaks form. Stir a large spoonful of whites into the mixture. Fold in the remaining egg whites. Divide the batter evenly amongst the prepared pans.

Bake for 25–30 minutes, until a toothpick inserted into the center comes out clean. Leave in the pan for 10 minutes to cool slightly. Turn out onto a wire rack and leave to cool completely.

Frosting: Combine the sugar and water in a medium heavy-based saucepan over low heat, stirring occasionally, until the sugar dissolves. Increase the heat and boil for 15–25 minutes, until the syrup reaches soft-ball stage or reads 240°F (115°C) on a candy thermometer.

Beat the egg whites and salt in a bowl with an electric mixer on medium speed until firm peaks form. Gradually pour in the hot syrup in a thin steady stream, beating constantly. Beat until glossy and very thick, about 5 minutes. Add the vanilla and beat to incorporate.

Transfer one-third of the frosting into the bowl with the soaking dried fruit. Add the pecans and stir to combine.

Place one of the cakes on a serving plate and spread half of the filling over the top, leaving a $3/4$ inch (2 cm) border. Cover with another cake and spread with the remaining filling. Put the remaining cake on top.

Spread the frosting over the entire cake, using a spatula to create decorative peaks. Chill for 1 hour to set slightly. Slice and serve.

Serves: 8
Preparation: 30 minutes
Cooking: 10 minutes
Level: 2

. . . . .

This classic roulade is a thin foam (sponge) cake baked in a jelly roll pan, then filled with raspberry preserves and cream and rolled. Originally from Central Europe, it is now popular all over the world. Feel free to experiment with the filling; try using another type of fruit preserves, a chocolate hazelnut spread, buttercream, or fresh fruit for a change.

SWISS ROLL

3	large eggs
3/4	cup (150 g) superfine (caster) sugar
2	tablespoons hot milk
3/4	cup (120 g) all-purpose (plain) flour
2	tablespoons unsalted butter, melted
1/2	cup (150 g) raspberry preserves (jam), warmed
	Whipped cream, to serve (optional)

Preheat the oven to 350°F (180°C/gas 4). Grease the base and sides of a 10 x 12-inch (25 x 30-cm) jelly-roll (Swiss roll) pan. Line with parchment paper, extending the paper 1½ inches (4 cm) above the sides of the pan.

Beat the eggs and ½ cup (100 g) of sugar in a bowl with an electric mixer on medium speed until very pale and thick. Stir in the milk. Sift in the flour, one-third at a time. Add the butter and gently fold it in. Spoon the batter into the prepared pan.

Bake for 10 minutes, until the cake springs back when lightly pressed. Cover the pan with a piece of parchment paper and a clean, slightly damp kitchen cloth and leave for 20 minutes to cool slightly.

Cut another piece of parchment paper slightly larger than the pan. Lay the paper on a work surface and dust evenly with the remaining ¼ cup (50 g) of superfine sugar. Turn the cake out onto the paper sprinkled with sugar. Peel away the paper and let cool completely.

Spread the raspberry preserves over the cooled cake.

With the longest side facing you and using the paper as a guide, roll to enclose the preserves. Turn seam-side down.

Slice and serve each portion with a dollop of whipped cream, if desired.

. . .

If you liked this recipe, you will love these as well.

ORANGE CHIFFON CAKE

ANGEL FOOD CAKE

PASSION FRUIT FOAM CAKE

Serves: 8

Preparation: 30 minutes
+ 1½ hours to cool
& to chill

Cooking: 15–20 minutes

Level: 3

. . . . .

This sinfully rich and delicious cake is flourless, and therefore gluten-free. It makes a great dessert if you are entertaining guests who don't eat gluten.

CHOCOLATE & RASPBERRY ROULADE

Roulade

7   ounces (200 g) good quality bittersweet dark chocolate, coarsely chopped
¼   cup (60 ml) water
5   large eggs, separated
    Pinch of salt
½   cup (100 g) firmly packed light brown sugar
    Unsweetened cocoa powder, to dust

Filling

1   cup (250 ml) heavy (double) cream
1   tablespoon confectioners' (icing) sugar
1   cup (150 g) fresh raspberries

Roulade: Preheat the oven to 350°F (180°C/gas 4). Grease the base and sides of a 10 x 12-inch (25 x 30-cm) jelly-roll (Swiss roll) pan. Line with parchment paper, extending the paper 1½ inches (4 cm) above the sides.

Melt the chocolate and water in a heatproof bowl set over a saucepan of barely simmering water, ensuring the base of the bowl is not touching the water. Stir until smooth. Set aside to cool.

Beat the egg yolks and sugar in a bowl with an electric mixer on medium-high speed until pale and thick. Fold in the cooled chocolate mixture.

Beat the egg whites and salt in a bowl with an electric mixer on medium speed until soft peaks form. Fold one large spoonful of the egg whites into the chocolate mixture. Gently fold in the remaining egg whites until just combined. Spoon the mixture into the prepared pan.

Bake for 15–20 minutes, until the cake springs back when lightly pressed. Cover the pan with a piece of parchment paper and a clean, slightly damp kitchen cloth and leave for 20 minutes to cool slightly.

Cut another piece of parchment paper slightly larger than the pan. Lay the paper on a work surface and dust evenly with cocoa. Turn the cake out onto the paper dusted with cocoa. Peel away the paper on the cake and leave to cool completely.

Filling: Whip the cream and confectioners' sugar in a bowl with an electric mixer on high speed until firm peaks form. Spread the cream over the cooled cake, leaving a ¾ inch (2 cm) border. Sprinkle with the raspberries.

With the longest side facing you and using the paper as a guide, roll to enclose the filling. Turn seam side down and chill for one hour before serving. Slice and serve.

tarts & pies

This chapter features 28 tarts and pies.
It includes recipes for elegant tartlets,
alongside many classic larger tarts and pies,
including tarte tatin, pumpkin pie, French
flan, and lemon meringue pie.

Serves: 6
Preparation: 30 minutes
    + 1 hour to chill
Cooking: 40–45 minutes
Level: 2

CUSTARD TARTLETS

Sweet Pastry

1 cup (150 g) all-purpose (plain) flour

$1/3$ cup (75 g) unsalted chilled butter, diced

$1/8$ teaspoon salt

$1/4$ cup (30 g) confectioner's (icing) sugar

1 large egg, lightly beaten

Custard

3 large eggs

$1/4$ cup (50 g) superfine (caster) sugar

2 teaspoons vanilla extract (essence)

1 cup (250 ml) single cream

Freshly grated nutmeg

Sweet Pastry: Combine the flour, butter, and salt in a food processor and blend until the mixture resembles coarse crumbs. Add the confectioners' sugar and pulse to combine. With the motor running, gradually beat in the egg.

Turn the pastry out onto a clean work surface and, using your hands, bring the mixture together to form a dough. Wrap in plastic wrap (cling film) and chill in the refrigerator for at least 30 minutes.

Lightly grease and flour six 2½-inch (6-cm) fluted or plain tartlet pans with removeable bases.

Roll the pastry out between two sheets of parchment paper to about ¼ inch (5 mm) thick. Cut out circles 1 inch (2.5 cm) larger than the prepared tartlet pans and use them to line the pans. Trim off and discard the excess pastry. Prick the bases with a fork and chill for 30 minutes.

Preheat the oven to 350°F (180°C/gas 4).

Place the tartlet pans on a baking sheet. Line the pastry cases with parchment paper and fill with baking weights, uncooked rice, or dried beans. Bake for 10 minutes, until the edges are golden. Remove the paper and baking weights and bake for 5 more minutes, until the pastry is just cooked through. Set aside.

Decrease the oven temperature to 300°F (150°C/gas 2).

Custard: Beat the eggs, sugar, and vanilla in a bowl with an electric mixer on medium speed until well mixed. Heat the cream in a small saucepan over medium-low heat until scalding. Gradually pour into the egg mixture, stirring constantly until combined.

Pour the custard into the cooked pastry cases. Grate a generous amount of nutmeg over each tartlet.

Bake for 25–30 minutes, until just set.

Leave on the baking sheet to cool slightly. Transfer to a wire rack and let cool to room temperature. Serve at room temperature or chilled.

Serves: 6
Preparation: 30 minutes
    + 1½ hours to chill
Cooking: 20–30 minutes
Level: 2

. . . . .

These little tartlets make an eyecatching dessert for a special dinner party. They are also convenient because you can prepare them a few hours before your guests arrive and chill until ready to serve.

STRAWBERRY TARTLETS

Pastry Cases

1	quantity sweet pastry (see page 172)
1	large egg white, lightly beaten, to brush
3	cups (450 g) strawberries

Crème Patissiere

3	large egg yolks
⅓	cup (70 g) superfine (caster) sugar
¼	cup (30 g) all-purpose (plain) flour
2¼	cups (560 ml) milk
1	vanilla pod, halved lengthwise and seeds scraped

Apricot Glaze

½	cup (160 g) apricot preserves (jam)
2	tablespoons water

Pastry Cases: Prepare the pastry as explained on page 172. Lightly grease and flour six ¾-inch (2-cm) deep, 3-inch (8-cm) fluted or plain tartlet pans with removeable bases.

Roll the pastry out between two sheets of parchment paper to about ¼ inch (5 mm) thick. Cut out circles 1 inch (2.5 cm) larger than the prepared pans and use them to line the pans. Trim off any excess pastry. Prick the bases with a fork and refrigerate for 30 minutes.

Preheat the oven to 350°F (180°C/gas 4).

Crème Patissiere: Beat the egg yolks and sugar in a bowl with an electric mixer on medium speed until pale and thick. Stir in the flour. Heat the milk and vanilla pod and seeds in a small saucepan over medium-low heat until scalding. Gradually pour the milk into the egg mixture, whisking constantly, until combined. Return the mixture to the pan and simmer over medium-low heat, whisking constantly, until it comes to a boil. Continue whisking while boiling for 1 minute. Transfer to a bowl and remove the vanilla pod. Cover the surface with a piece of parchment paper to prevent a skin from forming. Chill until cooled, about 30 minutes.

Place the tart pans on a baking sheet. Line the pastry cases with parchment paper and fill with baking weights, uncooked rice, or dried beans. Bake for 15 minutes, until the edges are golden. Remove the paper and baking weights. Brush the pastry with egg white and bake for 8 minutes, until the pastry is cooked through and golden brown. Transfer to a wire rack and let cool completely.

Spoon the crème patissiere into the cooled pastry cases. Cut the strawberries to size, halving the small and quartering the large ones. Arrange decoratively, cut-side down, on top of the crème patissiere.

Apricot Glaze: Heat the apricot preserves and water in a small saucepan over low heat, stirring occasionally, until syrupy. Strain through a fine-mesh sieve. Brush over the tarts to glaze, taking care not to disturb the strawberry arrangement. Chill until set, about 30 minutes. Serve chilled.

CHOCOLATE RASPBERRY TARTLETS

Pastry Cases

1 quantity chocolate pastry (see page 180)

Filling

8 ounces (250 g) dark chocolate

1/2 cup (120 ml) heavy (double) cream

2 tablespoons butter

1 tablespoon kirsch

2 cups (300 g) fresh raspberries

Pastry Cases: Prepare the pastry as explained on page 180. Press into a ball, wrap in plastic wrap (cling film), and chill for 30 minutes.

Preheat the oven to 350°F (180°C/gas 4). Butter twelve 2-inch (5-cm) fluted tartlet pans. Divide the dough into four pieces. Roll out one piece (keep the remaining pieces in the refrigerator) on a lightly floured work surface to about 1/8 inch (3 mm) thick. Cut out three disks slightly larger than the tartlet pans. Place in the pans. Repeat with the remaining dough.

Fill with pie weights and bake until the dough is firm, 12–15 minutes. Let cool completely on a wire rack.

Filling: Stir the chocolate in a double boiler over barely simmering water until melted. Remove from the heat and gradually stir in the cream, butter, and kirsch. Beat until smooth, then let cool. Spoon some chocolate filling into each tartlet case. Top with raspberries, and serve.

Serves: 12 Preparation: 45 minutes + 1 hour to chill Cooking: 12–15 minutes Level: 2

WHITE CHOCOLATE TARTLETS

Pastry Cases

2 quantities sweet pastry (see page 172)

Cherries

1/2 cup (120 ml) dry red wine

1/2 cup (100 g) sugar

3 cups (450 g) fresh cherries, pitted

Filling

8 ounces (250 g) white chocolate, coarsely chopped

8 ounces (250 g) ricotta cheese

8 ounces (250 g) mascarpone

Pastry Cases: Prepare and bake as explained on page 172.

Cherries: Put the wine and sugar in a saucepan over low heat. Cook and stir until the sugar dissolves. Bring to a boil. Add the cherries and simmer, stirring often, for 3–4 minutes, until the syrup thickens. Set aside to cool for 30 minutes.

Filling: Melt the chocolate in a double boiler over barely simmering water. Set aside for 10 minutes to cool.

Beat the chocolate, ricotta, and mascarpone in a bowl until smooth. Divide the ricotta mixture among the pastry cases and chill for 30 minutes. Top with the cherries and syrup, and serve.

Serves: 12 Preparation: 45 minutes + 1 hour to chill Cooking: 30 minutes Level: 2

Serve these wicked tartlets with a glass of very dry champagne for a special dessert celebration.

Cherries and white chocolate go wonderfully well together. Use frozen cherries for the topping when fresh cherries are out of season.

Serves: 6
Preparation 30 minutes
  + 1 hour to chill
Cooking: 13–15 minutes
Level: 2

. . . . .

This recipe makes 12 small tartlets, enough for six people for dessert. For a change, you can make lime curd tartlets by replacing the lemon juice and zest in the curd with the same quantity of freshly squeezed lime juice and zest.

LEMON CURD TARTLETS

Pastry Cases
1   quantity sweet pastry (see page 172)
1   large egg white, lightly beaten, to brush

Lemon Curd
3   large egg yolks
$\frac{1}{3}$ cup (70 g) superfine (caster) sugar
$\frac{1}{4}$ cup (60 ml) freshly squeezed lemon juice
     Finely grated zest of 1 unwaxed lemon
$\frac{1}{4}$ cup (60 g) unsalted butter, diced

Pastry Cases: Prepare the pastry as explained on page 172. Lightly grease and flour a twelve-cup patty or muffin pan.

Roll the pastry out between two sheets of parchment paper to about $\frac{1}{4}$ inch (5 mm) thick. Cut out circles using a $2\frac{3}{4}$-inch (7-cm) fluted cookie cutter. Line the prepared cups. The pastry will seem a little large but it will shrink slightly. Prick the bases with a fork and chill for 30 minutes.

Preheat the oven to 350°F (180°C/gas 4).

Lemon Curd: Whisk the egg yolks and sugar in a medium heatproof bowl until light and fluffy. Mix in the lemon juice and zest. Set the bowl over a saucepan of barely simmering water, ensuring the base of the bowl is not touching the water and cook, and whisk constantly, until thick, about 5 minutes. Add the butter one piece at a time, whisking between each addition, until incorporated.

Remove the bowl from the heat and set aside to cool slightly. Cover the surface of the lemon curd with a piece of parchment paper and refrigerate until cooled, about 30 minutes.

Bake the tartlets for 10 minutes, until the edges are golden. Brush with egg white and bake for 3–5 minutes more, until cooked through and golden brown. Place on a wire rack and let cool completely.

Spoon the lemon curd into the cooled pastry cases. Serve chilled or at room temperature.

ORANGE RICOTTA TART

LEMON TART

LEMON MERINGUE PIE

. . . . .

Salt, caramel, and chocolate go surprisingly well together, as this recipe will prove.

CHOCOLATE & SALTED CARAMEL CUPS

Chocolate Pastry

1   cup (150 g) all-purpose (plain) flour

1/3   cup (50 g) unsweetened cocoa powder

1/2   cup (120 g) chilled unsalted butter, diced

1/2   cup (75 g) confectioners' (icing) sugar

1   large egg, lightly beaten

1/2   teaspoon vanilla extract (essence)

Salted Caramel Filling

1   cup (200 g) superfine (caster) sugar

1/4   cup (60 ml) heavy cream

1/4   cup (60 g) unsalted butter

1   tablespoon sea salt flakes + extra, for sprinkling

Chocolate Ganache

4   ounces (120 g) bittersweet dark chocolate, coarsely chopped

1/4   cup (60 ml) heavy (double) cream

Chocolate Pastry: Place the flour and cocoa in a food processor and pulse to combine. Add the butter and blend until the mixture resembles coarse crumbs. Add the sugar and pulse to combine. With the motor running, add the egg and vanilla. Turn out onto a clean work surface and, using your hands, bring the mixture together to form a dough.

Lightly grease a 24-cup mini muffin pan with butter.

Divide the dough into twenty-four even pieces. Press a portion into each muffin cup to line, creating an even pastry case about 1/8 inch (3 mm) thick. Prick the bases with a fork. Refrigerate for 30 minutes.

Preheat the oven to 350°F (180°C/gas 4).

Bake the pastry cases for 10–15 minutes, until cooked through. Set aside to cool.

Salted Caramel Filling: Sprinkle the sugar in an even layer into a dry heavy-based pan. Cook over medium heat until the sugar begins to dissolve and caramelize in spots, about 5 minutes. Swirl the pan, but do not stir, to help dissolve all the sugar. Continue cooking until it turns into an even, amber-colored caramel. Remove from the heat and whisk in the cream, butter, and salt, taking care as the hot caramel will steam and bubble up. Set aside to cool slightly.

Divide the caramel evenly among the pastry cases.

Chocolate Ganache: Combine the chocolate and cream in a heatproof bowl and set over a saucepan of barely simmering water, ensuring the base of the bowl does not touch the water. Stir occasionally, until the chocolate melts to make a smooth sauce.

Pour over the caramel to fill the pastry cases. Slide the back edge of a knife over the top of the cups, to create a smooth flat surface.

Let stand at room temperature or refrigerate to set.

Serve at room temperature for a soft caramel center, or chilled for a firm center.

Makes: 24
Preparation: 30 minutes
    + 12 hours to chill
Cooking: 15–20 minutes
Level: 2

· · · · ·

These little pies are a tradition at Christmas time in Britain, and in many parts of the Commonwealth. Their history can be traced back to the Middle Ages when they did, as their name suggests, contain meat (mince). Nowadays they are made of a mixture of spiced mixed dried fruit and nuts.

CHRISTMAS MINCE PIES

Filling

1	medium green cooking apple, such as a Granny Smith, coarsely grated
$1/2$	cup (100 g) light brown sugar
$1/2$	cup (90 g) raisins
$1/2$	cup (90 g) golden raisins (sultanas)
$1/4$	cup (45 g) currants
$1/4$	cup (40 g) candied mixed peel
$1/4$	cup (30 g) slivered almonds
2	tablespoons butter
$1/4$	cup (60 ml) brandy
$1/2$	teaspoon ground nutmeg
$1/2$	teaspoon ground cinnamon
$1/2$	teaspoon mixed spiced
	Finely grated zest and juice of 1 lemon

Pastry

2	cups (300 g) all-purpose (plain) flour
$1/2$	cup (50 g) almond meal (finely ground almonds)
$1/2$	cup (75 g) confectioners' (icing) sugar + extra, to dust
7	ounces (200 g) chilled unsalted butter, diced
1	large egg yolk + 1 large egg, beaten
1–2	tablespoons chilled water

Filling: Combine all the ingredients in a large bowl and mix well. Cover with plastic wrap (cling film) and refrigerate for 12 hours. Stir occasionally, so that fruit soaks evenly.

Pastry: Place the flour, almond meal, and confectioners' sugar in a food processor and pulse to combine. Add the butter and pulse until the mixture resembles coarse crumbs. Mix the egg yolk with 1 tablespoon of the water in a small bowl. With the motor running, add the egg mixture.

Turn out onto a clean work surface and, using your hands, bring the mixture together, adding a little of the remaining water if necessary, to form a dough. Shape into two disks, one using two-thirds of the dough and the other the remaining third. Wrap in plastic wrap and chill in the refrigerator for at least 30 minutes.

Preheat the oven to 350°F (180°C/gas 4). Lightly grease two 12-cup patty or muffin pans with butter.

Roll the larger disk of pastry out between two sheets of parchment paper to about $1/8$ inch (3 mm) thick. Cut out twenty-four rounds using a 3-inch (8-cm) cookie cutter. Line the prepared cups with pastry.

Divide the filling evenly among the pastry cases.

Roll out the remaining pastry between two sheets of parchment paper and cut out twenty-four $2^{1}/_{2}$-inch (6-cm) rounds. Place on top of the filling, pinching the edges to seal.

Brush with egg and bake for 15–20 minutes, until golden. Leave in the pans for 10 minutes to cool slightly.

Place on a wire rack and let cool completely. Dust with confectioners' sugar, and serve.

Makes: 12
Preparation: 30 minutes
Cooking: 18–20 minutes
Level: 1

. . . . .

These pretty little tarts, known as pastels de nata in their homeland of Portugal, are simple to make. You can use storebought puff pastry, or try our recipe on page 224. If making our pastry recipe, you will only need about one-third of the recipe. Make a small batch, or freeze the excess for another recipe.

PORTUGUESE TARTS

1¼	cups (250 g) superfine (caster) sugar
2	lemon slices
2	cinnamon sticks
½	cup (120 ml) water
1	cup (250 ml) semi-skimmed milk
¼	cup (30 g) all-purpose (plain) flour
2	tablespoons cornstarch (cornflour) cornflour
½	teaspoon vanilla extract (essence)
3	large egg yolks + 1 large egg
12	ounces (375 g) storebought or homemade puff pastry (see page 224)
	Confectioners' (icing) sugar and ground cinnamon, to dust

Combine the sugar, lemon, and cinnamon sticks in a pan with the water and bring to a boil.

Mix the flour, cornstarch, and vanilla with a small amount of milk to make a smooth paste. Bring the rest of the milk to a boil, then pour it into the flour mixture, whisking constantly. Pour back into a clean pan and bring to a simmer, whisking until the mixture thickens.

Remove the cinnamon sticks and lemon then stir the sugar and flour mixtures together. Whisk in the eggs. Bring back to a simmer and whisk until smooth. Pour into a pitcher (jug), cover the surface with plastic wrap (cling film), and let cool.

Heat the oven to 450°F (220°C/gas 7). Butter a 12-cup muffin pan

Roll out the puff pastry on a clean work surface lightly dusted with flour and confectioners' sugar. Cut the pastry in half and lay one sheet on top of the other. Roll the pastry sheets up like a Swiss roll and cut the roll into twelve slices about ½ inch (1 cm) thick.

Lay each of the pastry slices flat on the work surface and roll them out into 4-inch (10-cm) disks. Press a pastry disk into each of the cups of the prepared muffin pan. Divide the custard among the pastry cases.

Bake for 18–20 minutes, until the custard has puffed up and is pale gold and the pastry is crisp and golden.

Let cool in the pan. Dust with the cinnamon and confectioners' sugar just before serving.

CUSTARD TARTLETS

STRAWBERRY TARTLETS

FRENCH FLAN

Serves: 6
Preparation: 30 minutes
    + 2-7 hours to set
    & chill
Cooking: 25-30 minutes
Level: 1

. . . . .

For a slightly different look and flavor, replace the raspberries in this recipe with small, wild strawberries or sliced ordinary ones.

RASPBERRY CREAM CHEESE TART

Crust

1⅓	cups (200 g) all-purpose (plain) flour
½	cup (120 ml) cold unsalted butter, cut into small pieces
⅓	cup (70 g) sugar
¼	teaspoon salt
	Fresh cream, to serve (optional)

Filling

8	ounces (250 g) cream cheese, softened
¼	cup (50 g) sugar
5	cups (750 g) fresh raspberries
¼	cup (75 g) seedless red currant jelly

Crust: Preheat the oven to 350°F (180°C/gas 4). Pulse the flour, butter, sugar, and salt in a food processor until moist crumbs form.

Transfer the dough to a 9-inch (23-cm) tart pan with a removeable bottom. Press evenly into the bottom and up the sides of the pan. Chill until firm, about 30 minutes.

Prick all over with a fork. Bake for 25–30 minutes, until golden. Let cool completely in the pan.

Filling: Beat the cream cheese and sugar in a bowl until smooth. Spread evenly over the cooled crust. Arrange the berries in tight concentric circles over the cream cheese.

Heat the jelly over low heat until liquid. Brush over the berries. Let set for 30 minutes. Chill in the pan for 1-6 hours. Slice and serve with fresh cream, if liked.

. . .

If you liked this recipe, you will love these as well.

STRAWBERRY TARTLETS

CHOCOLATE RASPBERRY TARTLETS

BERRYFRUIT PIE

Serves: 8–10
Preparation: 45 minutes
    + 1½–12½ hours to
    chill
Cooking: 20–25 minutes
Level: 2

• • • • •

This delicious French tart is a classic all over France and you will find it in every bakery and wayside stopover. The sweet, creamy custard baked into the flaky pastry makes it the ultimate comfort food.

FRENCH FLAN

Almond Pastry
⅓   cup (90 g) unsalted butter, softened
½   cup (75 g) confectioners' (icing) sugar
⅛   teaspoon salt
3   tablespoons almond meal (finely ground almonds)
1   large egg
1   cup (150 g) all-purpose (plain) flour

Filling
3⅓   cups (850 ml)) whole milk
¾   cup (150 g) sugar
1   vanilla bean, split and seeds scraped
⅔   cup (100 g) cornstarch (cornflour)
3   large egg yolks

Almond Pastry: Beat the butter, confectioners' sugar, and salt in a bowl until pale and creamy. Beat in the almond meal, followed by the egg. Sift in the flour and beat until just combined.

Scoop the pastry into a large sheet of plastic wrap (cling film) and form into a disk, wrapping in the plastic. Chill in the refrigerator for at least an hour, or overnight.

Butter a 9-inch (23-cm) springform pan. Roll out the pastry on a lightly floured work surface to about ⅛ inch (3 mm) thick. Place in the prepared pan, allowing it to come up the sides by about 1¼ inches (3 cm). Chill for at least 30 minutes.

Preheat the oven to 450°F (230°C/gas 8).

Filling: Combine the milk, half the sugar, and the vanilla in a large saucepan over medium heat and bring to a boil. Remove from the heat and set aside.

Whisk the cornstarch, egg yolks, and remaining sugar in a large heatproof bowl until smooth. Discard the vanilla pod from the milk and pour the hot milk over the egg mixture, whisking constantly. Continue whisking until smooth and very thick. It will be a little thicker than a normal pastry cream.

Pour the custard into the prepared crust and smooth the top with a small spatula. Bake for 20–25 minutes, until just sent but not browned.

Let cool in the pan on a wire rack, then release the sides of the pan. Serve warm or at room temperature.

• • •

If you liked this recipe, you will love these as well.

GATEAU BASQUE   CUSTARD TARTLETS   PORTUGUESE TARTS

ORANGE RICOTTA TART

Crust

1   quantity sweet pastry (see page 192)

Filling

1   large egg + 1 large egg yolk

1   cup (250 g) ricotta cheese, drained

$1/2$ cup (75 g) confectioners' (icing) sugar

2   teaspoons finely grated untreated orange zest

1   tablespoon orange liqueur

$1/2$ cup (120 ml) heavy (double) cream

Crust: Prepare the sweet pastry and pre-bake the crust as explained on page 192.

Filling: Preheat the oven to 350°F (180°C/gas 4). Combine the egg, egg yolk, ricotta, confectioners' sugar, and orange zest and liqueur in a medium bowl. Whip the cream in a small bowl until soft peaks form. Fold the cream into the ricotta mixture and spoon into the prepared tart crust.

Bake for 20 minutes, until golden and set. Let cool, then chill for at least 4 hours. Serve with extra whipped cream, if desired.

Serves: 8   Preparation: 45 minutes + 5 hours to chill   Cooking: 40 minutes   Level: 2

CHOCOLATE HAZELNUT TART

Crust

1   quantity sweet pastry (see page 192)

Chocolate Hazelnut Filling

12   ounces (350 g) dark chocolate, coarsely chopped

$1^1/4$ cups (300 ml) heavy (double) cream

$1/2$ cup (100 g) hazelnuts, lightly toasted and coarsely chopped

    Unsweetened cocoa powder, to dust

Crust: Prepare the sweet pastry and pre-bake the crust as explained on page 192.

Chocolate Hazelnut Filling: Melt the chocolate and cream in a double boiler over barely simmering water, stirring occasionally until smooth. Stir in the hazelnuts.

Pour the filling into the prepared tart case and refrigerate until set, about 1 hour. Dust with cocoa just before serving.

Serves: 8   Preparation: 45 minutes + 1 hour to chill   Cooking: 20 minutes   Level: 2

Be sure to use very fresh ricotta cheese and to drain off all the fluid before using it. You can change the flavor of this tart by replacing the orange zest and liqueur with the same quantity of mandarin zest and liqueur, or lemon zest and limoncello.

The crisp buttery crust melds with the nutty chocolate filling to create a taste explosion.

Serves: 8–10

Preparation: 45 minutes
+ 1 hour to chill

Cooking: 60–70 minutes

Level: 2

Pine nuts are the edible seeds of several different varieties of pine trees. They are rich in healthy oils and vitamins, especially vitamins B and E. They are also quite rich in calories, providing lots of energy. This tart is ideal to serve on winter days after skiing or other sporting events.

PINE NUT TART

Sweet Pastry

2	cups (300 g) all-purpose (plain) flour
2/3	cup (150 g) unsalted chilled butter, diced
1/8	teaspoon salt
1/2	cup (75 g) confectioner's (icing) sugar
2	large eggs, lightly beaten

Filling

1/2	cup (120 g) salted butter
1/2	cup (120 ml) honey
1/2	cup (100 g) superfine (caster) sugar
1/2	cup (120 ml) heavy (double) cream
1	large egg + 1 large egg yolk
1 1/2	cups (270 g) pine nuts
	Finely grated zest of 1 unwaxed lemon

Sweet Pastry: Combine the flour, butter, and salt in a food processor and blend until the mixture resembles coarse crumbs. Add the confectioners' sugar and pulse to combine. With the motor running, gradually add the egg.

Turn the pastry out onto a clean work surface and, using your hands, bring the mixture together to form a dough. Wrap in plastic wrap (cling film) and chill in the refrigerator for at least 30 minutes.

Lightly grease and flour a 9-inch (23-cm) tart pan with a removeable base.

Roll the pastry out between two sheets of parchment paper to about 1/4 inch (5 mm) thick. Line the base of the prepared tart pan, trimming off excess pastry. Refrigerate for 30 minutes.

Preheat the oven to 350°F (180°C/gas 4).

Place the tart on a baking sheet. Line the pastry case with parchment paper and fill with baking weights, uncooked rice, or dried beans. Bake for 15 minutes, until the edges are golden. Remove the paper and baking weights and bake for 5 more minutes, until the pastry is cooked through. Set aside.

Filling: Stir the butter, honey, and sugar in a medium saucepan over medium-low heat until the sugar dissolves. Increase the heat and simmer for 2 minutes. Transfer to a heatproof bowl and set aside to cool slightly.

Whisk the cream, egg, egg yolk, and lemon zest in a small bowl. Gradually pour into the cooled honey mixture, whisking to combine.

Decrease the oven temperature to 325°F (170°C/gas 3). Spread the pine nuts over the pastry base and pour in the filling.

Bake for 40–50 minutes, until set and golden brown.

Place on a rack and leave to cool to room temperature. Slice and serve.

Serves: 8–10
Preparation: 45 minutes
    + 1 hour to chill
Cooking: 65 minutes
Level: 2

. . . . .

If you are short of time, use drained canned pears instead of poaching your own.

PEAR & FRANGIPANE TART

Poached Pears
3	cups (750 ml) water
1½	cups (300 g) sugar
	Freshly squeezed juice of ½ lemon
2	strips unwaxed orange zest
4	medium pears, peeled

Crust
1	quantity sweet pastry (see page 192)
⅓	cup (110 g) apricot preserves (jam)
1	tablespoon water

Frangipane Filling
¾	cup (150 g) superfine (caster) sugar
⅔	cup (150 g) unsalted butter, softened
2	large eggs
1½	cups (150 g) almond meal (ground almonds)
1	tablespoon all-purpose (plain) flour

Poached Pears: Stir the water, sugar, lemon juice, and orange zest in a medium saucepan over medium heat until the sugar dissolves. Decrease the heat and add the pears. Cut out a circle of parchment paper large enough to cover the pears and set a plate or saucepan lid over the top, to keep them submerged. Simmer on low until just tender, about 20 minutes. Remove from the heat and leave in the poaching liquid to cool.

Crust: Prepare the sweet pastry and pre-bake the crust as explained on page 192.

Decrease the oven temperature to 325°F (170°C/gas 3).

Frangipane Filling: Beat the sugar and butter in a bowl with an electric mixer on medium speed until pale and creamy. Add the eggs one at a time, beating until just combined after each addition. Add the almond meal and flour and beat to combine. Spread the filling over the pastry base.

Cut the pears in half lengthwise, remove the stems, and scoop out the cores. Slice thinly. Arrange the pears around the tart, fanning the slices out from the center to the edge.

Bake for 45 minutes, until golden brown and firm to the touch.

Heat the apricot preserves and water in a small saucepan over low heat, stirring occasionally, until syrupy. Strain through a fine-mesh sieve and brush over the hot tart.

Place on a rack and leave to cool at room temperature. Slice and serve.

. . . . .

Bakewell tarts are a traditional English dessert. There are many stories about their origin but a likely claim comes from the town of Bakewell, in Derbyshire, where the tart is said to have been invented at the local White Horse Inn (now known as The Rutland Arms) in 1820.

BAKEWELL TART

Pastry Crust

1   quantity sweet pastry (see page 192)

Filling

$3/4$ cup (150 g) superfine (caster) sugar

$1/2$ cup (120 g) unsalted butter, softened

3   large eggs

$1^1/2$ cups (150 g) almond meal (ground almonds)

$1/4$ cup (30 g) all-purpose (plain) flour

1   teaspoon almond extract

$1/3$ cup (110 g) raspberry preserves (jam), warmed

$1/4$ cup (25 g) flaked almonds

Pastry Crust: Prepare the pastry as explained on page 192. Lightly grease and flour a 9-inch (23-cm) tart pan with removable base.

Roll the pastry out between two sheets of parchment paper to about $1/4$ inch (5 mm) thick. Line the base of the prepared tart pan, trimming off excess pastry. Prick the base with a fork and chill for 30 minutes.

Preheat the oven to 350°F (180°C/gas 4).

Place the tart on a baking sheet. Line the pastry case with parchment paper and fill with baking weights, uncooked rice, or dried beans. Bake for 15 minutes, until the edges are golden. Remove the paper and baking weights and bake for 5 minutes, until the pastry is cooked through and golden. Set aside.

Decrease the oven temperature to 325°F (170°C/gas 3).

Filling: Beat the sugar and butter in a bowl with an electric mixer on medium speed until pale and creamy. Add the eggs one at a time, beating until just combined after each addition. Add the almond meal, flour, and almond extract and stir to combine.

Spread the raspberry preserves over the pastry base. Spread the filling over the top and sprinkle with flaked almonds.

Bake for 35–40 minutes, until golden brown and firm to the touch.

Place on a wire rack to cool. Dust with confectioners' sugar. Slice and serve warm or at room temperature.

. . .

If you liked this recipe, you will love these as well.

PINE NUT TART

PEAR & FRANGIPANE TART

LINZERTORTE

Serves: 8–10
Preparation: 30 minutes
  + 1 hour to chill
Cooking: 50–55 minutes
Level: 3

. . . . .

Be sure to use organic or unwaxed lemons in this tart.
If not, the zest may be contaminated with chemicals.

LEMON TART

Pastry Crust

1   quantity sweet pastry (see page 192)

Filling

3   unwaxed lemons
6   large eggs
1¼   cups (250 g) superfine (caster) sugar
½   cup (120 ml) heavy (double) cream
     Confectioners' (icing) sugar, to dust

Pastry Crust: Prepare the pastry as explained on page 192. Lightly grease and flour a 9-inch (23-cm) tart pan with removable base.

Roll the pastry out between two sheets of parchment paper to about ¼ inch (5 mm) thick. Line the base of the prepared tart pan, trimming off excess pastry. Prick the base with a fork and chill for 30 minutes.

Preheat the oven to 350°F (180°C/gas 4).

Place the tart on a baking sheet. Line the pastry case with parchment paper and fill with baking weights, uncooked rice, or dried beans. Bake for 15 minutes, until the edges are golden. Remove the paper and baking weights and bake for 5 minutes, until the pastry is cooked through and golden. Set aside.

Decrease the oven temperature to 300°F (150°C/gas 2).

Filling: Finely grate the zest of two of the lemons and set aside. Juice all three of the lemons and strain through a fine-mesh sieve.

Whisk the eggs, sugar, and lemon zest in a large bowl until smooth. Add the lemon juice and cream and whisk to combine. Pour the filling into the pastry case and bake for 30–35 minutes, until the center is just set.

Place on a wire rack and let cool to room temperature.

Dust the top of the tart with an even layer of confectioners' sugar and caramelize to a dark amber using a kitchen blow torch, or under the overhead broiler (grill) in the oven.

Slice and serve at room temperature or chilled.

. . .

If you liked this recipe, you will love these as well.

LEMON CURD TARTLETS

ORANGE RICOTTA TART

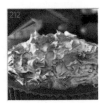
LEMON MERINGUE PIE

Serves: 8–10
Preparation: 30 minutes
+ 1 hour to chill
Cooking: 35–40 minutes
Level: 1

· · · · ·

This pie comes from the Austrian city of Linz. Made with short, crumbly pastry based on nuts and flour, it can be filled with raspberry, red current, or apricot preserves (jam).

LINZERTORTE

Pastry

1 1/3 cups (200 g) all-purpose (plain) flour

1 cup (100 g) almond meal (ground almonds)

3/4 cup (150 g) superfine (caster) sugar

1/2 teaspoon ground cinnamon

1/4 teaspoon ground cloves

2/3 cup (150 g) chilled unsalted butter, diced

Finely grated zest of 1 unwaxed lemon

1 large egg, lightly beaten

Filling

3/4 cup (240 g) good quality raspberry preserves (jam)

1 large egg, lightly beaten, to brush

1/2 cup (50 g) flaked almonds

Pastry: Combine the flour, almond meal, sugar, cinnamon, and cloves in a food processor and pulse to combine. Add the butter and lemon zest and blend until mixture resembles coarse crumbs. With the motor running, gradually add the egg.

Turn out onto a clean work surface and knead to form a dough. Shape the dough into two disks, one using three-quarters of the dough and the other the remaining quarter. Wrap in plastic wrap (cling film) and chill in the refrigerator for at least 30 minutes.

Lightly grease a 9-inch (23-cm) springform cake pan and line with parchment paper.

Roll the larger disk of dough out between two sheets of parchment paper to about 2/3 inch (1.5 cm) thick. Line the base of the prepared pan, pressing the dough 3/4 inch (2 cm) up the sides.

Roll the remaining dough out very thinly between two sheets of parchment paper to make a rectangle measuring about 10 x 8-inches (25 x 20-cm). Leaving the pastry on the parchment, slide onto a platter or baking sheet. Using a fluted pastry wheel cut into 2/3 inch (1.5 cm) wide strips. Refrigerate both the pastry base and strips for 30 minutes.

Preheat the oven to 350°F (180°C/gas 4).

Filling: Spread the raspberry preserves over the pastry base. Lay the pastry strips over the top to form a lattice pattern, pressing down gently around the edges to seal. Brush the pastry with the beaten egg. Sprinkle the flaked almonds around the edge to create a decorative border.

Bake for 35–40 minutes, until the pastry is golden brown. Leave to cool in the pan for 15 minutes. Loosen the pan sides, place on a wire rack and let cool to room temperature.

Slice and serve.

Serves: 8–10

Preparation: 30 minutes

Cooking: 65–70 minutes

Level: 2

. . . . .

Tarte tatin is an upside-down apple tart believed to have been invented by mistake at the Hotel Tatin in the French town of Lamotte-Beuvron in the 1880s. According to legend, one of the owners, Stephanie Tatin, was making an ordinary apple tart but left the apples and sugar to cook for too long. She tried to remedy the mistake by placing the pastry over the top, and the tarte tatin was born.

TARTE TATIN

$1/2$ quantity puff pastry (see page 224)

4 tart cooking apples, such as Granny Smith

Freshly squeezed juice of 1 unwaxed lemon

$1/2$ cup (100 g) superfine (caster) sugar

2 tablespoons water

2 tablespoons butter, diced

Pinch of ground cinnamon

Crème fraîche, to serve

Prepare the pastry as explained on page 224.

Preheat the oven to 400°F (200°C/gas 6).

Roll the pastry out on a floured work surface to about $1/4$ inch (5 mm) thick. Cut out a 10-inch (25-cm) round. Lay on a plate or baking sheet. Prick thoroughly with a fork and refrigerate.

Peel and quarter the apples. Cut off the base to remove the core and leave a flat surface. Place in a bowl, drizzle with lemon juice, and toss to coat.

Sprinkle the sugar into the base of a heavy-based 9-inch (23-cm) ovenproof frying pan. Drizzle with the water and cook over medium heat until the sugar begins to dissolve and caramelize in spots. Swirl, but do not stir, to help all of the sugar dissolve. Cook until an even caramel color, 5–10 minutes. Add the butter and swirl to melt and combine. Sprinkle with cinnamon.

Arrange the apples cut-side up in the pan, packing them in tightly. Cook for 10 more minutes, until the caramel begins to darken.

Place the pastry round over the apples and, using the back of a teaspoon, tuck the edges in around the apple. Take care not to burn your fingers on the hot caramel.

Bake for 25–30 minutes, until the pastry is puffed and dark golden brown and apples are tender. Leave to stand for 5 minutes.

Wearing oven mitts or using a kitchen towel, carefully invert onto a serving plate. Slice and serve warm with crème fraîche.

. . .

If you liked this recipe, you will love these as well.

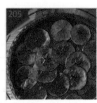

FRENCH APPLE TART   PLUM CROSTATA   APPLE PIE

. . . . .

This tart makes a perfect family dessert. Serve warm with a scoop or two of your favorite ice cream or a dollop or two of yogurt.

FRENCH APPLE TART

Pastry Crust

1   quantity sweet pastry (see page 192)

Filling

6   tart cooking apples, such as Granny Smith

3   tablespoons unsalted butter

1   tablespoon water

1/4   cup (50 g) superfine (caster) sugar

2   tablespoons confectioners' (icing) sugar

Apricot Glaze

1/3   cup (110 g) apricot jam

1   tablespoon water

1   tablespoon dark brandy

Pastry Crust: Prepare the sweet pastry and pre-bake the crust as explained on page 192.

Preheat the oven to 400°F (200°C/gas 6).

Filling: Peel, core, and coarsely chop four of the apples and place in a medium saucepan. Add 2 tablespoons of the butter and the water and cook with the lid on over low heat, stirring occasionally so it doesn't color, until softened, 5–10 minutes.

Add the sugar and cook uncovered, stirring occasionally, until all the liquid has evaporated leaving a thick apple purée, 5–10 minutes. Remove from the heat and set aside to cool.

Peel the remaining apples and slice very thinly. Remove the seeds from each slice.

Spread the apple purée inside the pastry case. Arrange the apple slices slightly overlapping over the top.

Finely chop the remaining butter and sprinkle over the apple. Dust with confectioners' sugar.

Bake for 20–25 minutes, until the tips of the apple begin to color golden brown.

Apricot Glaze: Heat the apricot preserves, water, and rum in a small saucepan over low heat, stirring occasionally, until syrupy. Strain through a fine-mesh sieve and brush over the hot tart.

Slice and serve warm or at room temperature.

APPLE & CUSTARD TEA CAKE

TARTE TATIN

APPLE PIE

Serves: 8
Preparation: 30 minutes
    + 1 hour to chill
Cooking: 30–40 minutes
Level: 1

· · · · ·

Another delicious pie to serve as a family dessert or when entertaining casually. Add a dollop of yogurt, custard, or cream to each portion when you serve.

PLUM CROSTATA

Pastry Crust

½ quantity sweet shortcrust pastry (see page 208)

Filling

1½ pounds (750 g) ripe plums, halved, pitted (stoned), and thickly sliced

¼ cup (50 g) sugar

2 tablespoons all-purpose (plain) flour

½ teaspoon ground cinnamon

Finely grated zest of 1 unwaxed lemon

2 tablespoons butter

1 large egg, lightly beaten, to glaze

Raw sugar, to sprinkle

Pastry Crust: Prepare the pastry as explained on page 208.

Preheat the oven to 400°F (200°C/gas 6). Lightly grease a large baking sheet and line with parchment paper.

Roll the pastry out between two sheets of parchment paper to make a 12-inch (30-cm) circle about ¼ inch (5 mm) thick. Place on the prepared baking sheet.

Filling: Combine the plums, sugar, flour, cinnamon, and lemon zest in a medium bowl and stir to combine. Pile the plum mixture into the center of the pastry circle, leaving a 3-inch (8-cm) border, and dot with butter.

Fold the pastry edges over the fruit to partially cover, creating pleats as you fold. Brush the pastry with egg and sprinkle with the raw sugar.

Bake for 30–40 minutes, until the pastry is golden brown and the fruit is tender with bubbling juices.

Leave on the baking sheet for 10 minutes, to cool to slightly.

Slice and serve warm.

· · ·

If you liked this recipe, you will love these as well.

PLUM & ALMOND SHEET CAKE   TARTE TATIN   FRENCH APPLE TART

Serves: 8

Preparation: 30 minutes
 + 1 hour to chill

Cooking: 45–50 minutes

Level: 2

. . . . .

Serve this classic pie to finish a special family meal or when entertaining friends casually.

APPLE PIE

Sweet Shortcrust Pastry

2²/₃ cups (400 g) all-purpose (plain) flour

1 cup (250 g) unsalted chilled butter, diced

¼ teaspoon salt

⅓ cup (50 g) confectioner's (icing) sugar

¼ cup (60 ml) iced water

1 large egg yolk, lightly beaten

Filling

8 medium tart green cooking apples, such as Granny Smith

Finely grated zest and juice of ½ unwaxed lemon

2 tablespoons butter

½ cup (100 g) superfine (caster) sugar

¼ cup (45 g) raisins

1 teaspoon ground cinnamon

1 large egg, lightly beaten, to glaze

2 tablespoons raw sugar, to sprinkle

Sweet Shortcrust Pastry: Combine the flour, butter, and salt in a food processor and blend until the mixture resembles coarse crumbs. Add the confectioners' sugar and pulse to combine. Mix the water and egg yolk in a small bowl. With the motor running, gradually add the egg mixture.

Turn out onto a clean work surface and use your hands to bring the mixture together, adding a little extra water if necessary, to form a dough. Wrap in plastic wrap (cling film) and chill for 30 minutes.

Lightly grease a 9-inch (23-cm) pie pan with butter. Divide the pastry into two disks, one using two-thirds of the pastry and the other the remaining one-third.

Roll the larger disk out between two sheets of parchment paper to about ¼ inch (5 mm) thick. Line the base of the prepared pie pan. Chill for 30 minutes.

Filling: Peel, quarter, and thickly slice the apples. Place in a large bowl as they are cut. Add the lemon juice and toss to coat to prevent browning.

Melt the butter in a large saucepan over low-medium heat, add the apples, lemon zest, sugar, raisins, and cinnamon and cook, stirring occasionally, until just softened, about 5 minutes. Drain, reserving the juice. Return the liquid to the pan and gently simmer until syrupy, about 2 minutes. Pour the syrup over the apples and stir to combine. Set aside to cool.

Preheat the oven to 400°F (200°C/gas 6). Spoon the cooled filling into the pie base.

Roll out the remaining pastry between two sheets of parchment paper to make a disk large enough to cover the top of the pie dish. Lay the pastry over the filling and cut a small hole in the center to allow steam to escape during baking. Brush with the beaten egg and sprinkle with the raw sugar.

Bake for 40–45 minutes, until the golden brown. Set aside for 10 minutes to cool slightly. Slice and serve.

Serves: 8

Preparation: 20 minutes
  + 1 hour to chill

Cooking: 30–40 minutes

Level: 2

· · · · ·

During the winter months when fresh apricots are out of season, you can make this pie using well-drained canned apricot halves.

APRICOT LATTICE PIE

Pastry Crust

1 quantity sweet shortcrust pastry (see page 208)

Filling

2 pounds (1 kg) apricots, halved and pitted

$\frac{1}{2}$ cup (50 g) almond meal (finely ground almonds)

$\frac{1}{2}$ cup (100 g) sugar

  Finely grated zest of $\frac{1}{2}$ unwaxed orange

1 large egg, lightly beaten, to glaze

Pastry Crust: Prepare the pastry as explained on page 208.

Lightly grease a 9-inch (23-cm) pie pan with butter.

Divide the pastry into two disks, one using two-thirds of the pastry and the other the remaining third.

Roll the larger disk out between two sheets of parchment paper to about $\frac{1}{4}$ inch (5 mm) thick. Line the base of the prepared pie pan. Refrigerate for 30 minutes.

Preheat the oven to 400°F (200°C/gas 6).

Filling: Combine the apricots, almond meal, sugar, and orange zest in a large bowl, stirring to combine. Spoon into the pie base.

Roll out the remaining pastry between two sheets of parchment to make a rectangle measuring about 10 x 8-inch (25 x 20-cm). Using a fluted pastry wheel, cut into $\frac{2}{3}$-inch (1.5-cm) wide strips.

Arrange the strips of pastry about 1 inch (2.5 cm) apart across the filling and then over the top in the opposite direction. Weave the strips in and out of each other, to create a lattice pattern. Brush the pastry all over with the egg.

Bake for 30–40 minutes, until the pastry is golden brown and the fruit is tender with bubbling juices.

Set aside for 10 minutes, to cool to slightly. Slice and serve.

· · ·

If you liked this recipe, you will love these as well.

LINZERTORTE

TARTE TATIN

APRICOT DANISH PASTRIES

Serves: 8

Preparation: 30 minutes
+ 3 hours to chill

Cooking: 35 minutes

Level: 2

. . . . .

Another classic pie that is always a winner. To vary, you can replace half the lemon juice with freshly squeezed pink grapefruit juice.

LEMON MERINGUE PIE

Pastry Crust

1/2 quantity sweet shortcrust pastry (see page 208)

Filling

1 cup (200 g) superfine (caster) sugar

1 1/4 cups (310 ml) water

3/4 cup (180 ml) lemon juice

Finely grated zest of 2 unwaxed lemons

1/3 cup (50 g) cornstarch (cornflour)

4 large egg yolks

1/4 cup (60 g) salted butter, diced

Meringue Topping

1 cups (200 g) superfine (caster) sugar

4 large egg whites

Pastry Crust: Prepare the pastry as explained on page 208.

Lightly grease and flour a 9-inch (23-cm) pie pan.

Roll the pastry out between two sheets of parchment paper to about 1/4 inch (5 mm) thick. Line the base of the prepared pan, trimming off excess pastry. Prick the base with a fork. Refrigerate for 30 minutes.

Preheat the oven to 350°F (180°C/gas 4).

Line the pastry case with parchment paper and fill with baking weights, uncooked rice, or dried beans. Bake for 15 minutes, until the edges are golden. Remove the paper and baking weights and bake for 5 more minutes, until the pastry is cooked through. Set aside.

Filling: Combine the sugar with 3/4 cup (180 ml) of the water and the lemon juice and zest in a medium saucepan and gently simmer over medium-low heat, stirring occasionally, until the sugar dissolves, 3–5 minutes.

Blend the cornstarch with the remaining water in a small bowl. Whisking constantly, gradually pour the cornstarch into the hot lemon liquid. Cook, whisking constantly, until thick, 3–5 minutes. Whisk in the egg yolks and butter. Pour the filling into the pastry case. Cover and refrigerate until set, about 2 hours.

Preheat the oven to 400°F (200°C/gas 6).

Meringue Topping: Beat the egg whites in a bowl with an electric mixer on medium speed until soft peaks form. Gradually add the sugar, beating constantly on high speed until the sugar has dissolved and thick, glossy peaks form.

Spoon the meringue over the lemon filling, creating small peaks with the back of a spoon or spatula.

Bake for 5 minutes, until the meringue peaks are golden.

Place on a rack and let cool to room temperature. Slice and serve.

Serves: 8
Preparation: 45 minutes
   + 1 hour to chill
Cooking: 55–60 minutes
Level: 2

. . . . .

Like walnuts, pecans are a good source of protein and healthy unsaturated fats. They also contain vitamin E and a range of B vitamins, as well as a range of phytochemicals.

CHOCOLATE PECAN PIE

Chocolate Pastry

1¼ cups (180 g) all-purpose (plain) flour

¼ cup (30 g) unsweetened cocoa powder

½ cup (120 g) unsalted chilled butter, diced

⅛ teaspoon salt

⅓ cup (50 g) confectioner's (icing) sugar

2 large egg yolks, lightly beaten

1-2 tablespoons iced water

Filling

¾ cup (180 ml) light corn (golden) syrup

½ cup (100 g) firmly packed light brown sugar

3 large eggs, lightly beaten

2 tablespoons unsalted butter, melted

1 teaspoon vanilla extract (essence)

2 cups (250 g) pecans, lightly toasted

3 ounces (90 g) good quality semi-sweet dark chocolate, finely chopped

Chocolate Pastry: Place the flour and cocoa in a food processor and pulse to combine. Add the butter and salt and blend until the mixture resembles coarse crumbs. Add the sugar and pulse to combine. With the motor running, add the egg yolks and 1 tablespoon of the water. Turn out onto a clean work surface and use your hands bring the mixture together, adding a little of the remaining water if necessary, to form a dough. Wrap in plastic wrap (cling film) and refrigerate for 30 minutes.

Lightly grease and flour a 9-inch (23-cm) pie pan.

Roll the pastry out between two sheets of parchment paper to about ¼ inch (5 mm) thick. Line the base of the prepared pan, pinching the edges to make a decorative boarder. Prick the base with a fork. Refrigerate for 30 minutes.

Preheat the oven to 350°F (180°C/gas 4).

Line the pastry case with parchment paper and fill with baking weights, uncooked rice, or dried beans. Blind bake for 10 minutes. Remove the parchment and baking weights and bake for 5 more minutes. Set aside.

Decrease the oven temperature to 325°F (170°C/gas 3).

Filling: Whisk the corn syrup, brown sugar, eggs, butter, and vanilla together in a medium bowl until combined.

Coarsely chop 1½ cups (185 g) of the pecans. Scatter the chopped pecans and chocolate over the pie base. Pour in the filling. Arrange the remaining pecan halves decoratively on top.

Bake for 40–50 minutes, until just set.

Place on a rack and leave to cool to room temperature. Slice and serve chilled or at room temperature.

Serves: 8

Preparation: 45 minutes
+ 1 hour to chill

Cooking: about 1½ hours

Level: 2

. . . . .

Serve this classic American pie at Thanksgiving, or at any time during the fall and winter when pumpkins are at their best.

PUMPKIN PIE

Pastry Crust

½ quantity sweet shortcrust pastry (see page 208)

Filling

1¼ pounds (600 g) pumpkin, peeled, seeded, and cut into large chunks

¾ cup (150 g) firmly packed light brown sugar

3 large eggs, lightly beaten

1 teaspoon ground cinnamon

1 teaspoon ground ginger

½ teaspoon ground nutmeg

⅛ teaspoon ground cloves

1½ cups (375 ml) heavy (double) cream

Pastry Crust: Prepare the pastry as explained on page 208.

Lightly grease and flour a 9-inch (23-cm) pie pan.

Roll the pastry out between two sheets of parchment paper to about ¼ inch (5 mm) thick. Line the base of the prepared pan, trimming off excess pastry. Prick the base with a fork. Refrigerate for 30 minutes.

Filling: Steam the pumpkin until tender, 10–15 minutes. Transfer to a bowl and mash coarsely with a fork. Press through a sieve to make a smooth purée. Set aside.

Preheat the oven to 350°F (180°C/gas 4).

Line the pastry case with parchment paper and fill with baking weights, uncooked rice, or dried beans. Bake for 15 minutes, until the edges are golden. Remove the paper and baking weights and bake for 5 more minutes, until the pastry is cooked through. Set aside.

Decrease the oven temperature to 325°F (170°C/gas 3).

Add the sugar, eggs, ground cinnamon, ginger, nutmeg, and cloves to the pumpkin purée and whisk to combine. Mix in the cream and pour into the pastry case, spreading evenly.

Bake for 1 hour, until just set.

Place on a rack and leave to cool to room temperature. Slice and serve chilled or at room temperature.

. . .

If you liked this recipe, you will love these as well.

APPLE PIE   CHOCOLATE PECAN PIE   BERRYFRUIT PIE

Serves: 8
Preparation: 30 minutes
  + 3 hours to chill
Cooking: 15–20 minutes
Level: 2

. . . . .

Another classic French tart. Serve chilled or at room temperature.

TARTE AU CHOCOLAT

Sweet Tart Pastry

1¹/₃ cups (200 g) all-purpose (plain) flour

¹/₄ teaspoon salt

¹/₃ cup (50 g) confectioners' (icing) sugar

¹/₂ cup (120 g) cold unsalted butter, cut in small cubes

1 large egg yolk

1–2 tablespoons water, as required

Chocolate Filling

1²/₃ cups (400 ml) heavy (double) cream

12 ounces (350 g) dark chocolate (70% cacao), coarsely chopped

1 tablespoon Cointreau or brandy

Sweet Tart Pastry: Sift the flour, salt, and confectioners' sugar into a medium bowl. Cut in the butter with a pastry blender until the mixture resembles fine bread crumbs. Add the egg yolk and knead lightly until the ingredients come together. Add enough water to obtain a smooth, firm dough. Press into a log, wrap in plastic wrap (cling film), and chill in the refrigerator for at least 30 minutes.

Preheat the oven to 400°F (200°C/gas 6). Lightly oil a 9-inch (23-cm) tart pan with a removeable bottom.

To line the pan, unwrap the dough and place on a lightly floured work surface. Roll the dough out until it is about 2 inches (5 cm) larger than the tart pan. Roll the dough loosely onto the rolling pin and unroll it evenly over the tart pan. Press the pastry evenly around the bottom and sides of the pan. Pinch the edges to rise ¹/₈ inch (3 mm) above the edge of the pan. Prick the bottom with a fork. Chill for 30 minutes.

Line the tart shell with parchment paper and fill with pie weights or dried beans. Bake for 10 minutes, remove the parchment and weights, and bake for 5–10 minutes, until light brown and dry to the touch. Remove from the oven and leave to cool.

Chocolate Filling: Pour the cream into a heavy-based saucepan and bring slowly to a boil. As soon as the first bubbles appear, remove from the heat and stir in the chocolate. Add the Cointreau and stir until all the chocolate has melted. Whisk until smooth, then let cool for 15 minutes.

Pour into the pastry shell and leave to set for at least 2 hours. Slice and serve.

CHOCOLATE MERINGUE PIE

Pastry Crust

1 quantity chocolate pastry (see page 215)

Filling

5 ounces (150 g) dark chocolate, chopped

1/4 cup (60 ml) heavy (double) cream

1 teaspoon vanilla extract (essence)

1/4 cup (60 g) butter

1/3 cup (70 g) sugar

4 large egg yolks

1 1/2 cups (150 g) ground almonds

Meringue

3 large egg whites

3/4 cup (150 g) sugar

Pastry Crust: Prepare the chocolate pastry and pre-bake as explained on page 215.

Filling: Melt the chocolate, cream, and vanilla in a double boiler over barely simmering water. Beat the butter and sugar in a bowl with an electric mixer on medium speed until creamy. Add the egg yolks, chocolate mixture, and almonds. Spread over the pastry and bake for 10 minutes.

Meringue: Beat the egg whites in a bowl with an electric mixer on medium speed until frothy. Gradually add the sugar, beating until smooth, glossy peaks form. Spoon the meringue over the filling and bake for 15 minutes, until just golden.

Serve at room temperature.

Serves: 8–10 Preparation: 50 minutes + 1 hour to chill Cooking: 30 minutes Level: 3

BERRYFRUIT PIE

Crust

1 quantity sweet shortcrust pastry (see page 208)

Filling

6 cups (900 g) mixed berries

1/2 cup (70 g) sugar

3 tablespoons all-purpose (plain) flour

1 teaspoon ground cinnamon

1/2 teaspoon ground nutmeg

1 large egg, beaten

Confectioners' (icing) sugar, to dust

Crust: Prepare the shortcrust pastry. Divide into two pieces, one slightly larger than the other. Wrap in plastic wrap (cling film) and refrigerate for 1 hour. Roll out the larger piece of pastry on a floured work surface to 1/8 inch (3 mm) thick. Line the base and sides of a 9-inch (23-cm) pie pan with the pastry. Chill for 30 minutes.

Filling: Preheat the oven to 400°F (200°C/gas 6). Combine all the berries, sugar, flour, cinnamon, and nutmeg in a bowl. Pour the filling into the pie pan. Roll out the remaining piece of pastry and cover the filling. Cut slits in the top to allow steam to escape during baking. Brush with the beaten egg.

Bake for 40 minutes, until golden brown. Serve warm, dusted with confectioners' sugar.

Serves: 8 Preparation: 45 minutes + 1 hour to chill Cooking: 40 minutes Level: 2

This attractive pie is suitable for all sorts of special occasions, including formal dinner parties.

You can use any mix of berries in this pie. Try blackberries, red or black currants, or raspberries.

pastries

This chapter includes classic pastries based on four basic doughs: puff pastry dough, croissant dough, strudel dough, and choux pastry dough. It also features a range of delicious recipes using storebought filo (phyllo) pastry.

Makes: about 3 pounds
(1.5 kg) of dough

Preparation: 1 hour
+ 6–18 hours to chill

Level: 3

. . . . .

Puff pastry can be stored in the refrigerator for up to two days or in the freezer for up to two months.

Making puff pastry is a time-consuming process so it is best to make it in larger batches and store some in the freezer to have at hand when required. See page 25 for step-by-step instructions.

PUFF PASTRY

$3^{1}/_{3}$ cups (500 g) all-purpose (plain) flour, + extra, to dust

1 teaspoon salt

2 cups (500 g) + $^{1}/_{2}$ cup (120 g) chilled unsalted butter, diced

1 cup (250 ml) iced water

1 tablespoon freshly squeezed lemon juice

Combine the flour, salt, and $^{1}/_{2}$ cup (120 g) of butter in a food processor and pulse until the mixture resembles coarse crumbs. Stir the water and lemon juice in a bowl. Gradually add the lemon water, pulsing to combine. Turn the dough out onto a clean work surface and knead to bring together. Shape into a ball. Cut a deep cross in the top. Wrap in plastic wrap (cling film) and chill for 2 hours.

Working in a cool kitchen, take the 2 cups (500 g) of butter out of the refrigerator. Let sit for 20 minutes, until slightly softened but still firm.

Generously dust the butter with flour and place between two sheets of parchment paper. Using a rolling pin, roll out into a 7-inch (18-cm) square, about $^{2}/_{3}$ inch (1.5 cm) thick. Dust with flour occasionally to prevent it from sticking. Wrap and, depending on the temperature of your kitchen, either stand at room temperature or refrigerate. You want the butter to be the same consistency as the pastry when you roll it out.

Lightly flour a work surface and place the pastry on top. Using a lightly floured rolling pin, roll out into a 12-inch (30-cm) square. Place the square of butter in the center and rotate so it faces you like a diamond with the corners pointing to the sides of the dough. Take the corners of the pastry and fold in to meet in the center of the butter, slightly overlapping to completely enclose. Press down firmly across the seams with a rolling pin to seal. Roll out lengthwise to about three times in length to make a $^{1}/_{2}$ inch (1 cm) thick, 12 x 24-inch (30 x 60-cm) rectangle.

With the longest end facing you, fold the left third of the pastry into the center over the middle third. Fold the right third over to cover the two layers, as if folding a letter to put into an envelope. Press lightly to seal. Turn the pastry 90 degrees clockwise, so that the seams are now pointing to the left and right of you. Roll out again to make a $^{1}/_{2}$ inch (1 cm) thick, 12 x 24-inch (30 x 60-cm) rectangle and fold letter-style as before. This completes the first two turns. The pastry requires six turns in total. Wrap in plastic wrap and chill for 30 minutes. Repeat the rolling and folding two more times, chilling for 30 minutes in between. At the end, wrap in plastic wrap and chill for at least 2 hours, or overnight. Leave at room temperature for 20–30 minutes before rolling, so that it is rollable but not soft.

Serves: 8
Preparation: 45 minutes
    + 1 hour to chill
Cooking: 13–15 minutes
Level: 3

· · · · ·

Mille-feuille, also known as gâteau Napoleon or custard slice, is a classic French dessert. It takes some time to prepare (especially if you are making your own puff pastry), but is well worth the effort.

CLASSIC MILLE-FEUILLE

Pastry

¹⁄₄ quantity homemade puff pastry (see page 224) or 14 ounces (400 g) ready-to-roll storebought puff pastry

Crème Patissiere

3 large egg yolks

¹⁄₃ cup (70 g) superfine (caster) sugar

2 teaspoons vanilla extract (essence)

3 tablespoons all-purpose (plain) flour

1¹⁄₂ cups (375 ml) milk

Fondant Frosting

8 ounces (250 g) soft white fondant frosting

¹⁄₄ cup (60 ml) hot water

2 tablespoons unsweetened cocoa powder

Pastry: Grease and line a large baking sheet with parchment paper. Dust a work surface lightly with flour. Roll the pastry into a 12-inch (30-cm) square about ¹⁄₈ inch (3 mm) thick. Cut into three equal rectangles and place on the prepared sheet. Prick well with a fork. Chill for 30 minutes.

Preheat the oven to 400°F (200°C/gas 6).

Crème Patissiere: Beat the egg yolks, sugar, and vanilla in a medium bowl with an electric mixer on medium speed until pale and creamy. Stir in the flour. Heat the milk in a small saucepan over medium-low heat until scalding. Gradually pour the milk into the egg mixture, stirring constantly until combined. Return to the pan and cook over medium-low heat, whisking constantly, until the mixture comes to a boil. Keep whisking while it boils for 1 minute, then transfer to a bowl and set aside to cool slightly. Cover the surface with plastic wrap (cling film) and refrigerate until cooled, about 30 minutes.

Take the pastry out of the refrigerator. Place a piece of parchment paper on top and cover with another baking sheet. Bake for 10 minutes. Remove the top baking sheet and paper and bake for a 3–5 minutes, until crisp and golden brown. Transfer to a rack and let cool completely.

Trim the edges of the pastry to straighten. Stack the pastry pieces on top of each other, spreading crème patissiere between each layer.

Fondant Frosting: Put the fondant in heatproof bowl and set over a saucepan of barely simmering water, ensuring the base of the bowl does not touch the water. Add the hot water and heat, stirring occasionally, until smooth.

Place the cocoa in a small bowl and blend with enough water to make a smooth paste. Add ¹⁄₄ cup (60 ml) of the fondant, mixing well.

Pour the frosting over the top layer of pastry, spreading evenly. Spoon the chocolate fondant into a ziplock bag and snip off one corner. Pipe lines across the white fondant about 1 inch (2.5 cm) apart. Run a toothpick through the lines to create the classic pattern. Refrigerate until set, at least 15 minutes. Slice to serve.

Serves: 8
Preparation: 45 minutes
  + 1½ hours to chill
Cooking: 30 minutes
Level: 3

. . . . .

Another divine French pastry cake. It is believed to have originated in the French town of Pithiviers, near Orleans, in northwestern France.

PITHIVIERS

Almond Cream

½	cup (120 g) unsalted butter, softened
¾	cup (150 g) superfine (caster) sugar
2	cups (200 g) almond meal (finely ground almonds)
1	tablespoon dark rum

Pastry

⅓	quantity homemade puff pastry (see page 224) or 1 pound (500 g) ready-to-roll storebought puff pastry
1	large egg, lightly beaten
	Confectioners' (icing) sugar, to dust

Almond Cream: Beat the butter and sugar in a bowl with an electric mixer on medium speed until pale and creamy. With the mixer on low speed, gradually beat in the almond meal and rum. Cover the bowl with plastic wrap and refrigerate until required.

Pastry: Grease a large baking sheet and line with parchment paper. Lightly dust a work surface with flour. Cut the pastry into two equal portions. Roll out one piece at a time, to make two 10-inch (25-cm) disks, about ¼ inch (3 mm) thick. Use a plate or cake pan as a guide.

Lay one of the pastry disks on the prepared sheet. Use a knife to mark a border about ⅔ inch (1.5 cm) in all around the edge. Prick well inside the border with a fork. Spread the almond cream in an even layer inside the border. Brush the border with egg. Cover with the remaining pastry disk, pressing firmly around the edges to seal. Brush the top of the pastry with egg. Chill for 30 minutes.

Preheat the oven to 400°F (200°C/gas 6).

Using the point of a sharp knife and working from the center to the outside edge, score the pastry with curved lines. Cut a small hole out of the center so steam can escape during cooking.

Bake for 15 minutes. Decrease the oven temperature to 350°F (180°C/gas 4) and bake for 10 minutes, until crisp and golden brown. Dust with confectioners' sugar and bake for 5 more minutes, until the sugar melts to form a glaze. Leave on the sheet to cool completely.

Transfer to a serving plate. Slice and serve at room temperature.

. . .

If you liked this recipe, you will love these as well.

CLASSIC MILLE-FEUILLE

ALMOND JALOUSIE

GALETTES DES ROIS

PALMIERS

$^2/_3$ cup (140 g) sugar + extra, to sprinkle

$^1/_4$ quantity homemade puff pastry (see page 224) or 14 ounces (400 g) ready-to-roll storebought puff pastry

Sprinkle half the sugar over a work surface. Place the pastry on top and sprinkle with the remaining sugar. Roll out into a 12 x 16-inch (30 x 40-cm) rectangle, about $^1/_8$ inch (3 mm) thick. Sprinkle with extra sugar if necessary to prevent the pastry from sticking to the work surface. Trim the edges to straighten. With the long end facing you, roll the two short ends to meet in the middle. Wrap in plastic wrap (cling film) and chill for 30 minutes.

Preheat the oven to 400°F (200°C/gas 6). Grease two large baking sheets and line with parchment paper. Sprinkle with extra sugar. Using a sharp knife, trim the ends of the pastry log and cut into fifteen $^1/_2$-inch (1.5-cm) thick slices. Lay on the prepared sheets and sprinkle with sugar.

Bake for 15–20 minutes, until golden brown. Turn over and bake for 3–4 minutes, until crisp and caramelized to a deep golden brown. Leave on the sheets to cool slightly. Transfer to a wire rack to cool completely.

Makes: 15 Preparation: 20 minutes + 30 minutes to chill Cooking: 18–24 minutes Level: 2

ECCLES CAKES

3 tablespoons butter

3 tablespoons light brown sugar

$^1/_4$ cup (90 g) currants

3 tablespoons mixed peel, finely chopped

$^1/_2$ teaspoon pumpkin pie (mixed) spice

$^1/_4$ teaspoon ground nutmeg

$^1/_4$ quantity homemade puff pastry (see page 224) or 14 ounces (400 g) ready-to-roll storebought puff pastry

1 egg white, beaten
Demerara sugar, to sprinkle

Heat the butter and sugar in a small saucepan until the butter melts and the sugar dissolves. Remove from the heat, add the currants, mixed peel, spice, and nutmeg and stir to combine. Set aside to cool.

Grease two large baking sheets and line with parchment paper. Roll out the pastry to $^1/_8$ inch (3 mm) thick. Using a 4-inch (10-cm) pastry cutter, cut out twelve disks. Place on one of the prepared sheets and chill for 30 minutes. Preheat the oven to 400°F (200°C/gas 6).

Spoon heaped teaspoons of filling onto the center of the pastry disks. Wet the edges slightly with water. Working around the edge, pinch and fold the pastry together, bringing it into the center to enclose the filling. Turn over so the folds are underneath. Use a rolling pin flatten to $^1/_4$ inch (5 mm) thick. Brush with egg and sprinkle with sugar. Chill for 15 minutes.

Make three slashes across the tops. Bake for 15–20 minutes, until golden brown. Cool slightly on the sheets. Transfer to a rack to cool completely.

Makes; 12 Preparation: 45 minutes + 15 minutes to chill Cooking: 15–20 minutes Level: 2

Palmier is the French word for palm tree, which is what these delicious little pastries are thought to resemble. Serve them with coffee for a special breakfast or brunch.

Eccles cakes come from the English town near Manchester of the same name. They have been sold there since 1793.

Serves: 8

Preparation: 20 minutes
    + 45 minutes to chill
    & set

Cooking: 20–25 minutes

Level: 2

. . . . .

Jalousie is a French pastry that can be filled with a sweet fruit or nut filling. Our recipe has a delicious almond filling.

ALMOND JALOUSIE

Almond Filling

1/2   cup (100 g) superfine (caster) sugar

1/3   cup (90 g) salted butter, softened

2   large egg yolks

1   cup (160 g) blanched almonds, lightly toasted and finely ground

2   tablespoons all-purpose (plain) flour

2   teaspoons almond extract (essence)

Pastry

1/3   quantity homemade puff pastry (see page 224) or 1 pound (500 g) ready-to-roll storebought puff pastry

1   large egg, lightly beaten, to glaze

1/4   cup (25 g) flaked almonds, to sprinkle

Frosting

1/2   cup (75 g) confectioners' (icing) sugar

2   teaspoons milk

Almond Filling: Beat the butter and sugar in a bowl with an electric mixer on medium speed until pale and creamy. Add the eggs yolks one at a time, beating until just combined after each addition. With the mixer on low speed, gradually add the ground almonds, flour, and almond extract. Cover the bowl with plastic wrap and chill until required.

Pastry: Grease a large baking sheet and line with parchment paper. Lightly dust a clean work surface with flour. Roll out the pastry to make a 10 x 12-inch (25 x 30-cm) rectangle, about 1/4 inch (5 mm) thick. Cut in half to make two even rectangles. Lay one of the rectangles on the prepared sheet for the base and place the other on a board or another baking sheet. Rest both in the refrigerator for 30 minutes.

Preheat the oven to 400°F (200°C/gas 6).

Use a knife to mark a border about 2/3 inch (1.5 cm) in all around the edge. Spread the almond filling over the pastry inside the border.

Roll out the remaining pastry to slightly larger and thinner than the base. Lightly dust with flour and fold in half lengthwise. Make 1 1/2-inch (4-cm) long cuts about 3/4 inch (2 cm) apart along the folded edge. Open the pastry sheet out.

Brush the pastry border with water. Lay the cut pastry top over the filling, pressing down on the edges to seal. Trim to an even size and crimp the edges with a fork. Brush the top of the pastry with egg and sprinkle with flaked almonds.

Bake for 20–25 minutes, until puffed and golden brown. Leave on the baking sheet to cool completely.

Frosting: Sift the confectioners' sugar into a small bowl, add the milk, and stir until smooth. Drizzle the frosting back and forth across the top of the pastry and set aside for 15 minutes to set.

Slice and serve.

Serves: 8

Preparation: 30 minutes
+ 30 minutes to chill

Cooking: 20–25 minutes

Level: 2

. . . . .

The Galette des Rois is a traditional French cake baked around Epiphany (6 January). Like the English Twelfth Night Cake, this pastry also has a hidden dried bean. The person who receives the bean in their slice of cake becomes king for the day and must offer the next cake. You can make one large cake, or several smaller ones.

GALETTES DES ROIS

Pastry

1/3 quantity homemade puff pastry (see page 224) or 1 pound (500 g) ready-to-roll storebought puff pastry

1 large egg, lightly beaten, to glaze

Filling

1/2 cup (120 g) unsalted butter, softened

1/3 cup (70 g) superfine (caster) sugar

3/4 cup (75 g) ground almonds

3 large egg yolks, lightly beaten

1 tablespoon kirsch or other brandy

1/2 teaspoon almond extract (essence)

1 dried bean

Pastry: Preheat the oven to 400°F (200°C/gas 6). Lightly grease two large baking sheets.

Roll out the pastry on a lightly floured work surface to 1/4 inch (3 mm) thick. Using a 4-inch (10-cm) pastry cutter, cut out sixteen disks. Place on the prepared sheets and chill for 30 minutes.

Preheat the oven to 400°F (200°C/gas 6).

Filling: Beat the butter and sugar in a bowl with an electric mixer on medium speed until pale and creamy. Add the ground almonds, egg yolks, brandy, and almond extract, beating until just blended. Hide the bean in the filling.

Spread the filling on half the pastry disks leaving a 3/4-inch (1-cm) border. Lightly brush the borders with some of the beaten egg. Cover with the remaining disks of pastry. Press down on the edges to seal.

Using a sharp knife, score the pastry in a swirl pattern, starting from the center and working outward. Do not cut through to the filling.

Glaze the top of the pastry with the remaining beaten egg, taking care not to brush the edges as this will stop the pastry from rising.

Bake for 20–25 minutes, until puffed and golden brown. Serve warm or at room temperature.

. . .

If you liked this recipe, you will love these as well.

CLASSIC MILLE-FEUILLE

PITHIVIERS

ALMOND JALOUSIE

Makes: 9
Preparation 30 minutes
+ 30 minutes to chill
& cool
Cooking: 35–45 minutes
Level: 1

. . . . .

Cooks have been baking turnovers for centuries. With their sweet fruit fillings, these versatile little pies can be served anytime, from breakfast and brunch to dessert.

APPLE TURNOVERS

Filling

12	ounces (350 g) Granny Smith apples, peeled, cored, and sliced into $1/2$-inch (1-cm) cubes
12	ounces (350 g) Golden Delicious apples, peeled, cored, and sliced into $1/2$-inch (1-cm) cubes
$1/4$	cup (60 ml) water
3	tablespoons sugar
1	teaspoon freshly squeezed lemon juice

Pastry

$1/3$	quantity homemade puff pastry (see page 224) or 1 pound (500 g) ready-to-roll storebought puff pastry
1	large egg, lightly beaten, to glaze

Filling: Put both types of apple in a medium saucepan with the water, sugar, and lemon juice. Bring to a boil over medium heat, stirring occasionally so that the sugar dissolves. Cover, reduce the heat to low, and simmer until the apples are very tender, stirring frequently, 10–12 minutes. Remove from the heat. Gently mash the apples with a fork, leaving a few chunks. Let cool completely. Cover and refrigerate.

Preheat the oven to 400°F (200°C/gas 6). Line two large baking sheets with parchment paper.

Pastry: Roll out the pastry on a lightly floured work surface into a 15-inch (38-cm) square. Cut into nine 5-inch (13-cm) squares. Place a heaped tablespoon of filling in the center of each square. Lightly brush the edges of the pastry with beaten egg. Fold half the pastry over the filling to form a triangle. Press the edges together with your fingertips to seal. Lightly brush with beaten egg.

Using a sharp knife, make three small slits in the top of each triangle to allow steam to escape during baking. Place the triangles on the prepared baking sheets. Chill until firm, about 15 minutes.

Bake the turnovers for 15 minutes. Reverse the baking sheets from top to bottom, reduce the oven temperature to 350°F (180°C/gas 4), and continue baking for 10–15 minutes, until puffed and golden brown.

Let cool for at least 15 minutes before serving. Serve warm or at room temperature.

. . .

If you liked this recipe, you will love these as well.

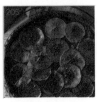
FRENCH APPLE TART

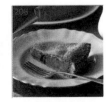
APPLE PIE

APPLE STRUDEL

PASTRY HEARTS & FLOWERS

1/3 quantity homemade puff pastry (see page 224) or 1 pound (500 g) ready-to-roll storebought puff pastry

1 cup (300 g) raspberry preserves (jam)

Preheat the oven to 400°F (200°C/gas 6). Line two large baking sheets with parchment paper.

Roll out the pastry on a lightly floured work surface to a 1/8 inch (3 mm) thick. Use heart- and flower-shaped cookie cutters to stamp out hearts and flowers. Use the offcuts of pastry to make stems and leaves for the flowers. Spoon 2 teaspoons of raspberry preserves onto each heart and flower. Transfer to the prepared baking sheets, spacing well.

Bake for 10–12 minutes, until the pastry is crisp and golden. Let the pastries cool on the baking sheets for 10 minutes, then transfer to wire racks and let cool completely.

Once cooled, carefully lift the pastries off the parchment paper using a metal spatula. Serve at room temperature.

Serves: 10–12 Preparation: 15 minutes Cooking: 10–12 minutes Level: 1

CARAMELIZED PEAR GALETTES

8 ounces (250 g) storebought puff pastry, thawed if frozen

2 small, ripe organic pears, halved, cored, and thinly sliced to make a fan shape (leave joined at the stalk end)

2 tablespoons slivered almonds

4 tablespoons (60 ml) dulce de leche

1 egg, lightly beaten, to glaze

Preheat the oven to 400°F (200°C/gas 6). Grease a large baking sheet.

Roll out the pastry on a lightly floured work surface to a 1/8 inch (3 mm) thick. Using a saucer as a guide, cut out four circles. Place on the prepared baking sheet and prick all over with a fork.

Press the pear halves, peel-side up, into the pastry circles. Sprinkle with the almonds and drizzle with the dulce de leche. Brush the pastry with the beaten egg.

Bake for 20–25 minutes, until the edges of the pastry are puffed and golden and the pears are tender. Serve warm.

Serves: 4 Preparation: 15 minutes Cooking: 20–25 minutes Level: 2

You can vary these little pastries by using a different flavored preserve (jam), or bake without a topping and spread with Nutella when cool.

Dulce de leche is a confection prepared by slowly heating sweetened milk to create a creamy caramel. You can buy dulce di leche in many supermarkets and baking stores, and also from online suppliers.

Makes: about 1¼
    pounds (1.2 kg)
    of dough
Preparation: 1 hour
    + 8–16 hours to chill
Level: 3

. . . . .

Croissant dough can be stored in the refrigerator for
up to 48 hours, or in the freezer for up to 2 months.

CROISSANT DOUGH

4   cups (600 g) strong
     white flour + extra,
     to dust
¼   cup (50 g) superfine
     (caster) sugar
2   teaspoons salt
½   ounce (15 g/2
     sachets) instant
     dried yeast or 1
     ounce (30 g) fresh
     yeast
1½   cups (375 ml)
     lukewarm milk
1½   cups (375 g) chilled
     unsalted butter

Combine the flour, sugar, and salt in the bowl of a stand mixer fitted with a dough hook. If using instant dried yeast, sprinkle it into the bowl. Mix on low speed to combine. If using fresh yeast, mix with a little of the milk in a small bowl. Set aside until foamy, about 5 minutes. Add the milk and yeast mixture and mix on low for 1–2 minutes, until the dough comes away from the sides of the bowl. Increase the speed to medium-low and mix until the dough is soft and smooth, 2–3 minutes. If mixing and kneading by hand, mix the ingredients in a large bowl. Turn out onto a lightly floured work surface and knead for 10–15 minutes, until soft and smooth. Cover and chill for 2 hours.

Working in a cool kitchen, take the butter out of the refrigerator. Let sit for 20 minutes, until slightly softened but still be firm. Generously dust the butter with flour and place between two sheets of parchment paper. Use a rolling pin to roll out into a 5 x 8-inch (13 x 20-cm) rectangle about ⅔ inch (1.5 cm) thick. Dust with flour to prevent it from sticking. Wrap in plastic wrap (cling film) and, depending on the temperature of your kitchen, either stand at room temperature or refrigerate. You want the butter to be about the same consistency as the pastry.

Lightly flour a work surface and flatten the dough. Using a floured rolling pin, roll into a 10-inch (25-cm) square about ½ inch (1 cm) thick. Place the butter in the center and rotate so it faces you like a diamond, with the corners pointing to the sides of the pastry. Take the corners of the dough and fold in to meet in the center slightly overlapping, to enclose the butter. Press down on the seams to seal.

Roll the dough into a 12 x 16-inch (30 x 40-cm) rectangle. With the longest end facing you, fold the left third into the center. Fold the right third over to cover both layers. Wrap in plastic wrap and chill for 1 hour.

Turn the dough 90 degrees clockwise, so that the seams point to the left and right of you. Roll out again and fold as before. Wrap and rest in the refrigerator for 1 hour. For the final time, turn and roll as before. This time, fold the two ends into the center to meet and fold together as if closing a book. Wrap and chill for at least 4 hours, or overnight. Leave at room temperature for 20–30 minutes to soften slightly before rolling.

Serves: 12
Preparation: 1½ hours
    + time for the dough
    + 1½-2 hours to
    prove
Cooking: 15–20 minutes
Level: 3

. . . . .

Croissants can be prepared and rolled in advance and frozen just before the proving stage. Take them out the night before you wish to cook them, thaw out in the refrigerator overnight, and prove and bake as usual.

Croissants can also be frozen after they are cooked. To serve, take them straight from the freezer and reheat in a hot oven for 5 minutes.

CROISSANTS

1   quantity croissant
     dough (see page
     241)
1   large egg, lightly
     beaten, to glaze

Prepare the croissant dough as explained on page 241. Cut the dough in half. Wrap one half in plastic wrap (cling film) and refrigerate.

Grease two large baking sheets and line with parchment paper. Make a triangular template with an 8 inch (20 cm) base and 10 inch (25 cm) sides out of card or thick plastic.

Lightly dust a clean work surface with flour and roll out the other half of the dough to make a 10 x 24-inch (25 x 60-cm) rectangle, about ¼ inch (5 mm) thick. Stop and rest the dough for 10 minutes if it becomes difficult to roll out.

Using the prepared template, mark out three triangles side by side along one of the longest sides of the rectangle. This will also create the start of another three triangles above. Trim the base and top edges straight. The smaller off-cuts at each end can be rolled up to make two mini croissants.

Make a ¾-inch (2-cm) cut in the center of the base of the triangles, to allow them to stretch when shaped. Stretch the base corners slightly and roll up, starting from the base to the tip. Wet the tip and tuck underneath. Pull the corners downward to create the classic crescent shape.

Arrange the croissants about 1½ inches (4 cm) apart on the prepared sheets. Set aside in a warm draft-free place to prove for 1½–2 hours, until puffy. Make sure it is not too hot or this will cause the butter to melt and the layers to merge. Repeat with the remaining dough.

Preheat the oven to 400°F (200°C/gas 6).

Brush the croissants with egg. Bake for 15–20 minutes, until puffed, flaky, and golden brown. Rotate the baking sheets halfway through for even baking. Transfer to a rack to cool slightly.

Serve warm or at room temperature.

Serves: 12

Preparation: 2 hours
+ time for the dough
+ 1½-2 hours to
prove

Cooking: 15–20 minutes

Level: 3

. . . . .

Pain aux raisins can be prepared and rolled in advance and frozen before the proving stage. Take them out the night before you wish to cook them and thaw out in the refrigerator. In the morning, prove and bake as usual.

Pain aux raisins can also be frozen after they are cooked. To serve, take them straight from the freezer and reheat in a hot oven for 5 minutes.

PAIN AUX RAISINS

Crème Patissiere

3   large egg yolks

½   cup (60 g) superfine (caster) sugar

1   teaspoon vanilla extract (essence)

2   tablespoons all-purpose (plain) flour

1   cup (250 ml) milk

Pastry

½   quantity croissant dough (see page 241)

1   cup (180 g) raisins, soaked in warm water for 20 minutes

1   large egg, lightly beaten, to glaze

Sugar Glaze

1   cup (150 g) confectioners' (icing) sugar

2   tablespoons water

1   teaspoon vanilla extract (essence)

Crème Patissiere: Beat the egg yolks, sugar, and vanilla in a bowl with an electric mixer on medium speed until pale and creamy. Stir in the flour. Heat the milk in a small saucepan over medium-low heat until scalding. Gradually pour the milk into the egg mixture, stirring constantly, until combined. Return to the pan and cook over medium-low heat, whisking constantly, until it comes to a boil. Keep whisking while it boils for 1 minute. Transfer to a bowl and set aside to cool slightly. Cover the surface with plastic wrap (cling film) and refrigerate until cooled, about 30 minutes.

Grease two large baking sheets and line with parchment paper.

Pastry: Lightly dust a work surface with flour and roll out the dough out to make a ¼-inch (5-mm) thick, 12 x 16-inch (30 x 40-cm) rectangle. Stop and rest the dough for 10 minutes if it becomes difficult to roll out.

Turn the dough so the shortest end is facing you. Spread evenly with the crème patissiere, leaving a ½-inch (1-cm) border around the edges. Drain the raisins and sprinkle evenly over the top. Roll up to make a log. Trim the edges and cut into 1½-inch (4-cm) thick slices.

Arrange the slices about 1½ inches (4 cm) apart on the prepared sheets. Flatten slightly with the palm of your hand. Set aside in a warm draft-free place to prove for 1½–2 hours, until puffy. Make sure it is not too hot or this will cause the butter to melt and the layers to merge.

Preheat the oven to 400°F (200°C/gas 6).

Brush the pain aux raisins with egg and bake for 15–20 minutes, until puffed, flaky, and golden brown. Rotate the baking sheets halfway through for even baking.

Sugar Glaze: Mix the confectioners' sugar, water, and vanilla in a small bowl to make a thin syrup. Brush over the warm pain aux raisins. Transfer to a rack to cool slightly.

Serve warm or at room temperature.

Serves: 16
Preparation: 1½ hours
    + time for the dough
    + 1½–2 hours to
    prove
Cooking: 15–20 minutes
Level: 3

· · · · ·

Pain au chocolat can be prepared and rolled in advance and frozen before the proving stage. Take out the night before you wish to bake them and thaw out in the refrigerator. In the morning, prove and cook as usual.

Pain au chocolate can also be frozen after they are cooked. To serve, take them straight from the freezer and reheat in a hot oven for 5 minutes.

PAIN AU CHOCOLAT

1	quantity croissant dough (see page 241)
12	ounces (350 g) dark chocolate, coarsely grated or chopped
1	large egg, lightly beaten, to glaze

Cut the croissant dough evenly in half. Wrap one half in plastic wrap (cling film) and refrigerate. Grease and line two large baking sheets with parchment paper.

Lightly dust a work surface with flour and roll out the other half of the dough to make a ¼-inch (5-mm) thick, 10 x 32-inch (25 x 80-cm) rectangle. If running out of working space, cut the dough in half and adjust the rolling size accordingly. Stop and rest the dough for 10 minutes if it becomes difficult to roll out. Trim the edges to straighten. Cut eight rectangles crosswise at 4 inch (10 cm) intervals.

Sprinkle about 2 tablespoon2 of chocolate across the short end of the rectangles to make a ½ inch (1 cm) thick line and fold over once to enclose. Place another 2 tablespoons of chocolate across the dough in front of the fold and fold over again to enclose, creating two lines of chocolate filling. Continue folding to make rectangular parcels.

Arrange the pain au chocolates about 1½ inches (4 cm) apart on the prepared sheets. Set aside in a warm draft-free place to prove for 1½–2 hours, until puffy. Make sure it is not too hot or this will cause the butter to melt and the layers to merge. Repeat with the remaining dough.

Preheat the oven to 400°F (200°C/gas 6). Brush the pain au chocolate with egg.

Bake for 15–20 minutes, until puffed, flaky, and golden brown. Rotate the baking sheets halfway through for even baking. Transfer onto a rack to cool slightly.

Serve warm or at room temperature.

CROISSANTS

PAIN AU RAISIN

APRICOT DANISH PASTRIES

Serves: 16

Preparation: 1½ hours
+ time for the dough
+ 1½-2 hours to
prove

Cooking: 15–20 minutes

Level: 3

. . . . .

These Danish pastries can be prepared and rolled in advance and frozen before the proving stage. Take them out the night before you wish to bake, thaw out in the refrigerator, and prove and cook as usual.

APRICOT DANISH PASTRIES

Pastry

1	quantity croissant dough (see page 241)
16	apricot halves
1	egg, lightly beaten, to glaze

Crème Patissiere

3	large egg yolks
¼	cup (60 g) superfine (caster) sugar
1	teaspoon vanilla extract (essence)
2	tablespoons all-purpose (plain) flour
1	cup (250 ml) milk

Apricot Glaze

| ¼ | cup (80 g) apricot preserves (jam) |
| 1 | tablespoon water |

Frosting

| ¾ | cup (120 g) confectioners' (icing) sugar |
| 3 | teaspoons milk |

Pastry: Cut the croissant dough evenly in half. Wrap each piece in plastic wrap (cling film) and chill.

Crème Patissiere: Beat the egg yolks, sugar, and vanilla in a medium bowl with an electric mixer n medium speed until pale and creamy. Stir in the flour. Heat the milk in a saucepan over medium-low heat until scalding. Gradually pour the milk into the egg mixture, stirring constantly, until combined. Return to the pan and cook over medium-low heat, whisking constantly, until it comes to a boil. Keep whisking while it boils for 1 minute. Transfer to a bowl. Set aside to cool slightly. Cover the surface with plastic wrap (cling film) and chill until cooled, about 30 minutes.

Grease two large baking sheets and line with parchment paper.

Lightly dust a clean work surface with flour and roll out one piece of dough to make a ¼-inch (5-mm) thick, 12 x 24-inch (30 x 60-cm) rectangle. If running out of working space, cut the dough in half and adjust the rolling size accordingly. Stop and rest the dough for 10 minutes if it becomes difficult to roll out. Cut eight 6-inch (15-cm) squares. Bring the corners into the center to meet, pressing to secure. Divide half of the crème patissiere among the pastries, placing a spoonful in the center on top of the corners. Place the apricot halves, flat-side down, on top.

Arrange about 1½ inches (4 cm) apart on the prepared sheets. Set aside in a warm draft-free place to prove for 1½–2 hours, until puffy. Make sure it is not too hot or this will cause the butter to melt and the layers to merge. Repeat with the remaining dough.

Preheat the oven to 400°F (200°C/gas 6). Brush the pastries with egg. Bake for 15–20 minutes, until puffed, flaky, and golden brown. Rotate the sheets around halfway through to ensure even baking.

Apricot Glaze: Warm the apricot preserves and water in a saucepan over low heat. Brush over the hot pastries. Leave on the sheets to cool slightly. Transfer to a rack to cool completely.

Frosting: Stir the confectioners' sugar and milk in a small bowl until smooth. Drizzle over the pastries and let stand for 10 minutes to set.

Makes: about 1 pound
(500 g) of dough
Preparation: 1 hour
+ 1½ hours to rest
Level: 3

. . . . .

The trick with strudel dough is rolling and stretching
it until it is paper thin. It should be almost transparent
and thin enough to read a newspaper through it.
See page 27 for step-by-step instructions.

STRUDEL DOUGH

2   cups (300 g) all-
    purpose (plain) flour
1   teaspoon salt
1   large egg
³/₄ cup (180 ml) warm
    water
1   tablespoon
    vegetable oil
    + extra, to coat
2   tablespoons
    unsalted butter,
    melted and cooled

Sift the flour and salt into a bowl and make a well in the center. Beat the
egg, water, and oil in a bowl then pour into the well. Using a fork, work
the flour into the liquid to make a sticky dough. Turn the dough out
onto a lightly floured work surface and knead until soft, smooth, and
elastic, about 5 minutes. Shape into two even balls and place in oiled
bowls, rolling to coat. Cover with plastic wrap (cling film) and set aside
to rest at room temperature for 1 hour.

Cover a kitchen table or island bench with a clean tablecloth and lightly
dust with flour. You need to be able to easily move around the table as
you stretch the dough out.

Using a rolling pin, roll out one of the dough balls as thinly as possible.
Brush with melted butter to prevent it from drying out. Cover with a
clean kitchen cloth and leave to rest for 30 minutes.

Working your way around the table, gently pull the edges of the dough
to stretch further until it is very thin. Lightly flour your hands and curl
your fingers to make loose fists. Place your hands with the backs facing
up underneath the dough and working from the center gently pull and
stretch the dough until it is paper thin. Patch up any tears or holes. Use
scissors to cut off the thick edges and trim to make a rough rectangle.
Sprinkle with melted butter and gentle brush or rub over with your
hands, taking care not to tear the pastry.

Use immediately. Once you have filled and rolled the first strudel, repeat
with the remaining dough ball.

PUFF PASTRY

CROISSANT PASTRY

CHOUX PASTRY

. . . . .

Apple strudel is a classic Viennese pastry, dating from the 18th century, if not earlier. It is considered the national dish of Austria.

APPLE STRUDEL

Pastry

1   quantity strudel dough (see page 251)

$1/4$ cup (60 g) unsalted butter, melted and cooled

Apple Filling

$1/3$ cup (60 g) raisins

2   tablespoons brandy

6   tart cooking apples, such as Granny Smith, peeled, cored, and thinly sliced

Finely grated zest and juice of $1/2$ unwaxed lemon

$1/2$ cup (100 g) firmly packed light brown sugar

$1/2$ cup (60 g) walnuts, finely chopped

1   teaspoon ground cinnamon

$1^1/2$ cups (120 g) fine fresh white bread crumbs

Confectioners' (icing) sugar, to dust

Fresh or whipped cream or ice cream, to serve

Pastry: Prepare the strudel dough as explained on page 251 up to and including the second resting stage of 30 minutes.

Apple Filling: Combine the raisins and brandy in a small bowl and set aside for 15 minutes to plump.

Put the apples in a medium bowl. Add the lemon zest and juice and toss to combine. Add the plumped raisins and any remaining brandy and the sugar, walnuts, and cinnamon. Stir to combine.

Preheat the oven to 400°F (200°C/gas 6). Grease two large baking sheets and line with parchment paper. Finish stretching the dough.

Sprinkle half of the bread crumbs 4 inches (10 cm) in from the edge of the short ends of the dough in a 4-inch (10-cm) thick strip, leaving a 2 inch (5 cm) border at the sides. Arrange half the apple mixture over the top. Fold the dough edge over the filling and brush with melted butter. Using the tablecloth as an aid, roll up completely, brushing the dough with melted butter at each turn. Trim the edges and tuck underneath. Transfer the strudel onto one of the prepared baking sheets, curving in a horseshoe shape to fit if necessary. Brush with melted butter and set aside. Repeat with the remaining dough and apple filling to make a second strudel.

Bake for 30–35 minutes, until crisp and golden brown. Leave on the sheet for 10 minutes, to cool slightly.

Dust with confectioners' sugar. Slice and serve warm or at room temperature with the cream or ice cream.

. . .

If you liked this recipe, you will love these as well.

TARTE TATIN

APPLE PIE

APPLE TURNOVERS

Makes: 18 pieces
Preparation: 40 minutes
    + 15 minutes to soak
Cooking: 35–45 minutes
Level: 2

. . . . .

Baklava is a delicious pastry made with layers of filo pastry and chopped nuts, honey, and spices. It is believed to be a very ancient dessert, perhaps dating back as far as the new Assyrian Empire in the 8th century BC.

PISTACHIO BAKLAVA

Baklava

2	cups (300 g) pistachios
2	cups (300 g) blanched almonds
1/2	cup (100 g) superfine (caster) sugar
1	teaspoon ground cinnamon
1/2	cup (120 g) unsalted butter, melted
1	(13-ounce/375-g) packet filo (phyllo) pastry

Syrup

1	cup (200 g) superfine (caster) sugar
1	cup (250 ml) water
1/2	cup (120 ml) honey
	Finely grated zest and juice of 1 unwaxed lemon
1	teaspoon rosewater

Baklava: Preheat the oven to 325°F (170°C/gas 3).

Grease the base and sides of a ³/₄-inch (2-cm) deep, 10 x 14-inch (25 x 35-cm) cake pan with butter.

Place the pistachios and almonds in a food processor and pulse until finely chopped. Add the sugar and cinnamon and blend to combine.

Unroll the pastry and divide it in half. Keep one half covered with a clean damp kitchen cloth. Use the other half of the pastry to line the prepared pan. Working with one sheet of pastry at a time, brush with butter and place in the prepared pan. Trim to fit the base of the pan. Spread the nut filling over the top and smooth to create an even surface. Cover with the remaining pastry sheets, brushing with butter between each layer. Trim to the size of the pan.

Score the first few layers of pastry, cutting crosswise and then diagonally at about 2 inch (5 cm) intervals to make diamond shapes. Drizzle with the remaining butter.

Bake for 35–45 minutes, until golden brown.

Syrup: Combine the sugar, water, honey, and lemon zest and lemon juice in a medium saucepan. Gently heat over low heat, stirring occasionally, until the sugar dissolves. Bring to a boil then boil gently for 3 minutes. Remove from the heat and stir in the rosewater.

Pour the hot syrup over the hot pastry and set aside for 15 minutes to soak. Cut the pastry into portions and serve at room temperature.

. . .

If you liked this recipe, you will love these as well.

NUTTY LEBANESE PASTRIES

MOROCCAN ALMOND PASTRIES

MOROCCAN ALMOND-FILLED SNAKE

NUTTY LEBANESE PASTRIES

Pastry
1   cup (250 g) unsalted butter
1   pound (500 g) fine semolina
1/2   cup (120 ml) rosewater
1/2   cup (120 ml) orange flower (blossom) water

Filling
1/2   cup (50 g) almonds
1/3   cup (30 g) walnuts
1/3   cup (30 g) pistachios
1/2   cup (100 g) sugar
1   tablespoon orange flower water
       Confectioners' (icing) sugar, to dust

Pastry: Melt the butter in a small pan over low heat. Put the semolina in a large bowl and stir in the butter. Cover and let rest overnight at room temperature. Next day, stir in the rosewater and orange blossom water and mix into a dough.

Preheat the oven to 350°F (180°C/gas 4). Lightly oil two baking sheets.

Filling: Combine the almonds, walnuts, and pistachios in a food processor and pulse briefly until coarsely ground. Transfer to a bowl with the sugar and orange flower water and mix well. Take heaped teaspoons of dough, shape into balls, and make hollows in the centers with your finger. Stuff a little of the filling into each hollow and seal the opening. Place on the baking sheets.

Bake for 10–15 minutes, until golden brown. Let cool on racks until firm. Dust with confectioners' sugar before serving.

Serves: 10–12 Preparation: 30 minutes + 12 hours to rest Cooking: 10–15 minutes Level: 2

MOROCCAN ALMOND PASTRIES

Syrup
1 1/2   cups (300 g) sugar
1 1/2   cups (370 ml) water
3   cinnamon sticks
1   vanilla bean

Filling
1 1/2   cups (250 g) whole almonds, toasted
1   teaspoon cinnamon
3   large eggs
1 1/2   cups (225 g) confectioners' (icing) sugar
1/4   teaspoon baking powder
12   sheets filo (phyllo) pastry
1/2   cup (180 g) butter

Syrup: Stir all the ingredients in a pan over medium heat until the sugar dissolves. Simmer for 5 minutes.

Filling: Finely chop the almonds and cinnamon in a food processor. Beat the eggs, confectioners' sugar, and baking powder in a bowl until thick. Beat in the almond mixture. Chill until thick, at least 3 hours.

Preheat the oven to 375°F (190°C/gas 5). Oil a baking sheet. Place a sheet of filo on a work surface. Brush with butter. Cut lengthwise into three 3 1/2-inch (9-cm) wide strips. Place a tablespoon of filling at a short end of one strip. Fold a corner of filo over the filling. Repeat the folding down the length of the strip to form a triangle. Brush with butter. Place on the baking sheet. Repeat with the remaining pastry, butter, and filling.

Bake for 15–20 minutes, until golden. Drizzle with syrup and let cool to room temperature before serving.

Serves: 10–12 Preparation: 30 minutes + 3 hours to chill Cooking: 15–20 minutes Level: 2

Serve these delicious little almond pastries for dessert with a cup of strong black coffee.

Almonds are grown all over the Middle East and the Mediterranean and are widely used in the cuisines of the region. Serve these sweet Moroccan pastries as a snack or dessert.

Serves: 8
Preparation 30 minutes
Cooking: 30–35 minutes
Level: 2

. . . . .

This dish is called *M'hanncha* (meaning "snake") in its native Morocco.

MOROCCAN ALMOND-FILLED SNAKE

Pastry

8 sheets filo (phyllo) pastry

¼ cup (60 g) unsalted butter, melted and cooled

Confectioners' (icing) sugar, to dust

Ground cinnamon, to dust

Almond Filling

2 cups (200 g) almond meal (finely ground almonds)

1 cup (150 g) confectioners' (icing) sugar

1 teaspoon ground cinnamon

1 large egg, separated

⅓ cup (90 g) butter, melted and cooled

2 tablespoons orange flower (blossom) water

Pastry: Preheat the oven to 350°F (180°C/gas 4). Grease and line a large baking sheet with parchment paper.

Almond Filling: Place the almond meal in a bowl, sift in the confectioners' sugar and cinnamon and stir to combine. Lightly beat the egg white, butter, and orange blossom water together in a small bowl. Pour into the almond mixture and stir to combine. Divide into four portions and roll into logs 2 inches (4 cm) shorter than a length of filo. Set aside.

Lay four of the filo sheets on a clean work surface and brush with melted butter. Arrange the sheets to make one long length, overlapping by approximately 1 inch (2.5 cm) at the short-sided ends, to join. Brush with melted butter and arrange the remaining sheets over the top to create a double-layered length. Lay the almond logs along the length of the filo, leaving a little space at the ends and roll up loosely to create an almond filled pastry roll. Ensure you roll it loosely otherwise it will split when cooking.

Twist one of the ends of the pastry log to seal and gradually begin to coil. Continue until the entire length is coiled, twisting the end to seal. Place on the prepared sheet and brush with melted butter.

Mix the egg yolk with one tablespoon of water in a small bowl and brush over the top of the pastry snake, to glaze. Bake for 30–35 minutes, until golden brown. Leave on the sheet to cool completely.

Transfer onto a serving plate and dust generously with confectioners' sugar. Dust lines of ground cinnamon coming out from the center out, like the spokes of a wheel over the top to decorate.

Slice and serve.

Serves: 14
Preparation: 30 minutes
Cooking: 40 minutes
Level: 2

• • • • •

Kataifi is a popular Middle Eastern pastry made with a special form of finely shredded filo (phyllo) pastry that is also called kataifi. Look for kataifi pastry in Middle Eastern markets and from online suppliers.

WALNUT KATAIFI

Pastry

1½ cups (185 g) walnuts, coarsely chopped

1 cup (150 g) almonds, coarsely chopped

½ cup (100 g) firmly packed light brown sugar

½ cup (80 g) fresh white bread crumbs

¼ cup (60 ml) freshly squeezed orange juice

1 large egg white, lightly beaten

1 teaspoon ground cinnamon

1 (13-ounce/375-g) packet kataifi pastry

1 cup (250 g) unsalted butter, melted

Syrup

3 cups (600 g) superfine (caster) sugar

2 cups (500 ml) water

½ cup (120 ml) honey

Finely grated zest and juice of 1 unwaxed lemon

1 cinnamon stick

Pastry: Preheat the oven to 350°F (180°C/gas 4).

Grease the base and sides of a ¾-inch (2-cm) deep 10 x 14-inch (25 x 35-cm) cake pan with a little of the butter.

Combine the walnuts, almonds, sugar, bread crumbs, orange juice, egg white, and cinnamon in a medium bowl and stir to combine.

Pull the kataifi pastry apart and divide into fourteen even portions. Cover with a clean damp kitchen cloth to prevent it from drying out. Working with one portion at a time, spread the strands out to make a square about ⅛ inch (3 mm) thick. Place a tablespoon of the filling along the center of the square. Fold the sides in and roll up to make a small parcel. Place in the prepared pan. Repeat with the remaining pastry and filling.

Pour the melted butter over the parcels in the pan. Bake for 40 minutes, until crisp and golden brown.

Syrup: Combine the sugar, water, honey, lemon zest and juice, cinnamon stick, and cloves in a medium saucepan. Heat over low, stirring occasionally, until the sugar dissolves. Increase the heat and boil until thickened slightly and syrupy, about 10 minutes.

Remove the cinnamon stick and pour the hot syrup over the pastries. Leave to stand to soak and cool.

Serve at room temperature.

• • •

If you liked this recipe, you will love these as well.

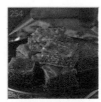

PISTACHIO BAKLAVA   MOROCCAN ALMOND PASTRIES   MOROCCAN ALMOND-FILLED SNAKE

Serves: 12
Preparation: 30 minutes
    + 1 hour to chill
Cooking: 20–25 minutes
Level: 2

· · · · ·

Rugelach is a traditional Jewish dessert. The pastry can be made with cream cheese or sour cream and fillings can include walnuts, chocolate, raisins, poppy seeds, and fruit preserves (jams).

RAISIN, CHOCOLATE & WALNUT RUGELACH

Pastry

8	ounces (250 g) cream cheese, softened
³/₄	cup (200 g) unsalted butter, softened
3	tablespoons confectioners' (icing) sugar
2	cups (300 g) all-purpose (plain) flour
1–2	tablespoons milk
1	large egg, lightly beaten, to glaze
2	tablespoons sugar
¹/₄	teaspoon ground cinnamon

Filling

1	cup (180 g) raisins, finely chopped
3	ounces (90 g) dark chocolate, coarsely grated
¹/₂	cup (60 g) walnuts, finely chopped
2	tablespoons brown sugar
¹/₂	teaspoon ground cinnamon
¹/₄	teaspoon ground nutmeg

Pastry: Beat the cream cheese, butter, and confectioners' sugar in a bowl with an electric mixer on medium until pale and creamy. Sift in the flour and beat to combine. Add just enough milk to bring the mixture together. Turn out onto a clean work surface and shape into four even disks. Wrap in plastic wrap (cling film) and chill for 30 minutes.

Filling: Combine the raisins, chocolate, walnuts, sugar, cinnamon, and nutmeg in a small bowl and mix well to combine.

Grease two large baking sheets and line with parchment paper.

Lightly flour a clean work surface and roll out one piece of pastry into a 10-inch (25-cm) disk about ¹/₄ inch (5 mm) thick. Sprinkle with a quarter of the filling. Using a pizza cutter or large sharp knife, cut the disk into six wedges.

With the wide edge facing you, roll up the wedges toward the point, tucking the ends underneath. Place on the prepared baking sheet. Repeat with the remaining dough and filling. Chill for 30 minutes.

Preheat the oven to 350°F (180°C/gas 4).

Brush the rugelach with egg. Combine the sugar and cinnamon in a small bowl and dust over the top.

Bake for 20–25 minutes, until golden brown. Leave on the baking sheets to cool slightly.

Transfer to a wire rack and let cool completely before serving.

PAN AU CHOCOLAT

PISTACHIO BAKLAVA

WALNUT KATAIFI

Makes: about 1 pound
      (450 g) of dough
Preparation: 30 minutes
Cooking: 1–2 minutes
Level: 2

. . . . .

Choux pastry is a light dough used to make éclairs, profiteroles, croquembouches, French crullers, beignets, St. Honoré cake, and gougères, among other things. It is made with butter, water, flour, and eggs. See page 24 for step-by-step instructions.

CHOUX PASTRY

1	cup (250 ml) water
1/3	cup (90 g) unsalted butter
	Pinch of salt
1	cup (150 g) all-purpose (plain) flour, sifted
4	large eggs

Place the water, butter, and salt in a medium saucepan over medium heat and bring to a boil. Add the flour and cook, stirring vigorously with a wooden spoon, until the dough begins to come away from the sides of the pan, 1–2 minutes.

Transfer the mixture to the bowl of a stand mixer fitted with a beater attachment. Beat for 1 minute, until cooled slightly, so as not to cook the egg. Add the eggs one at a time, beating between each addition, until the mixture is smooth and glossy and drops off a spoon. You may not need all of the eggs. You want the mixture to hold its shape when piped.

Alternatively, to mix by hand, set the hot mixture aside for 5 minutes to cool slightly so the egg doesn't cook when added. Add the first three eggs, one at a time, stirring vigorously to incorporate before the next addition. Add the remaining egg one tablespoon at a time until the mixture is smooth and glossy and drops off a spoon.

Use immediately.

. . .

If you liked this recipe, you will love these as well.

COFFEE CREAM
PROFITEROLES

CHOCOLATE ECLAIRS

PARIS-BREST

Makes: 12
Preparation: 1 hour
    + 30 minutes to cool
Cooking: 25–30 minutes
Level: 2

. . . . .

Profiteroles, also known as cream puffs, can be filled with the coffee cream in our recipe, but also with whipped cream, crème pastissiere, or ice cream. The tops can be frosted, dusted with confectioners' sugar, or left plain.

COFFEE CREAM PROFITEROLES

Pastry

½   quantity choux pastry (see page 264)

Coffee Cream

2   large egg yolks
3   tablespoons superfine (caster) sugar
1   teaspoon vanilla extract (essence)
2   tablespoons all-purpose (plain) flour
1   cup (250 ml) milk
2   tablespoons coffee flavored liqueur, such as Kahlua
1   teaspoon instant coffee powder, dissolved in 2 teaspoons water

Mocha Glaze

3½   ounces (100 g) dark chocolate, coarsely chopped
¼   cup (60 ml) light (single) cream
½   teaspoon instant coffee powder, dissolved in 1 teaspoon hot water

Pastry: Prepare the choux pastry as explained on page 264.

Preheat the oven to 400°F (200°C/gas 6). Grease a large baking sheet and line with parchment paper.

Spoon twelve walnut-size mounds of choux pastry onto the prepared baking sheet spacing 1½ inches (4 cm) apart. Flatten any peaks with wet fingertips. Sprinkle the sheet with water and bake for 15 minutes, until well puffed and golden. Decrease the oven temperature to 350°F (180°C/gas 4) and bake for 10–15 minutes more, until golden brown all over. Remove from the oven and use a small sharp knife to cut a small hole, about ½ inch (1 cm) in diameter, out of the base of the profiteroles. Place back on the sheets and return to the oven. Turn off and leave to cool with the door ajar.

Coffee Cream: Beat the egg yolks, sugar, and vanilla in a bowl with an electric mixer on medium speed until pale and creamy. Stir in the flour. Heat the milk in a small saucepan over medium-low heat until scalding. Gradually pour the milk into the egg mixture, stirring constantly, until combined. Return the mixture to the pan and cook over medium-low heat, whisking constantly, until it comes to a boil. Continue whisking while boiling for 1 minute. Remove from the heat and stir in the coffee liqueur and instant coffee mixture. Transfer to a bowl and set aside to cool slightly. Cover the surface with plastic wrap (cling film) and refrigerate until cooled, about 30 minutes.

Spoon the cooled coffee cream into a pastry (piping) bag fitted with a plain ½-inch (1-cm) nozzle. Poke the nozzle into the hole in the base of the profiteroles and fill with coffee cream.

Mocha Glaze: Combine the chocolate, cream, and coffee mixture in a small heatproof bowl and set over a saucepan of barely simmering water, ensuring the base of the bowl does not touch the water. Stir until smooth.

Dip the tops of the profiteroles into the glaze and place on a wire rack to set. Refrigerate until ready to serve.

Makes: 6
Preparation: 1 hour
    + time to cool & set
Cooking: 25–30 minutes
Level: 2

. . . . .

Like profiteroles, éclairs are made with choux pastry and can be completed with a variety of fillings and toppings. Chocolate éclairs are a classic dessert for special occasions.

CHOCOLATE ÉCLAIRS

Pastry
$1/2$ quantity choux pastry (see page 264)

Chocolate Fondant Frosting
7 ounces (200 g) soft white fondant frosting
$1/4$ cup (30 g) unsweetened cocoa powder
1–2 tablespoons water

Cream Filling
$1^{1}/_4$ cups (310 ml) heavy whipping cream
2 tablespoons confectioners' (icing) sugar
1 teaspoon vanilla extract (essence)

Pastry: Prepare the choux pastry as explained on page 264.

Preheat the oven to 400°F (200°C/gas 6). Grease a large baking sheet and line with parchment paper.

Spoon the choux pastry into a piping bag fitted with a $3/4$-inch (2-cm) plain nozzle. Pipe six thick 5-inch (13-cm) lengths of choux pastry about $1^{1}/_2$ inches (4 cm) apart on the prepared baking sheet. Flatten any peaks with wet fingertips. Sprinkle with water.

Bake for 15 minutes, until well puffed and golden. Decrease the oven temperature to 350°F (180°C/gas 4) and bake for 10–15 minutes more, until golden brown all over. Remove from the oven and use a small sharp knife to cut the eclairs in half horizontally. Place back on the sheets, cut-side up, and return to the oven. Turn off and leave to cool with the door ajar.

Chocolate Fondant Frosting: Place the fondant in a heatproof bowl and set over a saucepan of barely simmering water, ensuring the base of the bowl does not touch the water. Stir occasionally until smooth. Blend the cocoa in a small bowl with enough of the water to make a smooth paste. Stir into the fondant. Keep warm.

Cream Filling: Beat the cream, confectioners' sugar, and vanilla in a bowl with an electric mixer on medium speed until firm peaks form. Spoon into a pastry (piping) bag fitted with a fluted $3/4$-inch (2-cm) nozzle. Pipe cream onto the base of the éclairs.

Dip the tops of the éclairs in the fondant and lift out with an upward sweeping motion so that the excess drips off the end. Cover the bases with the lids and refrigerate until set, at least 15 minutes.

Refrigerate until ready to serve.

Serves: 8
Preparation: 1 hour
    + 30 minutes to cool
Cooking: 25–30 minutes
Level: 3

· · · · ·

The pastry was created in 1891 to celebrate a popular French bicycle race from Paris to Brest. Its round shape is said to represent a wheel. It has become a classic and is now found in pâtisseries all over France.

PARIS-BREST

Pastry

1	quantity choux pastry (see page 264)
1	large egg, lightly beaten, to glaze
1/2	cup (50 g) flaked almonds
	Confectioners' (icing) sugar, to dust

Praline

1/3	cup (70 g) superfine (caster) sugar
1/3	cup (50 g) blanched almonds

Crème Patissiere

3	large egg yolks
1/3	cup (70 g) superfine (caster) sugar
2	teaspoons vanilla extract (essence)
1/4	cup (30 g) all-purpose (plain) flour
1 1/2	cups (375 ml) milk

Pastry: Prepare the choux pastry. Preheat the oven to 400°F (200°C/gas 6). Grease a large baking sheet. Draw an 8-inch (20-cm) disk on a piece of parchment paper. Place disk-side down on the prepared baking sheet.

Spoon the pastry into a pastry (piping) bag fitted with a 3/4-inch (2-cm) plain nozzle. Pipe a ring of pastry over the marked disk. Pipe a second pastry ring on the inside so it is touching the first. Pipe a third pastry ring on top along the center seam where the two bottom rings meet. Brush with egg and scatter with the flaked almonds.

Sprinkle the baking sheet with water. Bake for 15 minutes, until well puffed and golden. Decrease the oven temperature to 350°F (180°C/gas 4) and bake for 10–15 minutes more, until golden brown all over. Remove from the oven and cut in half horizontally. Place back on the sheet, cut-side up and return to the oven. Turn off and let cool with the door ajar.

Praline: Lightly grease a baking sheet with vegetable oil. Sprinkle the sugar into a dry, heavy-based pan in an even layer. Cook over medium heat until the sugar begins to dissolve and caramelize, about 5 minutes. Swirl the pan, but do not stir, to help dissolve all the sugar. Continue cooking until it turns an even caramel color. Add the almonds and cook until it turns a deep amber, about 3 minutes. Pour onto the prepared baking sheet and set aside to cool.

Crème Patissiere: Beat the egg yolks, sugar, and vanilla in a bowl with an electric mixer on medium speed until pale and creamy. Stir in the flour. Heat the milk in a saucepan over medium-low heat until scalding. Gradually pour the milk into the egg mixture, stirring constantly, until combined. Return to the pan and cook over medium-low heat, whisking constantly until it comes to a boil. Keep whisking while it boils for 1 minute. Transfer to a bowl. Set aside to cool slightly. Cover the surface with plastic wrap (cling film) and chill until cooled, about 30 minutes.

Break the praline into small pieces. Chop in a food processor until finely ground. Stir into the crème patissiere. Spoon into a pastry (piping) bag fitted with a 3/4-inch (2-cm) nozzle. Pipe over the pastry base, cover with the lid, and dust with confectioners' sugar. Refrigerate until ready to serve.

Serves: 8–10
Preparation: 1¾ hours
Cooking: 35–45 minutes
Level: 3

. . . . .

This stunning cake is named for Saint Honoré, or Honoratus, Bishop of the French city of Amiens in early medieval times, who is the patron saint of bakers and pastry chefs. The cake is thought to have been created in 1846 by the famous pastry chef Chiboust.

ST HONORÉ

Base

1⅓ cups (200 g) all-purpose flour

1 tablespoon sugar

⅓ cup (90 g) cold unsalted butter + 1 tablespoon

1 large egg yolk + 1 large egg, lightly beaten

½ quantity choux pastry (see page 264)

Filling

2 cups (500 ml) milk

4 large egg yolks

¾ cup (150 g) sugar

½ cup (75 g) all-purpose (plain) flour

1 tablespoon dark rum

1 teaspoon vanilla extract (essence)

Caramel Glaze

1 cup (200 g) sugar

2 tablespoons water

Frosting

1 cup (150 g) confectioners' (icing) sugar

2 tablespoons water

1 tablespoon unsweetened cocoa powder

Base: Preheat the oven to 400°F (200°C/gas 6).

Combine the flour and sugar in a bowl. Use a pastry blender to cut in the butter until the mixture resembles coarse crumbs. Stir in the egg yolk until a smooth dough forms. Roll the dough out on a lightly floured surface to form a 10-inch (25-cm) round. Prick all over with a fork and place on a lightly greased baking sheet. Brush a little beaten egg around the edge.

Prepare the choux pastry. Fit a pastry (piping) bag with a plain ¾-inch (2-cm) tip and fill with half the pastry. Pipe around the edge of the pastry round. Brush some beaten egg over the top. Bake for 20–25 minutes, until golden. Cool completely on a rack.

Line a baking sheet with parchment paper. Fill a pastry bag with the remaining choux pastry. Pipe heaps the size of small nuts on the prepared sheet. Brush with the remaining beaten egg. Bake for 15–20 minutes, until golden. Cool the choux puffs completely on racks.

Filling: Warm the milk in a saucepan over low heat. Beat the egg yolks and sugar in a bowl with an electric mixer at high speed until pale and thick. Fold in the flour. Gradually stir in the hot milk. Transfer to a medium saucepan. Bring to a boil, stirring constantly. Remove from the heat and stir in the rum and vanilla. Set aside to cool completely.

Caramel Glaze: Warm the sugar and water in a saucepan over medium heat until the sugar has dissolved. Continue cooking, without stirring, until pale gold in color. Remove from the heat.

Spread the cooled filling in the pastry base. Dip the tops of the choux puffs in the caramel to glaze. Dip the bases of the puffs in the caramel and stick on the crown, pressing down lightly.

Frosting: Mix the confectioners' sugar and enough water to make a smooth frosting. Spoon half the frosting over the filling. Trace crossing diagonal lines on the frosting with a small knife. Stir the cocoa into the remaining frosting. Spoon the frosting into a pastry bag. Use the lines as a guide to pipe thin lines over the cake.

CHOUQUETTES

Pastry

$1/2$	cup (120 ml) water
$1/4$	cup (60 g) unsalted butter
2	teaspoons sugar
$1/2$	teaspoon salt
$1/2$	cup (75 g) all-purpose (plain) flour
2	large eggs

Topping

1	large egg
$1/2$	cup (40 g) pearl sugar

Pastry: Preheat the oven to 400°F (200°C/gas 6). Line a large baking sheet with parchment paper.

Boil the water with the butter and add the salt and the sugar. Carefully stir in the flour until smooth. Set aside to cool for a few minutes.

Whisk in the eggs one by one.

Spoon the batter into a pastry (piping) bag and pipe into walnut-size mounds onto the prepared baking sheet, spacing well.

Topping: Brush the tops with beaten egg and sprinkle with the pearls of sugar.

Bake for 20 minutes, until pale golden brown. Let cool on a wire rack before serving.

Serves: 4–6 Preparation: 30 minutes Cooking: 20 minutes Level: 2

PARTY ÉCLAIRS

Pastry

$1/2$	quantity choux pastry cases (see Chocolate Eclairs on page 264)

Filling

1	quantity crème patissiere (see page 271)

Frosting

$1^1/2$	cups (225 g) confectioners' (icing) sugar
2	tablespoons butter
$1/2$	teaspoon vanilla extract (essence)
1–2	tablespoons boiling water
	Red food coloring
	Colored candy

Pastry and Filling: Prepare the pastry cases following the instructions for chocolate éclairs. Prepare the crème patissiere and pipe into the éclair cases.

Frosting: Sift the confectioners' sugar into a bowl. Add the butter, vanilla, and enough water to make a creamy frosting. Add enough food coloring to make a bright red frosting.

Spread the tops of the éclairs with the frosting and decorate with the candy. Chill until ready to serve.

Serves: 6 Preparation: 1 hour + 30 minutes to cool Cooking: 25–35 minutes Level: 2

Chouquettes are a traditional French pastry and are often served as an afternoon snack.

You can dress éclairs up with brightly colored frostings and serve them as party food. For a childrens' party, make mini éclairs and use several different colored frostings.

desserts

Here you will find 24 delicious dessert ideas, ranging from crisp meringue cakes and tortes to baked custards and mouthwatering crisps (crumbles), cobblers, and clafoutis.

• • • • •

The meringue in this cake makes it very delicate. To serve, dip a serrated knife into very hot water, quickly dry, and slice carefully.

CHOCOLATE HAZELNUT DACQUOISE

Hazelnut Meringue

1$^1/_4$ cups (190 g) blanched hazelnuts

1$^1/_2$ cups (300 g) superfine (caster) sugar

6 large egg whites
Pinch of salt

Chocolate Ganache

1$^1/_2$ cups (375 ml) heavy (double) cream

12 ounces (350 g) bittersweet dark chocolate

Espresso Buttercream

1 cup (200 g) sugar

$^1/_3$ cup (90 ml) water

4 large eggs yolks

1$^1/_2$ cups (375 g) unsalted butter, diced and softened

$^1/_4$ cup (60 ml) espresso coffee, cooled

To Decorate

1 cup (100 g) flaked almonds

10 hazelnuts, toasted and skins rubbed off

Hazelnut Meringue: Preheat the oven to 250°F (130°C/gas $^1/_2$). Grease two baking sheets. Draw two 10 x 3-inch (25 x 8-cm) rectangles on two pieces of parchment paper (four in total). Place on the baking sheets to line.

Chop the hazelnuts in a food processor to a fine powder. Add $^1/_2$ cup (100 g) of sugar and blend to combine. Transfer to a large bowl. Beat the egg whites and salt in a bowl with an electric mixer on medium speed until soft peaks form. Add the remaining sugar one tablespoon at a time until thick and glossy. Fold the meringue into the hazelnut mixture. Spoon into a pastry (piping) bag fitted with a $^1/_2$-inch (1-cm) plain tip. Pipe into the marked rectangles. Bake for 1–1$^1/_4$ hours, until crisp on the outside, but not colored. Turn the oven off and leave with the door ajar until cooled.

Chocolate Ganache: Combine the cream and chocolate in a heatproof bowl and set over a saucepan of barely simmering water, ensuring the base of the bowl does not touch the water. Stir occasionally until smooth. Remove from the heat and let cool until thickened slightly, about 15 minutes.

Espresso Buttercream: Combine the sugar and water in a heavy-based saucepan over low heat, stirring occasionally, until the sugar dissolves. Increase the heat and boil until the syrup reaches the soft-ball stage or reads 240°F (115°C) on a candy thermometer, about 15 minutes. Beat the egg yolks until pale and thick. With the mixer on low, beat in the sugar syrup in a thin steady stream. Beat on medium until light and fluffy. Add the butter a cube at a time, beating on medium until smooth and creamy, about 5 minutes. Add the espresso and beat to combine.

Peel the meringues off the paper and place three on a rack over a baking sheet. Spread each one with $^1/_4$ cup (60 ml) of ganache. Spoon half the buttercream into a pastry (piping) bag fitted with a $^1/_2$-inch (1-cm) plain tip and pipe over the ganache to cover. Stack the coated meringues one on top of the other. Top with the remaining meringue. Spread with the remaining buttercream to cover. Chill until firm, about 2 hours.

Reheat the remaining ganache. Spread over the cake to cover. Press the flaked almonds into the sides. Arrange the hazelnuts down the center of the cake at intervals so it can be sliced into ten portions. Chill for 1 hour. Slice and serve.

Serves: 6–8
Preparation: 30 minutes
+ 30 minutes to chill
Cooking: 1–1¼ hours
Level: 2

. . . . .

Meringue is believed to have been invented in England. The earliest documented recipe for a baked "beaten-egg-white-and-sugar confection" is a handwritten recipe for "white bisket bread" by Lady Elinor Fettiplace in 1604 in Oxfordshire, which later appeared in the cookbook *Elinor Fettiplace's Receipt Book— Elizabethan Country House Cooking*.

MERINGUE TORTE
with blueberries & lemon curd cream

Meringue
4   large egg whites
     Pinch of salt
1   cup (200 g) superfine (caster) sugar
2   cups (300 g) blueberries
     Confectioners' (icing) sugar, to dust

Lemon Curd Cream
4   large egg yolks
½   cup (100 g) superfine (caster) sugar
⅓   cup (90 ml) freshly squeezed lemon juice
     Finely grated zest of 1 unwaxed lemon
⅓   cup (90 g) unsalted butter, diced
¾   cup (180 ml) heavy (double) cream

Meringue: Preheat the oven to 300°F (150°C/gas 2). Grease three large baking sheets. Draw 8-inch (20-cm) disks on three pieces of parchment paper and place them disk-side down on the baking sheets to line.

Beat the egg whites and salt in a bowl with an electric mixer on medium speed until soft peaks form. Gradually add the sugar, one tablespoon at a time, beating until the meringue is thick and glossy and the sugar has completely dissolved. Spoon into the center of the marked disks, dividing evenly, and spread out to an even thickness.

Put in the oven and decrease the temperature to 250°F (130°C/gas ½). Bake for 1–1¼ hours, until just crisp on the outside, but not colored. Turn the oven off and leave with the door ajar until cooled completely.

Lemon Curd Cream: Whisk the egg yolks and sugar in a medium heatproof bowl until light and fluffy. Mix in the lemon juice and zest. Set the bowl over a saucepan of barely simmering water, ensuring the base of the bowl is not touching the water and cook, whisking constantly until thick, about 5 minutes. Add the butter one piece at a time, whisking between each addition, until blended. Remove the bowl from the heat and set aside to cool slightly. Cover the surface with plastic wrap (cling film) and refrigerate until cooled, about 30 minutes.

Beat the cream in a medium bowl with an electric mixer until stiff peaks form. Stir one large spoonful of the cream into the cooled lemon curd. Fold in the remaining cream.

To assemble, place one of the meringue disks on a serving plate. Spread with one-third of the lemon curd cream and sprinkle with one-third of the blueberries. Repeat the layers, finishing with the lemon curd cream and blueberries. Dust with confectioners' sugar. Slice and serve.

MERINGUE TORTE
with chocolate hazelnut cream

Meringue
1	cup (200 g) sugar
1/2	cup (120 ml) water
5	large egg whites
1/8	teaspoon salt
1 2/3	cups (200 g) confectioners' (icing) sugar

Filling
2	cups (500 ml) heavy (double) cream
1/2	cup (120 g) chocolate hazelnut cream (such as Nutella), softened

Meringue: Preheat the oven to 250°F (130°C/gas 1/2). Line two baking sheets with parchment paper and mark four 9-inch (23-cm) circles on the paper. Cook the sugar and water in a saucepan over medium heat until the sugar has dissolved. Beat the egg whites and salt in a bowl with an electric mixer until frothy. Gradually add the hot sugar mixture and confectioners' sugar, beating until stiff, glossy peaks form. Spoon into a pastry (piping) bag with a 1/2-inch (1-cm) tip. Pipe into four spiral disks.

Bake for 2 hours, until crisp. Turn off the oven and leave the meringues in the oven with the door slightly ajar until cool. Remove the paper.

Filling: Beat the cream in a bowl until stiff. Fold in the chocolate hazelnut cream. Place a meringue round on a serving plate and spread with one-third of the filling. Repeat with two more rounds of meringue, finishing with a layer of filling. Crumble the remaining meringue into large pieces and place on top. Slice and serve.

Serves: 6–8 Preparation: 1 hour Cooking: 2 hours Level: 2

COFFEE LIQUEUR VACHERIN

Vacherin
5	large egg whites
1 1/2	cups (300 g) superfine (caster) sugar
1	tablespoon coffee liqueur

Coffee Cream
1 1/2	cups (375 ml) heavy (double) cream
2	tablespoons confectioners' (icing) sugar
2	tablespoons coffee liqueur
	Whole coffee beans, to decorate

Vacherin: Preheat the oven to 250°F (130°C/gas 1/2). Line a baking sheet with parchment paper and mark two 9-inch (23-cm) circles on the paper. Beat the egg whites in a bowl with an electric mixer on medium speed until frothy. Gradually beat in the sugar until stiff, glossy peaks form. Add the coffee liqueur. Spoon the mixture into a pastry (piping) bag fitted with a 1/2-inch (1-cm) tip and pipe into two spiral disks.

Bake for 1 hour, until crisp. Turn off the oven and leave the door ajar until the vacherins are cool, about 1 hour. Carefully remove the paper.

Coffee Cream: Beat the cream, confectioners' sugar, and liqueur in a bowl until stiff. Place a meringue layer on a serving plate. Spread with three-quarters of the cream. Top with the remaining meringue layer. Spoon the remaining cream into a pastry bag and decorate the top of the vacherin with 8–10 rosettes. Top each rosette with a coffee bean. Slice and serve.

Serves: 6–8 Preparation: 30 minutes Cooking: 1 hour Level: 2

Make sure that the hazelnut cream is softened so that it can be folded into the cream. Leave the jar at warm room temperature for a few hours beforehand.

Vacherin is a classic French dessert made by filling and stacking a number of disks of meringue. The meringue can be plain or flavored and is usually filled with whipped cream, often with the addition of fruit or other flavorings.

Serves: 6–8
Preparation: 30 minutes
Cooking: 1¼–1½ hours
Level: 2

Pavlova is a popular meringue dessert created in New Zealand in honor of the famous Russian ballet dancer Anna Pavlova during one of her tours to Australia and New Zealand in the 1920s.

MARSHMALLOW PAVLOVA
with fresh berries

Meringue
4	large egg whites
	Pinch of salt
1	cup (200 g) superfine (caster) sugar
1	tablespoon cornstarch (corn flour)
1	teaspoon white vinegar
1	teaspoon vanilla extract (essence)

Topping
1¼	cups (310 ml) heavy (double) cream
2	cups (300 g) strawberries, hulled and halved
1	cup (150 g) raspberries
1	cup (150 g) blueberries

Meringue: Preheat the oven to 300°F (150°C/gas 2). Grease a large baking sheet. Draw an 8-inch (20-cm) disk on a piece of parchment paper and place disk-side down on the prepared sheet.

Beat the egg whites and salt in a large bowl with an electric mixer on medium speed until soft peaks form. Gradually add the sugar, one tablespoon at a time, beating until the meringue is thick and glossy and the sugar has completely dissolved. Add the cornstarch, vinegar, and vanilla and beat to combine.

Spoon the meringue into the center of the marked disk and spread out to an even thickness. Sweep a spatula up the sides to create decorative waves.

Place the pavlova in the oven and decrease the temperature to 250°F (130°C/gas ½). Bake for 1¼–1½ hours, until just crisp on the outside, but not colored. Turn the oven off and leave with the door ajar until cooled completely.

Topping: Beat the cream in a medium bowl with an electric mixer on medium speed until stiff peaks form. Spread the cream over the top of the pavlova and sprinkle with the berries. Slice and serve.

· · ·

If you liked this recipe, you will love these as well.

CRISP PASTEL MERINGUES

MERINGUE TORTE WITH BLUEBERRIES & LEMON CURD CREAM

RASPBERRY & VANILLA VACHERIN

· · · · ·

You can vary the flavors of the ice cream in this pretty cake. Chocolate ice cream goes beautifully with the raspberry sorbet, for example.

RASPBERRY & VANILLA VACHERIN

Meringue

4	large egg whites
¼	teaspoon cream of tartar
¾	cup (150 g) superfine (caster) sugar
¼	cup (30 g) confectioners' (icing) sugar

Filling

4	cups (1 liter) good quality vanilla ice cream
3	cups (750 ml) raspberry sorbet
1	cup (150 g) fresh raspberries
	Confectioners' (icing) sugar, to dust

Chantilly Cream

1½	cups (375 ml) heavy (double) cream
2	tablespoons confectioners' (icing) sugar
1	teaspoon vanilla extract (essence)

Meringue: Preheat the oven to 300°F (150°C/gas 2). Grease three baking sheets. Draw 8-inch (20-cm) disks on two pieces of parchment paper and place on two baking sheets. Line the remaining sheet with plain paper.

Beat the egg whites and cream of tartar in a bowl with an electric mixer on medium speed until soft peaks form. Gradually beat in the superfine sugar, one tablespoon at a time, until thick and glossy. Sift in the confectioners' sugar and fold to combine. Spoon one-third of the meringue into a pastry (piping) bag fitted with a plain 1-inch (2-cm) tip. Pipe twelve 3-inch (8-cm) long fingers about 1 inch (2.5 cm) apart onto the unmarked paper. Spoon the remaining meringue into the bag and pipe in circles to fill the marked disks.

Decrease the temperature to 250°F (130°C/gas ½). Bake for 1–1¼ hours, until just crisp on the outside but not colored. Turn the oven off and leave with the door ajar, until cooled completely.

Filling: Grease an 8-inch (20-cm) springform pan and line with parchment paper. Let the ice cream stand at room temperature until softened, about 10 minutes. Put one of the meringue disks into the pan, trimming to fit if necessary. Spoon the ice cream on top, pressing down to remove any air pockets. Smooth the surface. Cover with plastic wrap (cling film) and chill until firm, 1–2 hours.

Let the sorbet stand at room temperature until softened, 5–10 minutes. Spoon over the ice cream. Place the remaining meringue disk on top. Cover and freeze until firm, about 1 hour.

Chantilly Cream: Beat the cream in a bowl until soft peaks form. Add the confectioners' sugar and vanilla and beat until firm peaks form. Spoon into a pastry bag fitted with a ¾-inch (2-cm) star tip.

Run a hot knife around the edge of the cake in the pan. Open the sides and transfer to a serving plate. Stick the meringue fingers around the edges, spacing evenly and securing with a little cream. Pipe cream decoratively between the fingers and on top. Freeze until required. Before serving, stand the cake at room temperature for 5 minutes. Decorate with raspberries and dust with confectioners' sugar. Slice with a hot knife.

Serves: 6
Preparation: 45 minutes
   + 30 minutes to cool
   & churning time
Cooking: 15 minutes
Level: 3

. . . . .

The name Baked Alaska was coined at Delmonico's Restaurant in New York City in 1876 to honor the recent acquisition of the northernmost American state. This dessert is also known as a Norwegian omelet.

MINI BAKED ALASKA

Strawberry Ice Cream

2	cups (500 ml) heavy (double) cream
1/2	vanilla bean, split lengthwise and seeds scraped
5	large egg yolks
1/2	cup (100 g) superfine (caster) sugar
2	cups (500 g) fresh strawberries, hulled
1	tablespoon strawberry liqueur

Meringue

3	large egg whites
1/2	cup (100 g) superfine (caster) sugar
1/4	cup (80 g) raspberry preserves (jam)
12	small ladyfingers (sponge fingers)

Strawberry Ice Cream: Combine the cream and vanilla bean and seeds in a medium saucepan over medium-low heat and bring to a boil. Remove from the heat and set aside.

Beat the egg yolks and sugar in a medium heatproof bowl with an electric mixer fitted on high speed until pale and creamy. Slowly pour one-third of the hot cream into the egg mixture, stirring until combined. Stir in the rest.

Place the bowl over a saucepan of barely simmering water and cook, stirring constantly with a wooden spoon, until the custard coats the back of the spoon. Remove from the heat, discard the vanilla bean, and cover with parchment paper to prevent a skin from forming.

Purée the strawberries and liqueur in a blender and strain through a fine-mesh sieve to remove the seeds. Stir the strawberry purée into the custard and refrigerate until cooled, about 30 minutes.

Pour the mixture into an ice-cream maker and churn according to the manufacturer's instructions. Transfer the ice cream to a freezer container, cover with parchment paper, and freeze until ready to serve.

Preheat the oven to 425°F (220°C/gas 7). Line a baking sheet with parchment paper.

Meringue: Beat the egg whites in a bowl with an electric mixer on medium speed until soft peaks form. Gradually add the sugar and beat until the mixture is glossy and forms stiff peaks.

Melt the preserves in a small saucepan over medium-low heat. Brush generously on one side of the ladyfingers. Sandwich two fingers together using a little meringue mixture as glue, and place side by side on the prepared sheet. Continue this process until you have six sponge finger bases. Place a scoop of the strawberry ice cream on top of each base. Cover completely with a large dollop of the meringue. Create decorative peaks using a spatula or the back of a spoon.

Immediately bake for 4 minutes, until the meringue is golden. Transfer to individual serving plates using a palette knife and serve immediately.

CANNELÉS

1	cup (250 ml) milk
2	tablespoons unsalted butter
½	cup (75 g) all-purpose (plain) flour
½	cup (100 g) + 1 tablespoon sugar
1	large egg + 1 large egg yolk
½	teaspoon vanilla extract (essence)
½	tablespoon rum

Bring the milk and butter to a boil together in a saucepan. Stir the flour and sugar together in a bowl. Beat the egg and egg yolk in a cup, and then stir into the flour mixture. Add the hot milk mixture, whisking until smooth. The batter should be thin and lump-free, like crepe batter.

Stir in the vanilla and rum. Cover the batter with plastic wrap (cling film), and chill in the refrigerator for 4 hours, or overnight.

Preheat the oven to 450°F (220°C/gas 8).

Pour the batter into the mini cannele mold, and bake for 5 minutes. Reduce the oven temperature to 350°F (180°C/gas 4), and continue baking until the cannelés are dark golden brown, about 45–50 minutes. Unmold the cakes, and let cool before serving.

Makes: 18 Preparation: 20 minutes + 4–12 hours to chill Cooking: 50–55 minutes Level: 1

FAR BRETON

2	cups (500 ml) milk
3	large eggs
½	cup (100 g) sugar
5	tablespoons butter, melted and cooled
½	teaspoon vanilla extract (essence)
¾	cup (120 g) all-purpose (plain) flour
1	cup (180 g) small pitted prunes
½	cup (120 ml) water
⅓	cup (40 g) raisins
¼	cup (60 ml) Armagnac or other brandy
	Confectioners' (icing) sugar, to dust

Whisk the milk, eggs, sugar, butter, and vanilla in a bowl until smooth. Add the flour and beat until just blended. Cover and chill for 3 hours.

Heat the prunes, water, and raisins in a small pan over medium heat until softened, about 10 minutes. Turn off the heat. Pour in the brandy. Using a long match, ignite the brandy. Let the flames burn off, shaking the pan occasionally. Transfer the prunes to a bowl and let cool.

Preheat the oven to 375°F (190°C/gas 5). Butter an 8-inch (20-cm) cake pan. Pour the batter into the pan. Spoon the prune mixture over the top. Bake for 1 hour, until puffed and golden. Cool in the pan on a rack.

Dust with confectioners' sugar just before serving.

Serves: 6–8 Preparation: 20 minutes + 3 hours to chill Cooking: 1 hour Level: 1

You will need an 18-cup mini cannele mold to make these traditional French cakes from Bordeaux.

Far Breton is a traditional dessert from Brittany, in northern France.

Serves: 6
Preparation: 30 minutes
+ 2½ hours to infuse,
& cool & 2–12 hours
to cool
Cooking: 50–55 minutes
Level: 1

· · · · ·

Crème caramel is simple to prepare and most people love it. It makes an ideal family dessert and can be prepared ahead of time and chilled until ready to serve.

CRÈME CARAMEL

Flavorless oil, such as almond, to grease

Caramel
½ cup (100 g) superfine (caster) sugar
¼ cup (60 ml) water

Custard
1½ cups (375 ml) heavy (double) cream
¾ cup (180 ml) milk
1 vanilla bean, split in half lengthwise, seeds scraped and reserved
2 large eggs + 2 large egg yolks
1 cup (200 g) superfine (caster) sugar

Preheat the oven to 300°F (150°C/gas 2). Line the base of a deep roasting pan with a clean kitchen cloth.

Lightly grease six ½-cup (120-ml) heatproof dariole molds or ramekins with a flavorless oil and arrange in the pan.

Caramel: Combine the sugar and water in a small saucepan and heat over low heat, stirring occasionally, until the sugar dissolves. Increase the heat to medium and simmer until the mixture caramelizes to a dark amber color, 5–10 minutes. Pour the caramel into the base of the prepared molds.

Custard: Combine the cream, milk, and vanilla bean and seeds in a small saucepan and bring to scalding point over medium-low heat. Set aside for 20 minutes to infuse.

Beat the eggs, egg yolks, and the sugar in a medium bowl with an electric mixer on medium speed until pale and thick. Gradually pour in the cream mixture, stirring with a wooden spoon to combine. Strain through a fine-mesh sieve into a pitcher (jug).

Pour the custard mixture into the caramel-lined molds. Pour enough boiling water into the roasting pan to come halfway up the sides of the molds. Carefully place the pan in the oven, taking care not to spill any water into the molds. Bake for 45 minutes, until just set. Remove the pan from the oven.

Remove the hot molds from the pan and set aside for 15 minutes to cool slightly. Refrigerate for at least 2 hours, or overnight, until set firm.

To serve, gently press your fingers on top of the crème caramels near the rim to release the seal. Invert onto serving plates.

Serves: 4
Preparation: 30 minutes
  + 3–13 hours to
  infuse, rest & chill
Cooking: 30 minutes
Level: 2

. . . . .

You will need a kitchen blowtorch to caramelize the sugar on the tops of these little custards. If you don't have one, then you can just as easily broil (grill) the custard tops to caramelize under the overhead broiler (grill) in the oven.

CRÈME BRÛLÈE

2⅓ cups (580 ml) heavy (double) cream
1 vanilla bean, split in half lengthwise, seeds scraped and reserved
6 large egg yolks
¼ cup (50 g) superfine (caster) sugar + extra, to sprinkle

Preheat the oven to 300°F (150°C/gas 2).

Line the base of a deep roasting pan with a clean kitchen cloth. Arrange four ¾-cup (180-ml) ovenproof ramekins on top.

Place the cream and vanilla bean and seeds in a small saucepan and bring to scalding point over medium-low heat. Set aside for 20 minutes to infuse.

Beat the egg yolks and sugar in a bowl with an electric mixer on medium speed until pale and thick. Gradually pour in the cream, stirring with a wooden spoon to combine. Strain through a fine-mesh sieve into a pitcher (jug).

Pour the custard mixture into the ramekins. Pour enough boiling water into the roasting pan to come halfway up the sides of the ramekins. Cut a piece of aluminum foil large enough to cover the ramekins, leaving the rest of the pan open.

Carefully place the pan in the oven, taking care not to spill any water into the ramekins. Bake for 30 minutes, until just set but still with a slight wobble in the center. Remove the pan from the oven.

Using a kitchen cloth, remove the hot ramekins from the pan and set aside for 15 minutes to cool slightly. Refrigerate for at least 2 hours or overnight, until set firm.

Prior to serving, remove the crème brûlèes from the refrigerator and stand at room temperature for 20 minutes.

Sprinkle the tops of the crème brûlèes with superfine sugar to create an even layer. Run a clean kitchen cloth around the rims to clean. Using a kitchen blowtorch, caramelize the sugar until dark brown. Serve.

Serves: 10-12
Preparation: 30 minutes
+ 15 minutes to cool
Cooking: 35-40 minutes
Level: 2

. . . . .

This cake comes from Mexico and Central America and is known in Spanish as *Pastel de tres leche.*

MEXICAN THREE-MILK PUDDING

Pudding

1¹/₂ cups (180 g) all-purpose (plain) flour

1¹/₂ teaspoons baking powder

Pinch of salt

5 large eggs, separated

1 cup (200 g) superfine (caster) sugar

1 teaspoon vanilla extract (essence)

¹/₄ cup (60 ml) milk

Confectioners' (icing) sugar, to dust

Milk Syrup

1 (14-ounce/400-ml) can sweetened condensed milk

1¹/₂ cups (375 ml) canned evaporated milk

³/₄ cup (180 ml) light (single) cream

1 tablespoon dark rum

1 teaspoon vanilla extract (essence)

Pudding: Preheat the oven to 350°F (180°C/gas 4). Line a 10-inch (25-cm) springform pan with parchment paper.

Sift the flour, baking powder, and salt into a small bowl. Beat the egg yolks, ³/₄ cup (150 g) of sugar, and vanilla in a bowl with an electric mixer on medium speed until pale and thick. With the mixer on low speed, add the flour mixture and milk alternately, beating until just combined.

Beat the egg whites in a bowl until soft peaks form. Gradually add the remaining ¹/₄ cup (50 g) of sugar, beating until thick and glossy. Fold a large spoonful of the whites into the yolk mixture. Fold in the remaining whites. Pour the mixture into the prepared pan.

Bake for 35–40 minutes, until springy to the touch and a toothpick inserted into the center comes out clean. Let cool in the pan for 15 minutes.

Milk Syrup: Place all the syrup ingredients in a medium bowl and whisk to combine. Poke holes in the cake with a skewer. Slowly pour the syrup over the cake, waiting for each addition to be absorbed before adding the next. Dust the cake with confectioners' sugar, slice, and serve.

FAR BRETON

STICKY DATE PUDDING

QUEEN OF PUDDINGS

Serves: 4

Preparation: 20 minutes
   + 3 minutes to stand

Cooking: 12 minutes

Level: 2

- - - - -

Chocolate fondant is created by slightly underbaking a chocolate cake so that the center is still runny although warmed through. Be warned tough, these are addictive!

CHOCOLATE FONDANTS

7   ounces (200 g) good quality dark chocolate, coarsely chopped

$1/2$ cup (120 g) unsalted butter, diced + extra melted butter

2   tablespoons espresso coffee

2   large eggs + 2 large egg yolks

$1/3$ cup (70 g) superfine (caster) sugar

3   tablespoons all-purpose (plain) flour

     Cream or ice cream, to serve

Preheat the oven to 350°F (180°C/gas 4).

Grease four $3/4$-cup (180-ml) ovenproof dariole molds or ramekins, brushing melted butter into the bases and around the insides. Refrigerate for 10 minutes. Brush the insides of the molds again and refrigerate until required.

Place the chocolate, butter, and coffee in a medium heatproof bowl and set over a saucepan of barely simmering water, ensuring the base of the bowl does not touch the water. Stir occasionally until smooth. Set aside to cool.

Beat the eggs, egg yolks, and sugar in a bowl with an electric mixer on medium speed until pale and thick. Pour in the cooled chocolate mixture and gently fold to combine. Sift the flour and gently fold into the batter.

Spoon the batter evenly into the prepared molds. Tap firmly on a work surface to remove any air bubbles. Slide the back of a knife or a spatula across the top, to create a flat surface. Place the molds on a baking sheet.

Bake for 12 minutes, until the edges are firm but the centers still wobble. Let stand for 3 minutes to cool slightly.

To serve, run a knife around the edges of the molds, taking care not to pierce the fondant. Invert onto serving plates.

Serve warm, with the cream or ice cream.

- - -

If you liked this recipe, you will love these as well.

CHOCOLATE CAKE

CHOCOLATE MUD CAKE

SELF-SAUCING CHOCO-LATE PUDDING

CHERRY CLAFOUTIS

3   large eggs + 2 large egg yolks

$^1/_2$ cup (100 g) superfine (caster) sugar

3   tablespoons (45 g) unsalted butter, melted and cooled

$^1/_3$ cup (50 g) all-purpose (plain) flour

1   cup (250 ml) milk

1   pound (500 g) pitted cherries

       Confectioners' (icing) sugar, to dust

Preheat the oven to 400°F (200°C/gas 6). Grease a 9-inch (23-cm) pie pan with butter.

Beat the eggs, egg yolks, and sugar in a medium bowl with an electric mixer on medium speed until pale and thick. Pour in the butter and beat to combine. Sift in the flour, folding it gently into the mixture. Gradually stir in the milk to make a smooth batter.

Spread the cherries evenly over the base of the prepared pie pan. Pour the batter over the top.

Bake for 20–25 minutes, until golden brown on top and the custard is just set. Set aside for 10 minutes, to cool slightly.

Dust with confectioners' sugar and serve warm.

Serves: 6   Preparation: 30 minutes + 10 minutes to rest   Cooking: 20–25 minutes   Level: 1

PEACH COBBLER

Fruit Base

3   pounds (1.35 kg) ripe peaches

$^1/_2$ cup (100 g) super-fine (caster) sugar

Topping

$1^1/_3$ cups (200 g) all-purpose (plain) flour

2   teaspoons baking powder

$^1/_3$ cup (90 g) chilled salted butter, diced

$^1/_3$ cup (70 g) superfine (caster) sugar

$^3/_4$ cup (180 ml) buttermilk

       Cream, ice cream, or custard, to serve

Fruit Base: Preheat the oven to 400°F (200°C/gas 6).

Cut the peaches in half, remove the pits (stones), and thickly slice. Place the peach slices and sugar in an 8-cup (2-liter) ovenproof dish and toss to coat. Set aside.

Topping: Sift the flour and baking powder into a bowl. Using your fingertips, rub in the butter until the mixture resembles coarse crumbs. Add the sugar and stir to combine. Gradually mix in the buttermilk to make a thick batter.

Drop dollops of the batter over the peach filling, leaving parts of the filling still exposed.

Bake for 30–35 minutes, until the cobbler is golden brown and the fruit underneath is bubbling. Stand in the dish for 10 minutes, to cool slightly.

Serve warm with cream, ice cream, or custard.

Serves: 6-8   Preparation: 20 minutes   Cooking: 30–35 minutes   Level: 1

Cherry clafoutis is a traditional French dessert from the Limousin region of France.

A cobbler is a dessert with a fruit base over which a batter or biscuity topping is spread or spooned to make a crust. Cobblers make great family desserts and are also good for casual entertaining.

Serves: 6

Preparation: 20 minutes
10 minutes to stand

Cooking: 30–35 minutes

Level: 1

Like a cobbler, a crisp, or crumble as it is known in the United Kingdom and the Commonwealth, is a fruit-based dessert covered with a topping. Most crisps are sweet and served for dessert, although there are also some savory recipes.

APPLE & RHUBARB CRISP

Fruit Base

6	medium green cooking apples, such as Granny Smith, peeled, quartered, and thickly sliced
6	sticks rhubarb, cut into 2-inch (5-cm) lengths
1/4	cup (50 g) sugar
2	tablespoons golden raisins (sultanas)
1	tablespoon water
	Finely grated zest of 1 unwaxed lemon
1/2	teaspoon ground cinnamon
	Cream, ice cream, or custard, to serve

Topping

1	cup (150 g) all-purpose (plain) flour
1	teaspoon baking powder
1	teaspoon ground cinnamon
1/2	cup (100 g) firmly packed light brown sugar
1/4	cup (25 g) old fashioned (rolled) oats
2/3	cup (150 g) salted butter, softened

Fruit Base: Preheat the oven to 400°F (200°C/gas 6).

Combine the apples, rhubarb, sugar, golden raisins, and water in a medium saucepan. Cover and cook over medium-low heat until softened, about 5 minutes. Remove from the heat, add the lemon zest and cinnamon, and stir to combine. Spread evenly in a medium ovenproof baking dish and set aside.

Topping: Sift the flour, baking powder, and cinnamon into a bowl. Add the brown sugar and oats and stir to combine. Using your fingertips, rub in the butter, until the mixture begins to clump together. Sprinkle the topping evenly over the fruit.

Bake for 25–30 minutes, until the topping is crisp and golden brown and the fruit is bubbling underneath. Let stand for 10 minutes to cool slightly.

Serve warm with the cream, ice cream, or custard.

. . .

If you liked this recipe, you will love these as well.

CHERRY CLAFOUTIS

PEACH COBBLER

RUSSIAN RASPBERRY PUDDING

Serves: 6
Preparation: 30 minutes
Cooking: 12 minutes
Level: 3

. . . . .

Serve these pretty soufflés for dessert on a special occasion. Be sure to try them first, as they can be a bit tricky to get right at the beginning. Serve as soon as they are baked, before they deflate.

RASPBERRY SOUFFLÉS

Soufflé Base

2	tablespoons unsalted butter, melted
3	large egg yolks
1/2	cup (100 g) superfine (caster) sugar + extra, to sprinkle
3	tablespoons all-purpose (plain) flour
1	cup (250 ml) milk
1	pound (500 g) fresh or frozen raspberries

Soufflé Meringue

4	large egg whites
	Pinch of cream of tartar
1/4	cup (50 g) superfine (caster) sugar
	Confectioners' (icing) sugar, to dust

Soufflé Base: Preheat the oven to 400°F (200° C/gas 6). Grease six 3/4-cup (180-ml) soufflé dishes, or ovenproof ramekins, by brushing melted butter into the bases and around the insides. Refrigerate for 10 minutes. Brush the inside of the dishes with butter again. Sprinkle with sugar and rotate to coat evenly. Gently tap to remove any excess sugar and set aside.

Beat the egg yolks and 1/4 cup (50 g) of the sugar in a bowl with an electric mixer on medium speed until pale and creamy. Sift in the flour. Heat the milk in a small saucepan over medium-low heat until scalding. Gradually pour the milk into the egg mixture, beating constantly on low speed, until combined. Return the mixture to the pan and cook over medium-low heat, whisking constantly, until it comes to a boil. Keep whisking and simmer for 1 minute. Transfer to a large bowl, cover the surface with plastic wrap (cling film), and set aside to cool.

Place the raspberries and remaining 1/4 cup (50 g) sugar in a small saucepan and gently simmer over low heat until softened into a thick purée, 3–5 minutes. Press through a fine-mesh sieve into a small bowl, discarding the seeds. Add the purée to the custard and whisk to combine. Cover with plastic wrap and set aside.

Soufflé Meringue: Beat the egg whites and cream of tartar in a medium bowl with an electric mixer on medium speed until soft peaks form. Gradually add the sugar one tablespoon at a time beating constantly until firm peaks form. Stir one large spoonful of the meringue into the base. Gently fold in the remaining meringue.

Spoon the mixture into the prepared molds. Tap once firmly on the work surface to ensure the mixture has filled the dish. Slide the back of a knife or a spatula across the top to create a flat surface. Run the tip of a small knife around the top of the molds to stop the soufflé from sticking so it can rise evenly. Place the dishes on a baking sheet.

Bake for 12 minutes, until well risen and golden. Dust with confectioners' sugar, and serve immediately.

Serves: 8
Preparation: 30 minutes
+ 40 minutes to
infuse, soak & cool
Cooking: 25–30 minutes
Level: 1

. . . . .

Panettone is a traditional Italian sweet bread. Originally from Milan, it is now served all over Italy and in many other parts of the world, mainly at Christmas time.

PANETTONE BREAD & BUTTER PUDDING

2   cups (500 ml) single (light) cream
1½   cups (375 ml) milk
1   cinnamon stick
2   strips unwaxed orange zest
2   strips unwaxed lemon zest
1   panettone, weighing about 1¼ pounds (600 g)
¼   cup (45 g) raisins
¼   cup (25 g) flaked almonds
4   large eggs
½   cup (100 g) superfine (caster) sugar
1   tablespoon raw sugar, to sprinkle
     Cream or ice cream, to serve

Preheat the oven to 350°F (180°C/gas 4).

Combine the cream, milk, cinnamon, and orange and lemon zests in a medium saucepan and bring to scalding point over medium-low heat. Set aside for 20 minutes to infuse.

Slice the panettone into ½-inch (1-cm) thick wedges. Arrange half of the slices in the base of a 6-cup (1.5-liter) ovenproof dish and sprinkle with half of the raisins and flaked almonds. Create another layer using the remaining panettone, raisins, and almonds.

Beat the eggs and sugar in a bowl with an electric mixer on medium speed until pale and thick. Gradually pour in the cream mixture, beating to combine. Strain through a fine-mesh sieve into a pitcher (jug).

Pour the custard mixture over the panettone, pressing the cake down slightly to cover. Let stand for 10 minutes to soak. Sprinkle with the raw sugar.

Place the dish in a deep roasting pan and pour in enough boiling water to come halfway up the sides. Carefully place the pan in the oven, taking care not to spill any water into the dish.

Bake for 25–30 minutes, until the top is golden brown and the custard just set. Carefully remove the pan from the oven. Using a kitchen cloth, remove the dish from the pan and stand for 10 minutes to cool slightly.

Serve warm with cream or ice cream.

MEXICAN THREE-MILK PUDDING

QUEEN OF PUDDINGS

PAIN AU CHOCOLAT PUDDING

. . . . .

Everyone will love this delicious dessert. It can definitely be classed as a comfort food and is great for family meals, casual gatherings of friends, and girls' nights in.

STICKY DATE PUDDING

Pudding

2	cups (400 g) pitted dried dates, coarsely chopped
1¹⁄₂	cups (375 ml) water
1	teaspoon baking soda (bicarbonate of soda)
³⁄₄	cup (150 g) firmly packed light brown sugar
¹⁄₃	cup (90 g) salted butter, softened
3	large eggs
1¹⁄₂	cups (225 g) all-purpose (plain) flour
1¹⁄₂	teaspoons baking powder
1	teaspoon ground ginger
1	teaspoon pumpkin pie (mixed) spice
	Cream or ice cream, to serve

Caramel Sauce

1¹⁄₂	cups (300 g) firmly packed light brown sugar
1	cup (250 ml) single (light) cream
¹⁄₂	cup (120 g) salted butter

Pudding: Preheat the oven to 350°F (180°C/gas 4). Grease an 8-inch (20-cm) square cake pan and line with parchment paper.

Combine the dates, water, and baking soda in a medium saucepan and bring to a boil over medium heat. Set aside to cool.

Beat the brown sugar and butter in a bowl with an electric mixer on medium speed until creamy. Add the eggs one at a time, beating until just combined after each addition. Add the date mixture and beat to combine. Sift in the flour, baking powder, ginger, and pumpkin pie spice and fold to combine. Spoon into the prepared pan.

Bake for 40–45 minutes, until golden brown and a toothpick inserted into the center comes out clean. Leave in the pan for 10 minutes to cool slightly.

Caramel Sauce: Combine the brown sugar, cream, and butter in a medium saucepan and simmer over medium-low heat, stirring occasionally, until smooth. Simmer until thickened into a rich sauce, 3–5 minutes. Strain through a fine-mesh sieve into a pitcher (jug).

Slice the pudding into portions and serve warm with the caramel sauce and cream or ice cream.

. . .

If you liked this recipe, you will love these as well.

FAR BRETON

CHOCOLATE FONDANTS

SELF-SAUCING PUDDING

LEMON DELICIOUS PUDDING

2/3 cup (140 g) superfine (caster) sugar

1/3 cup (90 g) unsalted butter, softened

Finely grated zest and juice of 3 unwaxed lemons

4 large eggs, separated

1/2 cup (75 g) all-purpose (plain) flour

2 cups (500 ml) milk

Confectioners' (icing) sugar, to dust

Cream or ice cream, to serve

Preheat the oven to 350°F (180°C/gas 4). Grease a 6-cup (1.5-liter) ovenproof dish with butter.

Beat the sugar, butter, and lemon zest in a bowl with an electric mixer on medium speed until pale and creamy. Add the egg yolks one at a time, beating until just combined after each addition. Sift in the flour and stir to combine. Gradually stir in the milk and lemon juice. Beat the egg whites in a bowl until soft peaks form. Stir one large tablespoon of the whites into the batter. Fold in the remaining whites and pour into the prepared dish.

Place the dish in a deep roasting pan and pour in enough boiling water to come halfway up the sides of the dish. Carefully place the pan in the oven, taking care not to spill any water into the dish.

Bake for 40 minutes, until golden brown. Remove the pan from the oven. Remove the dish from the pan and stand for 10 minutes, to cool slightly.

Dust with confectioners' sugar, and serve warm with cream or ice cream.

Serves: 6 Preparation: 15 minutes + 10 minutes to cool Cooking: 40 minutes Level: 1

SELF-SAUCING CHOCOLATE PUDDING

1 cup (150 g) all-purpose (plain) flour

1/3 cup (50 g) unsweet-ened cocoa powder

1 teaspoon baking powder

1 cup (200 g) firmly packed light brown sugar

1/2 cup (120 ml) milk

1/4 cup (160 g) unsalted butter, melted

1 large egg, beaten

1 teaspoon vanilla extract (essence)

1 1/2 cups (375 ml) boiling water

Cream, to serve

Preheat the oven to 350°F (180°C/gas 4). Grease a 6-cup (1.5-liter) ovenproof dish with butter.

Sift the flour, 3 tablespoons of cocoa, and the baking powder into a medium bowl. Add half of the brown sugar and stir to combine. Add the milk, butter, egg, and vanilla and stir to make a smooth batter. Pour into the prepared dish.

Combine the remaining cocoa and brown sugar in a small bowl. Sprinkle the cocoa mixture over the batter. Pour the boiling water over the top.

Bake for 35–40 minutes, until the top is firm and the sauce is bubbling up at the sides. Let stand for 10 minutes to cool slightly.

Serve warm, with cream or ice cream.

Serves: 6 Preparation: 15 minutes + 10 minutes to stand Cooking: 35–40 minutes Level: 1

Serves: 6
Preparation:
+ 40 mi
stand
Cookin
Lev

This mouthwatering dessert is as delicious to eat as it is simple to prepare.

. . . . .

Variations on this traditional British pudding have been made since the 17th century.

QUEEN OF PUDDINGS

2½ cups (625 ml) milk

2 tablespoons unsalted butter

Finely grated zest of 1 unwaxed lemon

4 large eggs, separated

½ cup (100 g) + 1 teaspoon superfine (caster) sugar

1 teaspoon vanilla extract (essence)

2 cups (160 g) fresh white bread crumbs

3 tablespoons raspberry preserves (jam)

Grease a 6-cup (1.5-liter) ovenproof dish with butter.

Combine the milk, butter, and lemon zest in a medium saucepan and bring to scalding point over medium-low heat. Set aside.

Beat the egg yolks, 2 tablespoons of the sugar, and the vanilla in a bowl with an electric mixer on medium speed until pale and thick. Gradually pour in the hot milk, beating to combine. Add the bread crumbs and stir to combine. Pour into the prepared dish, spreading in an even layer. Leave to stand for 20 minutes.

Preheat the oven to 350°F (180°C/gas 4).

Bake the bread crumb and custard base for 25–30 minutes, until just set. Remove from the oven and leave for 10 minutes to firm up slightly.

Beat the egg whites in a bowl with an electric mixer on medium speed until soft peaks form. Gradually add the sugar, one tablespoon at a time, beating constantly until firm glossy peaks form.

Spread the raspberry preserves over the base. Spoon the meringue on top, using the back of a spoon or spatula to create decorative peaks. Sprinkle with the remaining 1 teaspoon of sugar. Bake for 15–20 minutes, until the meringue is pale golden brown.

Let stand for 10 minutes to cool slightly. Serve warm.

. . .

If you liked this recipe, you will love these as well.

LEMON MERINGUE PIE

PANETTONE BREAD & BUTTER PUDDING

PAIN AU CHOCOLAT PUDDING

PAIN AU CHOCOLAT PUDDING

3   day-old pains au chocolat

$^1/_2$ cup (90 g) dark chocolate chips

$^1/_2$ cup (90 g) dried cherries

$1^1/_4$ cups (300 ml) milk

$1^1/_4$ cups (300 ml) light (single) cream

3   large eggs, beaten

5   tablespoons superfine (caster) sugar

$^1/_4$ cup (60 g) unsalted butter, melted

$^1/_2$ teaspoon vanilla extract (essence)

Preheat the oven to 350°F (180°C/gas 4). Butter a 4-cup (1-liter) shallow ovenproof dish. Slice the pains au chocolat across the chocolate filling about $^1/_2$-inch (1-cm) thick. Arrange the slices in the dish overlapping to fit. Sprinkle with the chocolate chips and dried cherries or cranberries.

Combine the milk and cream in a small saucepan and warm over medium heat. Bring near to boiling point. Whisk the eggs and sugar in a medium bowl. Slowly add the hot milk mixture and melted butter, whisking continuously until smooth. Add the vanilla and pour over the pain au chocolat in the dish. Let soak for 10 minutes.

Bake for 30–35 minutes, until the pudding is set and the top is golden. Serve hot or warm.

Serves: 4 Preparation: 15 minutes + 10 minutes to soak Cooking: 30–35 minutes Level: 1

RUSSIAN RASPBERRY PUDDING

3   cups (450 g) raspberries

$^1/_2$ cup (100 g) superfine (caster)

$^3/_4$ cup (180 ml) sour cream

2   large eggs

1   tablespoon all-purpose (plain) flour or potato flour

2-3   tablespoons confectioners' (icing) sugar

Preheat the oven to 300°F (150°C/gas 2). Pour the raspberries into a shallow 9-inch (23-cm) gratin dish and sprinkle with 2 tablespoons of the sugar. Bake for 5–8 minutes, until the raspberries are hot. Remove from the oven.

Beat the sour cream and eggs in a medium bowl with an electric mixer fitted with a whisk until combined. Beat in the flour and remaining sugar. Pour over the raspberries in the dish.

Bake for 40–45 minutes, until the topping is golden brown. Dust with the confectioners' sugar. Serve hot or at room temperature.

Serves: 4-6 Preparation: 15 minutes Cooking: 45–55 minutes Level: 1

If you have any leftover pain au chocolat (see our recipe on page 247), this recipe is an excellent way to use them up.

This delicious pudding can be made in a jiffy. It is perfect for busy weeknight dinners.

Serves: 10
Preparation: 45 minutes
+ 2 hours or
overnight to prove
Cooking: 45–50 minutes
Level: 2

· · · · ·

Kulich is a tall, sweet yeast bread. It is traditionally baked and served at Easter time in Russia and other Orthodox Christian countries, such as Georgia, Romania, and Serbia. The bread is baked at home and taken to Church on Easter Sunday to be blessed by the priest.

You will need a 6-inch (15-cm), 7-inch (18-cm) tall cylindrical pan to bake it. A 2$\frac{1}{4}$-pound (1 kg) coffee can works well for this.

KULICH

Kulich

$\frac{1}{3}$ cup (90 ml) rum

$\frac{1}{3}$ cup (60 g) raisins

$\frac{1}{3}$ cup (60 g) golden raisins (sultanas)

$\frac{1}{3}$ cup (60 g) currants

1 cup (250 ml) milk

$\frac{3}{4}$ cup (180 g) unsalted butter

Pinch of saffron threads

4 cups (600 g) strong white flour

1 cup (200 g) superfine (caster) sugar

$\frac{1}{2}$ teaspoon salt

$\frac{1}{2}$ ounce (14 g/2 sachets) instant dried yeast or 1 ounce (30 g) fresh yeast

4 large eggs, lightly beaten

1 teaspoon vanilla extract (essence)

$\frac{1}{4}$ cup (40 g) slivered almonds

3 tablespoons mixed peel, finely chopped

Frosting

1$\frac{1}{2}$ cups (225 g) confectioners' (icing) sugar

2 teaspoons fresh lemon juice

Pink food coloring

Colored sprinkles (100's & 1000's), to decorate

Combine the rum, raisins, golden raisins, and currants in a small bowl and set aside for 30 to minutes to plump.

Heat the milk, butter, and saffron in a small saucepan over low heat until the butter melts. Combine the flour, sugar, and salt in a stand mixer fitted with a dough hook. If using dried yeast, sprinkle it into the bowl. Mix on low speed to combine. If using fresh yeast, blend with a little of the warmed milk mixture in a bowl. Add the milk mixture, yeast mixture (if using fresh yeast), eggs, and vanilla to the flour and mix on low until the dough comes away from the sides of the bowl, 3–4 minutes. Rest for 15 minutes. Increase the speed to medium and mix until smooth and elastic.

If mixing by hand, stir the ingredients in a large bowl with a wooden spoon. Turn out onto a floured work surface and knead for 5–10 minutes. Rest for 15 minutes. Knead for 5–10 minutes, until smooth and elastic.

Place the dough on a floured work surface and knead in the rum mixture, slivered almonds, and peel. Shape into a ball. Grease a bowl with oil. Place the dough in the bowl, cover with a clean cloth, and set aside in a warm, draft-free spot to prove until doubled in size, about 1 hour. Alternatively, cover with plastic wrap (cling film) and prove in the refrigerator overnight.

Preheat the oven to 400°F (200°C/gas 6). Grease and line the base and sides of a 6-inch (15-cm), 7-inch (18-cm) tall, cylindrical mold with parchment paper, extending the paper 4 inches (10 cm) above the rim.

Transfer the dough to a floured work surface. Knead briefly, then shape into a fat log and place inside the prepared pan. Cover with a clean cloth and set aside in a warm place to prove until increased in size by two-thirds, about 1 hour. The dough should be almost up to the rim of the pan.

Bake for 10 minutes. Decrease the oven temperature to 350°F (180°C/gas 4) and bake until golden brown, 35–40 minutes. Leave in the mold for 10 minutes. Turn out onto a rack and let cool completely.

Frosting: Mix the confectioners' sugar, lemon juice, and enough water to make a smooth frosting. Tint pink with food coloring. Pour over the cooled kulich and scatter with sprinkles. Let set before serving.

index